LEADERSHIP,
LOVE, AND
AGGRESSION

ALLISON DAVIS

*Civilization
is a process—whose
purpose is to combine single
human individuals, and after that
families, then races, peoples
and nations, into one
great unity, the
unity of
mankind.*

SIGMUND FREUD,
*Civilization and
Its Discontents*

HARCOURT BRACE JOVANOVICH, PUBLISHERS

LEADERSHIP, LOVE, AND AGGRESSION

SAN DIEGO NEW YORK LONDON

Library of Congress Cataloging in Publication Data
Davis, Allison, 1902–
Leadership, love, and aggression.
Bibliography: p.
1. Afro-Americans—Biography. 2. Afro-Americans—
Psychology. 3. Afro-American leadership. I. Title.
E185.96.D28 1983 973'.0496073'0922 [B] 82-21342
ISBN 0-15-149348-0

Designed by Jacqueline Schuman
Printed in the United States of America

First edition

A B C D E

Contents

Acknowledgments

I am indebted to H. Thomas James, president of the Spencer Foundation, and to the board of that foundation for the opportunity to write *Leadership, Love, and Aggression*. Dr. James has encouraged me throughout five years of research and writing.

I am indebted also to John E. Corbally, president of the John D. and Catherine T. MacArthur Foundation, for providing an emergency presidential grant to enable me to complete this work, and to James Furman, executive vice president of the MacArthur Foundation.

A writer is most fortunate if he finds an understanding publisher. In William Jovanovich, I have met such a man. I also am indebted to Peter Jovanovich, who has directed the publication of this book, and to my editor, Marie Arana-Ward.

My lifelong friend Sterling A. Brown, poet, critic, essayist, and teacher, suggested that I show the typescript of this book to Michael R. Winston, professor of history and director of the Moorland-Spingarn Research Center at Howard University. Dr. Winston sent it to Mr. Jovanovich, and thus I am happily indebted to him.

Edward H. Levi, distinguished president emeritus of the University of Chicago and former attorney general of the United States, has encouraged and assisted my research for many years, as has my friend John T. Wilson, president emeritus of the University of Chicago. Most of all, I am indebted to the University of Chicago itself, where I have taught and done research during forty years.

Ralph Wingate Tyler, much admired dean of American social scientists, benefactor and advisor of hundreds of social scientists at the University of Chicago, and founder of the Center for Advanced

Study in the Social Sciences, has encouraged and aided me throughout the forty years since he appointed me to the faculty of the University of Chicago.

This book originated in a theoretical paper on leadership and aggression, which Jeanne Spurlock, M.D., deputy director of the American Psychiatric Association, invited me to read at an annual meeting of that association.

During 1980 and 1981, Mr. Mark Dean served as my graduate research-assistant in history. I thank him for his conscientious work.

I am primarily indebted to my wife Lois Mason Davis, to my sister Dorothy Davis Lucas, to my brother John Aubrey Davis, professor emeritus and former chairperson of the department of political science in the City College of the University of New York, and to my friend Professor Leon Forrest, poet and novelist of the highest level. For five years, my wife has worked unselfishly day after day, month after month, in researching and typing endless versions of my writing. Many of my thoughts on Wright and King originated with my sister, who has repeatedly offered her psychological perceptiveness and her gift for language. My brother, always an illuminating critic, is a man of keen psychological insight from whom I have profited, especially in my studies of Martin Luther King, Jr., and Frederick Douglass. I have been helped also by his wife Mavis Wormley Davis, who referred me to Dickson J. Preston's *Young Frederick Douglass, The Maryland Years,* in which I found the pivotal evidence on Douglass's white kin.

I also am indebted to my friend Charles Prudhomme, M.D., the dean of American Negro psychiatrists, and former colleague of Harry Stack Sullivan. Dr. Prudhomme battled for forty years to establish the rights of Negro psychiatrists to practice in white hospitals, and has paved the way for younger Negro psychiatrists who now are professors in northern medical schools. He is a man greatly admired by his colleagues, by his students, and by me.

None of those to whom I have expressed my gratitude, however, should be regarded as being responsible for any of the possible errors in this book.

My sons, Gordon Jamison Davis and Allison Stubbs Davis, as always, have given me their unfailing support. I am indebted also to my friend Richard Pollak for his advice on publishing.

I wish to acknowledge my specific indebtedness to International Publishers, who have granted me permission to quote liberally from Philip S. Foner's *The Life and Writings of Frederick Douglass* and W.E.B. Du Bois's *Autobiography,* and to The Citadel Press for permission to quote from Philip S. Foner's *Frederick Douglass.*

Finally, I owe a debt that cannot be paid to the men whom I have come to know better than anyone on earth: to Frederick Douglass, incomparable foe of all racism, white or black; to Richard Wright, a most able and insightful man; to W.E.B. Du Bois for his profoundly tragic understanding of the Negro psyche entombed in the American "glass cage"; and to Martin Luther King, Jr., for his magnificent appeal for peace and the unity of mankind. King indeed was the most admirable man I have known—the wisest leader of our time. I wish it were possible to express personally my indebtedness to him for what he has taught me about anger and hate; *and about love,* without which, as he and Freud have said, our spirits will sicken and die.

1

Transformations
of Aggression

A follower is bound emotionally to his leader by the process of identification. The most vivid instance I can recall of such a bond was my father's fervent admiration for Theodore Roosevelt. Indeed he risked his very life in 1904 to vote for "Teddy" in rural Democratic Virginia. Already marked in a town of 236 citizens as the owner of one of the largest farms in Prince William County, he further angered the whites by registering and voting. A brave man himself, he admired beyond reason Roosevelt's stand against the great economic trusts of his day. He dressed like Teddy, trimmed his mustache like his, and wore pince-nez like his. He accepted Roosevelt unquestioningly and adopted his political ideas as his own. Moreover, he attributed to Roosevelt many of his own virtues, which, in fact, Teddy lacked.

During the next three generations, many of us identified with Franklin Roosevelt, or Dwight Eisenhower, or John Kennedy, or even Richard Nixon. Germans identified with Hitler as their Fuehrer; Russians with Stalin. Identification with a leader can tie the follower to a tyrant and mass-murderer as firmly as to a figure like Martin Luther King, Jr., who was a lover of mankind. In either case, the follower assumes the ideals or goals of the leader, and relinquishes his own conscience in favor of the leader's morality.

But what, if anything, ties the leader to his followers? What motivates him? Above all, he wants to control and direct others. The leader's *handling of his own aggression* determines whether he and his group will work to build or to destroy. Since the follower identifies with the leader, he will prove sadistic if the leader is sadistic; masochistic if the leader is masochistic; or affiliative if the leader is capable of love—love of mankind. It is difficult, however, to name even a few leaders today who manifest love. It is all too easy to enumerate those who hate and destroy. Great political leaders who have been compassionate and humanitarian have been regarded, as a rule, as too "soft" to govern in a violently aggressive society such as ours. It seems, if they wish to be elected, their compassion for mankind is best hidden. Eventually they may be exalted, but only posthumously, as Lincoln was, by a national cult of repentance.

Clearly, no one can function as a leader without a drive to gain power over others and the willingness to bear the work and anxiety such responsibility for others entails. There are, of course, many other desires propelling a man or a woman to seek the position of leader; these may include wishes for economic and social status, for admiration, for attention, for domination, and for revenge, as well as for self-sacrifice. The desire to be loved completely was probably the deepest in political leaders such as Napoleon, Franklin Roosevelt, or Lyndon Johnson.

Aggression takes many forms. Anger is the simplest, most normal form of aggression. Yet anger itself is an extremely complex emotion. It takes a thousand protean transformations, ranging from realistic and conscious anger to anger that is completely unrealistic, unconscious, and irrational.

Realistic anger is the natural response to attack or basic frustration. In the face of attack, it is anger that mobilizes one to defend oneself. There is no reason to feel guilty about such anger.

To nourish resentment is another matter. Resentment is a smouldering fire—a chronic, repetitive anger. It may last years and be very general, as in the resentment of one's fate, or in long-harbored resentment against a parent who, one believes, did not love one enough. Such anger maintains itself year after year, decade after decade, without one's knowing why. What maintains such long-term resentment? How does childhood resentment reactivate itself year after year? Although the answer is not always readily apparent, it is an inner, unresolved conflict that keeps the resentment alive. The most universal conflict of this type exists between the wish to be loved and an angry desire to avenge a lack of love.

Abraham Lincoln suffered from such irrational anger.

Anger is often a psychological defense. When attacked, the immediate response is fear and not anger. But fear is painful; physically, it manifests itself in trembling, sweating, diarrhea, retching, stomach cramps, and vasomotor upsets. Emotionally, fear arouses shame and threatens one's self-esteem. Anger is the usual defense against fear. If a reckless driver nearly hits us, for instance, we feel in that moment a blinding spasm of fear—*a terror of death*. Immediately afterward, anger sweeps over us. The anger blots out our fear ("that s.o.b.!"); it is counterphobic (against fear).

We use such defensive anger daily to inhibit fear. When you feel most angry, and unaccountably so, look for the fear which has triggered it. It may be fear that your child, who stayed out until two or three in the morning, may have been hurt; fear that you have been unjust to your mate, et cetera. If we cannot face the fear, we unconsciously try to defend ourselves by anger.

Most groups in America today are angry. Beneath the anger, however, lies fear. The middle class is frightened by taxes and inflation, and by the continually rising cost of educating its children. "Hard hats" are frightened by unemployment, automation, and job insecurity; machine operatives by the new robots. In feeling frightened, each group has its bellyful of anger.

Anger is energy; it cannot be obliterated. It will find some outlet, whether conscious or unconscious. To swallow one's anger is to allow it to gnaw at the stomach, gut, or heart; and this could lead to ulcers, diverticulitis, or cardiac disease.

We channel our anger in several ways—all learned from early childhood. The child usually learns to *displace* his anger from his parents to his siblings. That is, he shifts his target from a dangerous object to a less dangerous one. As adults we do the same thing, displacing our anger from the powerful boss to the long-suffering wife; from the abusive husband to the helpless child.

The most benign way to handle anger is to sublimate it. In so doing, we consciously transform anger into socially constructive energy. What we call "initiative" really is sublimated aggression, redirected from its original goal of violence or verbal assault to economic or social competition. In a society such as ours, initiative proves tonic; it consists in putting one's best foot forward, striking out in one's own behalf. But many of us fear such competitive impulses and equate them with murderous attack. Nevertheless, one cannot avail oneself of life in any sense without striking out, without exploring, and taking the initiative.

Some of man's greatest achievements result from the sublimation of anger or aggression. Scientific inquiry and research are, essentially, attacks upon the stubborn forces of nature in the effort to analyze them, "break them down" into smaller components, "take them apart"—all plainly forms of sublimated aggression.

Art may sublimate anger. Sharp abrupt strokes of the brush release pent-up anger. In symphonic music, the crescendos and finales with their crashing cymbals plainly express triumphant anger and aggression. Pianists who habitually strike the keys with tremendous force are expressing their own anger, not necessarily toward the piano, but toward the original aggravation. By all odds, the most effective *catharsis of anger* is to compose, sculpt, paint, or write it out of one's system.

On the other hand, to project one's anger is less benign. To project is unconsciously to *attribute one's own anger* to another person, to thrust it onto him. The child who feels very angry with his mother may believe *she* is angry with him. The man who hates his fellow men believes *they* hate him. "I'm not angry and full of hate, *he* is!"

Most of us fear our own anger. As children we learn to feel anger is equivalent to murder. *But anger is only an emotion,* and as such cannot kill; it is not equivalent to murder. We may subconsciously wish to murder, but *wishes are not deeds.* Sticks and stones may kill, but *wishes cannot.* The neurotic person who equates anger with murder is like the self-punishing monk who, having imagined a naked woman, feels as guilty as if he had possessed her!

Anger nourished becomes hate; and hate has only one goal—to be avenged. Whereas anger may be resolved, hatred demands blood; it "sees red." And hate, unlike anger, is not abated by being expressed. The only therapy for hatred is through forgiveness.

Humans are masterful haters. Their hatred is not innate, however; it is learned in early family life, which is capable of generating both love and hate. The more love, apparently, the more hate. The battles which are most filled with hate take place between husband and wife, brother and brother. Murders are often love murders, involving family, lovers, or friends. This continual oscillation of the human spirit between love and hate, this deep ambivalence toward those we also love, is even more mysterious than the labyrinths of sex. We understand it best in the personalities and lives of actual individuals such as those discussed in this book.

With respect to the *manner* in which they handle their own aggression, leaders may be viewed as chiefly (1) sadistic, (2) masochistic, or (3) affiliative. For want of a better term, I shall call the last type of leader *reality-oriented,* since, as I shall show, he is attuned to basic aspects of both his external and his inner reality. Of course, no single leader will conform *exactly* to any one of these personality types, but will combine several. The three types are meant to be abstractions, and as such emphasize only the dominant drives in the overall motivational pattern.

THE SADISTIC LEADER

One motivation is to master and control other people—the lust for power. Among individuals of this motivational type, the normal aggressive and destructive drives, present in all human beings from early childhood, are intensified; they have in fact organized the individual's pattern of interactions with other human beings. Sadistic leaders are driven by a thirst, unquenchable by definition, for proof that they are loved and admired. They are found in every kind of institution. We are quite familiar with the lust for power and for acclaim among politicians, in whose complex personalities is usually found the feeling that other persons are instruments to be controlled, used—and discarded—as personal advantage dictates. Such exploitation, such sadism is common among leaders in business, in industry, in professional organizations, in school systems—in all competitive, hierarchical systems, including families and religious groups. In all institutions there are positions of power; in all, there are individuals driven by the desire to hold power and exert mastery.

Sadistic leaders, like members of dominant social classes, find ready rationalizations for their desire for autocratic power over others. In academic life, among the "aristocracy of intellect," as among the upper social classes everywhere, the defensive rationalization is that the majority of people are unlearned or incapable or recalcitrant, prey to their emotions, and therefore unable as a rule to develop into leaders themselves or to share in their own governing.

The least destructive form the sadistic leader assumes is that of a patriarch whose dogma is "father knows best!" Such leaders thrive upon *the dependency feelings of others, simply because most men wish to be protected and sheltered from the continual struggle which life demands.* Thus it happens that a group or nation of people, burdened by a longing for dependence upon some omniscient parent and the desire for a protector, falls under the power of a sadistic leader who, in turn, is motivated by the thirst for infinite love and acclaim, by the wish to manipulate others so he may satisfy his infantile craving to be the object of attention, admiration, and love.

THE REALITY-ORIENTED LEADER

A second type of leader is (1) relatively objective about the nature both of himself and of society, (2) driven chiefly by *affiliative* rather than destructive feelings toward others, and (3) controlled inwardly by principles which the culture recognizes as leading to its highest group goals. Morality and the loyalty to ideals will not in themselves make such a leader. Millions of highly conscientious and moral people devoted to principles are in fact emotionally punitive and sadistic, and lack insight into their own irrational and destructive drives.

This second type of leader—one thinks of Adlai Stevenson, Abraham Lincoln, and Frederick Douglass—is not caught in the grip of irrational wishes and unconscious conflicts; he is able to control both his sadistic and his self-destructive drives, and thereby is freed for a fuller use of his rational and creative resources. He will not constantly act out his unsolved inner conflicts in his relation with others, but is generally able to deal objectively both with the inner reality of his own emotions and with social and political realities. He wants not to master and use people to satisfy his own irrational drives, but instead to help them to identify and use their own abilities more fully in the service of themselves and society. There are very few such leaders in any institution because there are few people who possess real insight into themselves, and who are governed by an objective view of society and not by passion and prejudice.

This type of leader is not harried by irrational guilt—the guilt over things he has not done, but only wished or thought—and therefore he is not self-punishing. One thinks again of Adlai Stevenson, who may have been the only powerful voice in this Age of Despair to speak courageously for sanity, for cooperation by nations, and for keeping people from self-destruction by making them aware how illogical are their sadistic drives. Neither the jeers of the sadists and destroyers, nor the snide implications that he lacked a "manly" relish for violence, nor the despair of those weak enough to be caught in their own anger could drive Stevenson to succumb to worldwide madness. He held his ground; he spoke and stood for sanity at home and abroad. He was a fighter who believed in life and his ideas gave hope to a new generation in many countries.

LEADERSHIP, LOVE, AND AGGRESSION

The indomitable black antislavery leader Frederick Douglass came from the bottom of society. Stevenson came from the top. Douglass never was allowed to live with his mother and was never recognized openly by his white father. He saved himself from slavery—from a condition in which he, his mother, and brothers and sisters were whipped and forced to work harder than horses; and he fought his way to a position of international influence as an antislavery leader. Douglass was able to respond to reality and either channel or restrain his aggression. He fought with his fists to save his life when attacked by the slave driver and by white workmen in the Baltimore shipyards. Most slaves were supine or broken, but he defended himself. He was a realist who had learned that "such floggings are *seldom repeated* on such persons by overseers. *They prefer to whip those who are the most easily whipped*. The doctrine that submission to violence is the best cure for violence did not hold good as between slaves and overseers. *He was whipped oftener who was whipped easiest*. . . . 'You can shoot me,' said a slave to Rigby Hopkins, 'but you can't whip me,' and the result was that he was neither whipped nor shot." (Emphasis added.)

Douglass would quickly fight for self-preservation, but he was not suicidal. He rejected John Brown's invitation to join him in self-annihilation at Harpers Ferry. He was realistic, even cagey, about the brutal system into which he was born. Knowing his value as property, he correctly gauged that he would not be killed if he defended himself against whipping. He stood up also to his own fears, which were constantly aroused by his owner's threats of murder if he tried to escape. After trying to escape, after being caught and beaten, he tried again and succeeded. Douglass is a remarkable instance of a leader who, although essentially a man of reason, nevertheless has powerfully aggressive and self-asserting drives and thus is able to stand up against a most oppressive social system. Without these drives he would not have become a free man and, in course, the most influential leader of the antislavery movement.

THE MASOCHISTIC LEADER

A third type of leadership motivation, one rooted in learned and often unconscious masochistic drives, has been more common among Negro Americans. Black society, in reacting to the danger of physical and economic annihilation by the ruling white society, approved and institutionalized self-depreciating responses by blacks. Self-subordination was learned in childhood. Most Negro parents taught their children that in the face of whites self-defense and self-assertion were in effect suicidal. Parents preached, "Stay in your place." These values, reinforced by fear and often by violence, became part of the Negro child's moral code. The warning voice of his father and mother punished him if he wished or tried to obtain the rights and privileges of a white man.

Self-depreciation, then, was taught the Negro child by his own society as a means of self-preservation. The point is crucial. Self-subordination was not taught by the Negro parent as morally justified, but was taught and learned as a survival technique, a defense against an *immoral* society. To survive in the white man's economy under his unjust system of legal administration, one must bow one's head, swallow indignation and anger, and pretend to like one's oppressors. Of course, Negroes were like all other subordinate groups in being ambivalent about their oppressors. They both hated whites and wanted their acceptance.

HANDLING ANGER

To some people of every group the circumstance of being subjected to punishment and contempt is satisfying to their own basic drives of self-contempt and self-punishment. These are, of course, masochistic persons who, reacting to childhood experiences, have persisted in holding lacerating feelings of guilt, of unworthiness, ultimately, of a "need" to be punished.

A leader who himself is masochistic affords such persons a masochistic ideal with which they can identify. Thus, he gives them a cause to *avoid the struggle of the ego for life and mastery of reality.* Both sadism and masochism are present in all persons in childhood. The wish to attack and master, and the wish to *be* hit or mastered, are both forms of the aggressive drive. The analog is clear. Just as the life and death drives are always mingled, so the sadistic and masochistic drives interact in each person.

A basic problem of the Negro masses and of Negro leaders is how to transform and direct their anger into reform, in short, how to remedy the social and economic causes of their anger. Negroes always have borne anger toward whites because they have been systematically subordinated by whites in every type of relationship. But this anger, always present, had to be inhibited because the white society was all-powerful—or seemed so. The Negro suppressed his anger so strongly and over so long a period that, in many cases, it was hidden from himself.

Under the masochistic leader, the follower identifies with self-punishment and becomes sacrificed to the leader's wish for self-destruction. For this leader is driven chiefly by the unconscious desire to provoke attack upon himself, to kill himself—or, as he thinks, to "sacrifice himself for others." This is a death drive. When combined with rage against the dominant group, this motivation turns on itself. Rage expressed provokes its backlash, and the dominant group is caused to attack and destroy him and thus satisify his deepest drive for self-destruction.

The difference between "the true masochist—who always holds out his cheek wherever he sees a chance of receiving a blow" (Freud)—and the most effective black leaders of "nonviolent resistance" was that the resistance of the latter was self-assertive and self-enhancing. It included powerful forms of initiative—the protest and boycott—which replaced old black habits of self-subordination and self-contempt.

Among those discussed in this book, Frederick Douglass, enslaved and "imbruted" for twenty-one years, discovered the strength to speak for the downtrodden—for slaves, women, the Irish in Britain, the Chinese in California, the massacred and exploited American Indians. One has only to compare Douglass with his friends and colleagues William Lloyd Garrison and John Brown to appreciate the extent of his love for mankind. Garrison and Brown were principally haters; Douglass was, as Stephen M. Weissman has written, "more a man of love than hate."

William Edward Burghardt Du Bois, Harvard scholar and incorruptible champion of the Negro middle class, was angry and defiant unto death. A great polemicist and an even greater sociologist and essayist, he taught and led two generations of Negro college students, scholars, and professionals to fight racism by setting examples of their own achievement. He fought to free the oppressed, not only at home, but even in far-flung European colonies. Although he praised Gandhi and the young King, he seldom evinced compassion or a love of mankind, and felt too alone in the world—too rejected personally—to understand *ahimsa,* or "the community of love." Nevertheless, his gallant fight for liberty gave rise to a far greater leader, Martin Luther King, Jr. On the very day Du Bois died in Ghana, Dr. King, speaking before a quarter of a million people on the grounds of the Washington Monument and the Lincoln Memorial, said that Du Bois had inspired his own battle for civil justice.

The enraged Richard Wright claimed compassion for the lynched and the exploited—his best short stories inspire pity and terror for their tragedies. But his novels express no compassion; they are filled with hatred for the oppressors, and disdain for their Negro victims, Wright's own people.

King taught millions of Americans, regardless of color, to forbear violence and deal justly with those of another "race." His love of mankind was not facile cant, but the hard-won product of disciplined behavior. Both he and Gandhi suffered imprisonment, manhandling, and humiliation to learn this behavior and to persuade the other side to learn a reciprocal forbearance and acceptance. Such forbearance demands the most of one's followers, and of one's opponents. King taught that hatred is doomed to perpetuate itself, but that forbearance may lead to mutual understanding and, eventually, to reconciliation and justice between peoples. This is the *affiliative drive,* the desire to join with others as a social, political, and identity-forming community. The leader who is driven by this "love" seeks "one great unity, the unity of mankind."

2

Douglass, the Lion

This is the story of Frederick Douglass, the fiery and rebellious ex-slave who freed himself from all prejudice based upon sex, race, class, or nationality to become champion of all oppressed peoples. Always an activist, Douglass, "the lion," once thundered, "Those who profess to favor freedom and yet deprecate agitation . . . want crops without plowing . . . rain without . . . lightning . . . the ocean without the awful roar of its many waters. . . . This struggle may be a moral one, or it may be a physical one, but it must be a struggle. Power concedes nothing without a demand."

The most powerful speaker among the abolitionists, Douglass became a highly successful lecturer in both the United States and Europe. Today it is still astonishing that so defiant and independent a Negro should have been greatly admired by many of his powerful white contemporaries in his own country and abroad. It is paradoxical, too, that the later Negro leader Booker T. Washington chose the role of subservience yet admired Douglass enough to publish a favorable biography of him.

This is a psychological study of Douglass's childhood, adolescence, young adulthood, and prime of life, until his forty-second year. In that year he finally overcame any suicidal inclinations when he rejected John Brown's plan for armed insurrection at Harpers Ferry. With his anger behind him, the former slave was able to transform suicidal hate into constructive energy. By the time he was forty-two, Douglass was a leader of international stature. He had written two successful books, edited the best-known abolitionist newspaper, was the most influential reformer in America, and was to become adviser to President Lincoln and four later Presidents. By forty-two he had achieved complete independence and self-determination. Tracing this catharsis in Douglass's personality may well reveal his decisive conflicts and the devices by which he resolved them.

Douglass was named Frederick Augustus Washington Bailey by his mother, Harriet Bailey. As nearly as he could determine, he was born sometime during February 1817 on a dilapidated plantation in Talbot County, on the Eastern Shore of Maryland. Since his mother was hired out to a wealthy slaveholder twelve miles away, the boy had seen her only four or five times before her death when he was seven. He was not told when she had died or where she had been buried. His grandmother Betsey Bailey reared him in her cabin until he was claimed at six by his master.

His grandmother loved him; and though she favored and protected him as did most women in his life, she also taught him a strict moral code. It was a doctrine far more rigorous than his master's, and he adhered to it for the rest of his life. She taught him, too, how to get along with whites, for she herself had learned to gain favors from her master and had become his favorite slave. She hoped Fred might do the same. But as much as the boy wanted the love of his white father and master, he also felt he had just reason to hate him.

Everyone, including Douglass, has surrounded the identity of his white father with mystery. It was, of course, dangerous for him or his black family to say that his master was also his father. Fear of retaliation insured their silence.

Their white master was Captain Aaron Anthony, owner of three plantations in Tuckahoe and steward for the most powerful slaveowner in eastern Maryland, Colonel Edward Lloyd V. Although Captain Anthony never specifically acknowledged Douglass as his son, he sent him to Baltimore at age eight to escape the rigors of plantation work. Furthermore, his daugher, Lucretia, and her sister-in-law treated him as they would a member of the family. So Douglass had two families—one white and one black.*

---

*Fortunately, remarkably thorough research into state and Talbot County records by Dickson J. Preston (*Young Frederick Douglass: The Maryland Years*, 1980) has

None of his biographers has studied the central paradox in Douglass's personality—the conflicting hatred and love for a powerful father who treated him as a son at times, but never emancipated or publicly acknowledged him. Only Dr. Stephen Weissman, in a short article, has explored this early, ambivalent bond. Douglass's relationship with his father was a crucial reference point from which the boy developed a consuming fantasy, a dream of himself as a rebellious and vengeful hero, divinely called to free his people from the tyranny that his father represented. Throughout childhood and adolescence, Fred nourished this *fantasy of Titanistic revolt even as he lived with his white family, and loved his mistress Lucretia, his mistress Sophia, and her son, Tommy.*

There are other mysteries concerning Douglass. Here it will be enough just to mention one more—his physical appearance. Photographers made his face appear all shades: black, dark brown, light brown, bronze, copper, olive, and white. The degree of retouching may have depended upon the status of Douglass at the moment, or upon the purpose of a particular photograph. In his first autobiography, written as propaganda for the Massachusetts Anti-Slavery Society, his photograph makes him look almost black. In one taken much later and hung in his Anacostia home, he appears almost white!

Whatever doubt there may have been about these matters, there never was any question in his own mind about his mission in life.

---

turned up essential data on both the white and Negro families of Douglass. These data, overlooked by all other Douglass scholars, provide us with excellent evidence of the mutually close relations between Douglass and his white kin *through three generations.* It is also by far the best account of both the Anthony and the Lloyd families.

§ Douglass always sought but never discovered the exact date of his birth. He thought it had been in February 1817. However, if one accepts plantations records found by Preston, it actually was in February 1818 (the date assumed here to be correct). In that case, all other dates of events in his early life as represented by Douglass are incorrect by one year. At times his errors are much greater; for instance in his *Personal Narrative,* he claims he was sent back to the plantation four years after he was first sent to Baltimore. In fact, he was sent back less than a year later.

It was "Agitate! Agitate! Agitate!" That was his advice to young Negro Americans even in his last years.

Douglass escaped from slavery in 1838 at the age of twenty or twenty-one. Four years later he was well known as a lecturer and representative of the American Anti-Slavery Society. Three years subsequently he published *A Personal Narrative,* which won acclaim in the United States, Great Britain, and France. That year and the next he lectured throughout Britain, earning the admiration of leading orators and statesmen.

The incredible rapidity with which he attained this success as a writer and lecturer, however, was not so remarkable as his achievement in transforming his own anger and hatred toward whites. As Weissman has written, "He is someone I would like to have known personally, for somehow his writing and his work, *passionate and indignant as they were, were more acts of love than acts of hate.*" His greatest quality as he matured and accumulated power was his triumphant love for mankind in all conditions, in all countries. Not only did he become the chief spokesman for Negro slaves, but also he was the first prominent male in America to endanger his life in the fight for emancipation of women—he became a vice president of their Equal Rights Association. Douglass became the champion of the downtrodden everywhere! His life is a study in the healing of hatred.

Fred Douglass's master, Captain Aaron Anthony, was a lower-middle-class man who had started as pilot of a Chesapeake Bay sloop, but, by the time of Fred's birth had become the owner of three small plantations and thirty slaves in a desolate backwoods area on Maryland's Eastern Shore. Captain Anthony's status and power, however, were derived from his position as steward for thirteen plantations and over 600 slaves belonging to Colonel Edward Lloyd. Lloyd was the largest wheat grower in the state, and head of one of the oldest, most distinguished Episcopal families in Maryland.

Captain Anthony, as Lloyd's steward, then, wielded the power of life or death over hundreds of slaves, among whom were Fred, his mother, and his grandmother.

Although farm production in Talbot County was above average for Maryland as a whole, large-scale slavery had ceased to be profitable by 1800. By 1820, when Fred was two or three, large-scale owners were hiring out their slaves either to farmers who owned none or to employers in Baltimore who needed servants or artisans. This slump in the slave-owning economy was felt generally, and many planters were known to starve their slaves. The topic of his own starvation as well as that of his fellow slaves is recurrent in Douglass's account.

In his *Personal Narrative,* written when he was about twenty-five, Douglass, who had been out of slavery only four years and had never been to school, related horrors of life in slavery with such brilliance and dramatic force that he won the acclaim of Harriet Beecher Stowe, Senator Charles Sumner, William Lloyd Garrison, Gerrit Smith, and many other powerful and wealthy whites in England and America. [1]

He wrote a passionate and defiant account of the inhumanity of the slave system: the starvation of slaves, and the perversion of using men and women as chattel. His prose was designed to anger the Northern reader. This he achieved in vivid recollections of the bloody whippings of two women (one was flogged while her young children wept and cried for mercy), in other scenes of vindictive torture and murder, and by accounts of the sadistic sexual abuse of black women. [1]

To add to these depravities (which, in the interest of proselyting to gain adherents, his employers in the Massachusetts Anti-Slavery Society encouraged him to document), Douglass recounts an even more grisly tale: Douglass's grandmother had been a mammy to his master, yet eventually she "had peopled his plantation" as his paramour. Douglass points out that miscegenation between white masters and their Negro female slaves had been a common practice in the South for 300 years. His grandmother Betsey Bailey had been but one victim.

One of her five daughters, Harriet Bailey, became Fred's mother. The fact, then, was that the master, Anthony, had sexual relations not only with his own former mammy, but with at least two of her daughers: Fred's mother, Harriet, and Hester, the aunt whose whippings Fred often witnessed during Anthony's fits of sexual jealousy.

Incest thus numbers among the "dark and nameless crimes" with which Douglass charges his master. Perhaps it was for this reason that, as Douglass writes, his master frequently raved against recurrent apparitions and "demons" that tortured him. Whether such psychotic interludes began before the incest, or after, we do not know. But it is certain that even though such relationships were not regarded as incestuous by slave law, they were perceived as incestuous by the man's conscience. Consistent with Western societies, the *master's own childhood training* had certainly defined sexual intercourse with one's daughters as repugnant; eventually it would have been viewed so by his conscience.

Douglass pictures his early years as filled with loss—the early loss of his mother and grandmother. He relates the crimes of his father and master, whom he portrays as psychotic. At eight, however, he was suddenly and inexplicably sent away by this "murderous" old master to live in the relative safety of Baltimore, with a new mistress, who loved him. According to Weissman, "Shortly after the death of his slave mother, Douglass is given the special privilege and opportunity of going to live in Baltimore. This was both given and received as a disguised and disavowed form of affection and a specialness." The "tyrannical" and "cruel" master thus consigned the slave child to the land of opportunity! But Douglass insists he was rescued not by his father but by fate. He writes a long paean to divine Providence for having chosen him from among the slave boys on his master's plantations. In fact, the choice was not made by his master alone. Lucretia, his master's favorite child and only daughter, was party to the decision. He was given a reprieve, then, by his half-sister as well as by his father.

While Douglass distorts his account of his relationships with white kin, his story is basically true in one respect. *He was motivated powerfully by a personal feeling of rejection by his father and a need to defy and overcome the man.* Like other boys, Fred at five or six wove a hero-and-villain story, a myth, pitting his father against himself. The typical slave child's fantasy would have included an overestimation of the master, an assumption that he was all-powerful and all-knowing, both hateful and admirable. This was exactly Fred's image of his father. Long before he had seen this "old master," he had heard his grandmother speak of him "with every mark of reverence." She reminded him that he belonged to the master along with everyone else. His father's "name seemed ever to be mentioned with fear and shuddering."

In a father-fantasy, the boy's feelings toward the father typically change from fear and respect to hostility and rivalry. Douglass reports such a rejection of his father and an *exaltation of himself* as the father's heroic opponent.

The hero-myth which he created about himself as a boy was a defense against his own powerlessness. His dreams of becoming a hero amounted to fantasied compensation for his position as a motherless and fatherless child. In this fantasy, he dispensed with his original identity and original parents and assumed a new psychological identity.

In real life his self-confidence was the effect of the love and approbation he received from his grandmother during the most formative years of his life. From *her faith in him* he learned faith in himself. His achieving drive, however, came from fantasies of revenge against his father and a desire to overcome and displace him.

Later, in *My Bondage and My Freedom,* published seventeen years after his escape, Douglass revealed the truth about his ties with both his white father and his half-sister. He states that his master-father "could be kind, and at times, even showed an affectionate disposition." Moreover, "could the reader have seen him gently leading me by the hand—as he sometimes did—patting me on the head, speaking to me in soft caressing tones and calling me his 'little Indian boy,' he would have deemed him a kind old man, and really, almost fatherly." The fact that Douglass remembered these incidents after more than twenty-six years clearly shows the extent of his desire to be loved by his white father.

Similarly, his recollection of his master's daughter, Lucretia, is that of a kind young mistress—a merciful and motherly figure—who saved him from starvation, bound up his wounds, listened with pleasure to his serenades for bread, and recommended him to the loving care of her brother-in-law's wife in Baltimore, Sophia Auld. Of Lucretia, Douglas wrote:

> Miss Lucretia—as we all continued to call her long after her mar-riage—had bestowed upon me such words and looks—[as] taught me that she pitied me, if she did not love me. In addition to words and looks, she sometimes gave me a piece of bread and butter; a thing not set down in the bill of fare, and which must have been an extra ration, planned aside from either Aunt Katy or old master, solely out of the tender regard and friendship she had for me. Then, too, I one day got into the wars with Uncle Abel's son "Ike," and had got sadly worsted; in fact, the little rascal had struck me directly in the forehead with a sharp piece of cinder fused with iron from the old black-smith's forge, which made a cross in my forehead very plainly to be seen now. The gash bled very freely, and I roared very loudly and betook myself home. . . . Miss Lucretia . . . called me into the parlor quietly, acted the good Samaritan. With her own soft hand she washed the blood from my head and face, fetched her own balsam bottle, and with the balsam wetted a nice piece of white linen, and bound up my head.

These are words of love, the love of a little boy of five or six, as remembered by the man. Lucretia was his half-sister, and she seemed to treat him as such. She fed him when he was hungry; "I was the only one of the children to whom such attention was paid." He was also the only child to serenade his mistress.

When very hungry, I would go into the backyard and play under Miss Lucretia's window. When pretty severely pinched by hunger, I had a habit of singing, which the good lady very soon came to understand as a petition for a piece of bread. When I sung under Miss Lucretia's window, I was very apt to get well paid for my music.

What a changed picture! Instead of being the rejected son of his master, Douglass now admits he enjoyed a special status apart from other slave boys: He was actually loved by his white kin. And this love extended not only to two generations but to collateral kin. In short, just as Fred was not "abandoned" by his black mother and grandmother, as he had felt in *A Personal Narrative,* he was not rejected or disowned by his white family. He was reared in his master-father's plantation for several years with evidence of both love *and* rejection. He also was nurtured attentively by his first two mistresses.

In this second autobiography, *My Bondage and My Freedom,* his mother appears as a handsome woman "whose personal appearance and bearing are ineffaceably stamped upon my memory." Before, he had only the vaguest memory of her. Now, "She was tall and finely proportioned . . . had regular features . . . and was remarkably sedate in her manners." He even discloses that although only a hired field hand, his mother could read!

During these first five years, as we have said, the anchor of his trust and love was his grandmother Betsey Bailey, who later became the wife of a free Negro. In these first years with his grandmother, Douglass writes, he was "idyllically happy, and *led a carefree, unrestrained existence denied to the children of white slaveowners!*" (Emphasis added.) This is a tribute to his love for and gratitude to his grandmother, not to slavery.

Clearly, then, this second book reveals Douglass developing into a more balanced view of his childhood. The early loss of his mother no longer seemed a catastrophic blow by hostile fate; it was more than balanced by five years of indulgence from his grandmother.

Moreover, the defiance and resentment Douglass felt toward his master-father had been softened by tender memories of his father's attention and caresses even as he struggled through his madness to show love for the boy. In this book, Douglass also remembers many kindnesses from his master's only daugher, Lucretia, who was always steadfast in her loyalty.

Most warmly, he recalls his second mistress, Sophia Auld. During the first months of his stay in Baltimore, she loved him like a son. Even after her husband's warning not to teach the slave boy how to read, she persisted in her tenderness toward him. "I had a kind mistress at Baltimore who was almost a mother to me. She was in tears when we parted." These repressed memories of happier relationships with both white and black kin were finally remembered and expressed.

We now have enough facts about his early life to take tentative measure of his emerging personality. As a boy and as a man, Douglass had superior intellectual abilities and powerful emotions. At the center of his early personality were two intense needs: the first was to win acceptance and recognition from his white father and master; the second was to secure, and enjoy, the trust and love of a woman, since he had lost his mother and grandmother before the age of seven.

The first drive, his desire for recognition from his white father, was deeply conflicted and ambivalent. Later, with William Lloyd Garrison, he yearned again for love from a father figure, and felt the same hurt. With maturity, however, his defiance was mitigated, and he won influential friends among both white and black leaders. But the conflict was to arise often in his breaks with Garrison, Charles Sumner, and other powerful men.

The second nuclear conflict in his personality occurred between (1) an early distrust of women, rooted in his mother's disappearance and early death, and (2) a longing to trust and love them. With the love he received during childhood from his grandmother and two white mistresses, he developed a basic acceptance of and trust in women. There have been few historical figures so uniformly fortunate as Douglass in his relationships with women—in his two marriages as well as in his professional life. At the heart of Douglass's self-confidence lay the knowledge that in his first years he had been loved and admired by three women.

This trust in women proved lasting; women felt it and returned it. After his escape, it was Englishwomen who paid his purchase price and made him legally free. Women gave him money to start his newspaper, the *North Star*; two English sisters did the work of organizing it, proofreading it, promoting it, and raising funds to keep it alive. American women were equally helpful. His "old master's" granddaughter, Amanda, admired him so much that on her deathbed, it was he whom she called to reminisce about her dead mother—his former mistress Lucretia. His black wife gave him the money to escape, furnished their home in New Bedford, Massachusetts, worked as a washerwoman and shoemaker to support herself and the children during his first year and a half in Great Britain, and earned the respect and esteem of his white and black friends. Douglass wrote of her after her death, "Mother was the post in the center of my house and held us together." His Yankee secretary, Helen Pitts, whom he married when he was sixty-seven, proved equally devoted to him.

Douglass was fortunate to have resolved the sense of desertion he felt in the early disappearance of his mother. He was not so fortunate with respect to his feelings of rejection by his white father. This inner conflict was not solved in childhood or adolescence. He was often bitterly hostile toward his father, as he was toward his later masters. When a slave, his hostility toward white males nearly cost him his life on several occasions; and his second master, Thomas Auld, feared he would be killed by other whites on adjoining farms. White apprentices in Baltimore shipyards did try to kill him, and they nearly succeeded when he had the audacity to fight back.

How could such a man, defiant and embittered by bondage,

learn to harness his rage and his rancor, and convert his gifts into strong, self-controlled leadership? It is the next question addressed here.

Fred Douglass never forgot the childhood experience of witnessing his Aunt Hester's whippings at the hands of his enraged father. He was awakened by her screams. Peeping through cracks in the door of a kitchen closet where he was sleeping, he saw his aunt being lashed by Captain Anthony. The heart-stopping agony of her screams terrified him. He watched as the young woman was dragged into the kitchen and stripped.

> . . . leaving her neck, shoulders, and back entirely naked. [Her master] then told her to cross her hands, calling her at the same time a black bitch. [After she had crossed her hands] he tied them with a strong rope, and led her to a stool under a large hook in the joist, put in for the purpose. He made her get upon the stool, and tied her hands to the hook. Her arms were stretched up at their full length, so that she stood upon the ends of her toes. He then said to her, "Now you damned bitch I'll learn you how to disobey my orders!" . . . and soon the warm, red blood (amid heart-rending shrieks from her, and more horrid oaths from him) came dripping to the floor. I was so terrified . . . I dared not venture out till long after the blood transaction was over. I expected it would be my turn next.

To a slave child sex was no secret. Slaves had no bedrooms and no privacy, and Fred had often seen persons engaging in sexual intercourse. His immediate response, then, was to assume—as everyone on the plantation had been saying—that his master loved Hester and was sleeping with her. "Then why is he trying to kill her?" Fred wondered.

He knew, as did everyone else, that Hester preferred her black lover, Ned Roberts, and often ran off late at night to be with him. As he saw his aunt's tender flesh cut to bloody ribbons by the relentless whip, he must have wondered whether the same thing had happened to his grandmother and mother. He even imagined himself as the victim. Years later, he wrote that he had been "terrified" by the thought that his towering master might easily kill a little boy like himself.

During these early years he often saw Hester whipped. In time, fear for his own life was replaced by anger, and the desire to hurt his father. The anger was a defense: "I am not helpless. I can find ways to protect myself from him. If I can't win his favor and protection, I can outwit him. And in the future when I grow strong, I can get even with him."

The crucial difference between Fred and other slave boys was that his rage against the powerful white master did *not* translate into subservience, nor the accepted role as clown. Instead, Fred spun a fantasy of revenge. He fabricated a private myth that he was a disowned and defiant son who would rebel against his father, become a hero to his people, and lead them out of bondage. In this reaction he was normal, for every boy or adolescent is at times his own private "culture-hero"—bringer of fire, light, truth, justice. In the glory and bedazzlement of this fantasy, he forgets that it involves the killing of the father.

Thus, Douglass's drive and aspirations were spawned by a revengeful wish to bring his father to his knees. This wish was expressed thirteen years after his escape, when he wrote in a published open letter to his second master, Thomas Auld, Lucretia's widower, that he had surpassed him in life. He boasted that he had won powerful white friends in the North as well as in England, had prospered financially, written and published two books, owned and published an internationally recognized newspaper, and successfully learned the language and manners of a people with a culture far superior to that of his former masters in the backwoods of Tuckahoe. (That is, he had overcome his father figure.)

By the time he was eight, as mentioned earlier, Fred was sent to the freer life of Baltimore (1826). There his new young mistress, Sophia Auld, was far more openly affectionate than Lucretia Auld had been. Her face actually beamed with good will and affection.

"I wish I could describe the rapture that flashed through my soul as I beheld it." Again, this is the expression of a little boy's love, remembered vividly when Douglass was twenty-seven years old. Sophia was his ideal mother: "I was utterly astonished at her goodness. I scarcely knew how to behave toward her. She was entirely unlike any other white woman I had ever seen. . . . *Her face was made of heavenly smiles, and her voice of tranquil music.*" (Emphasis added.)

In fact, Sophia Auld became and remained his sociological mother. "Miss Lucretia," he wrote, comparing his two young mistresses, "was kind; but my new mistress, 'Miss Sophy,' surpassed her in kindness. . . ." In his second book, he remembered that Sophia had mothered him when he was eight—a late age for a boy to be so indulged.

> If little Thomas was her son, and her most dearly beloved child, she for a time at least made me something like his half-brother in her affections. If her dear Tommy was exalted to a place on his mother's knee, "Freddy" [Douglass] was honored by a place at his mother's side. Nor did he lack the caressing strokes of her gentle hand to convince him that though motherless, he was not friendless.

His new master, Hugh Auld, also was an improvement:

> He was never very cruel to me, according to the notion of cruelty in Maryland. The first year or two which I spent in his house, he left me almost exclusively to the management of his wife. She was my law-giver. In hands so tender as hers, and in the absence of the cruelties of the plantation, I became, both physically and mentally, much more sensitive to good and ill treatment; and, perhaps, suffered more from a frown from my mistress, than I formerly did from a cuff at the hands of Aunt Katy. Instead of the cold, damp floor of my old master's kitchen, I found myself on carpets; for the corn bag [to sleep on] in winter, I now had a good straw bed, well furnished with covers; for the coarse corn-meal in the morning, I now had good bread, and mush occasionally; for my poor tow-linen shirt, reached to my knees, I had good, clean clothes. I was really well-off. My employment was to run errands, and to take care of

Tommy; to prevent his getting in the way of carriages, and to keep him out of harm's way generally.

Although Hugh Auld had forbidden his wife to teach Fred how to read, the boy quickly learned how to get around his new master. He learned to read with the help of Irish boys in the streets. When the Aulds were out and he had the run of the house, he read whatever he liked. He "tested" Auld by making a place for himself in the attic, and when his master did not object, he carried up a barrel for a desk and a comfortable chair. He learned to write by copying on shipyard boards the letters he saw on the lumber, and then writing them on fences and in the sand. He learned most from little Tommy's copybooks.

> When my mistress left me in charge of the house I had a grand time. I got Master Tommy's copy books and a pen and ink, and in the sample spaces between the lines I wrote other lines as nearly like his as possible. The process was a tedious one, and I ran the risk of getting a flogging for marking the highly prized copy books of the oldest son. In addition to these opportunities, sleeping as I did in the kitchen loft, I contrived to get a flour-barrel up there and a chair, and upon the head of that barrel I have written, or endeavored to write, copying from the Bible and the Methodist hymn book, and other books which I had accumulated, till late at night, and when all the family were in bed and asleep. I was supported in my endeavors by renewed advice and by holy promises from the good father Lawson, with whom I continued to meet and pray and read the Scriptures. Although Master Hugh was aware of these meetings, I must say for his credit that he never executed his threats to whip me for having thus innocently employed my leisure time.

As always, Hugh Auld's bark proved more ferocious than his bite.

These constructive forms of aggression were constantly impeded by the slave system. It was illegal to give slaves books or newspapers, or to teach them how to read. It was illegal, too, for a slave to start a Sunday school and teach slaves to read the Bible, as Fred did several times. Just before his escape at twenty Douglass presided over a successful Sunday school with forty students—most of whom he had taught to read. It was illegal to bring the *Liberator* and other abolitionist papers into Maryland, but this interdiction only whetted Fred's appetite to learn about the abolitionists. It was, of course, also illegal for slave to possess and read books that could incite them to rebellion, but at twelve he saved fifty cents and bought a copy of the *Columbian Orator,* in which he read the great speeches of William Pitt, Fox, Lord Chatham, and Sheridan.

> The mighty power and heart-searching directness of truth, penetrating the heart of a slaveholder and compelling him to yield up his earthly interests to the claims of eternal justice, were finely illustrated in the dialogue, and from the speeches of Sheridan I got a bold and powerful denunciation of oppression and a most brilliant vindication of the rights of man.

During the first seven years he spent in Baltimore, "Father Lawson," an old black preacher with whom he spent most of his free time, greatly encouraged Douglass to pursue his heroic fantasies about himself and his future.

> His words made a very deep impression upon me, and I verily felt that some such work was before me, though I could not see how I could ever engage in its performance. The good Lord would bring it to pass in his own good time, [Lawson] said, and that I must go on reading and studying the Scriptures. This advice and these suggestions were not without their influence on my character and destiny. He fanned my already intense love of knowledge into a flame by assuring me that I was to be a useful man in the world. When I would say to him, "How can these things be? and what can I do?" his simple reply was, "Trust in the Lord." When I would tell him, "I am a slave, and a slave for life, how can I do anything?" he would quietly answer, "The *Lord* can make you free, my dear; all things are possible with Him; only have faith in God. If you want liberty, ask the Lord for it in faith, and He will give it to you."
>
> Thus assured and thus cheered on under the inspiration of hope, I worked and prayed with a light heart, believing that my life was under the guidance of a wisdom higher than my own. With all other blessings sought at the mercy seat, I always prayed that God

would, of His great mercy, and in His own good time, deliver me from my bondage.

But, in 1830, when he was twelve, his relatively easy life in the service of Hugh Auld's family was threatened after the death of his "old master" and owner-father, Aaron Anthony. Anthony died intestate, and as a result Fred had to be returned to Tuckahoe for evaluation and assignment according to an agreement among the heirs—Lucretia and her brothers.

". . . up to this time," Douglass wrote, "there had been no dark clouds arisen to darken the sky of that happy abode. It was a sad day to me when I left for the Eastern Shore to be valued and divided, as it was for my dear mistress and teacher and for little Tommy. We all three wept bitterly, for we were parting forever. No one could tell among which pile of chattels I might be flung."

Once more, however, Lucretia intervened at a decisive turning point for Fred. She made her husband, Thomas Auld, return the boy to Hugh and Sophia in Baltimore. "Captain Thomas Auld and Mrs. Lucretia at once decided on my return to Baltimore. They knew how warmly Mrs. Hugh Auld was attached to me, and how delighted Tommy would be to see me. . . ." These are not the words of a man unaware of his charm.

But if the death of his "old master" raised only a false cry of alarm for Fred, another blow was to follow. Shortly thereafter, his chief protector, Lucretia, died. He became the property of her widowed husband, Thomas Auld, who allowed his brother Hugh to keep Fred in Baltimore on the condition that he also keep a crippled slave girl, Henny—a cousin of Fred's. When Hugh and Sophia found that Henny was useless, they returned her to Thomas Auld. Thomas, who had inherited all of Lucretia's slaves but hated his role as master, became angry. He demanded Fred be sent back to him.

For the first six months, fifteen-year-old Fred lived with Thomas Auld and his upper-class bride, Rowena Hamilton, the daughter of a rich slaveholder on the Eastern Shore. Fred's sister, Eliza, his Aunt

Priscilla and the crippled Henny also lived in the same house. There were no separate slave quarters; nor had there been at his "old master's" house. These were not mansions; they were ordinary farmhouses, and contact between the white Aulds and the black Baileys was face to face and constant. For Fred, therefore, the words "white family" signified not only a unilocal, but also a patrilocal residence. The whites lived in the master's part of the house, and the slaves in the kitchen and pantry area. Slaves attended the "white service." Contact was so close, in fact, that Douglass could describe the religious exercise in which Thomas Auld was converted, including Auld's experiences in converts' "pen," the expression on his face, and, even, his single tear.

In Thomas Auld, Fred Douglass had a master quite different from his brother, Hugh Auld. Thomas had a sadistic streak; he was not a farmer, he had never been a landholder or a slaveowner, and he was very sensitive about his social standing compared to the Lloyds and the Hamiltons. His newly inherited slaves recognized the signs of the "climber," and called him "Captain" instead of "Master." Infuriated, he starved them. Fred's hunger was so constant and so intense that he would visit friends on the Hamilton plantation, where food was plentiful, to get a meal. For this, Thomas Auld would whip him. These were Fred's first whippings—whippings he decided to endure in place of starvation.

Observing the crippled girl, Henny, in the hands of his new master, Fred could see what to expect. Her hands and arms had been so severely burned in childhood that she could not use them. Thomas Auld's torture of Henny and brutality toward Fred permanently changed Fred's character. The account of Henny's life, therefore, is significant.

> It was not merely the agency of Master Thomas in breaking up our Sabbath-school that shook my confidence in the power of that kind of southern religion to make men wiser or better, but I saw in him all the cruelty and meanness after his conversion which he had exhibited before that time. His cruelty and meanness were especially

displayed in his treatment of my unfortunate cousin Henny, whose lameness made her a burden to him. I have seen him tie up this lame and maimed woman and whip her in a manner most brutal and shocking, and then with blood-chilling blasphemy he would quote the passage of scripture, "That servant which knew his lord's will and prepared not himself, neither did according to his will, shall be beaten with many stripes." He would keep this lacerated woman tied up by her wrists to a bolt in the joist, three, four and five hours at a time. He would tie her up early in the morning, whip her with a cowskin before breakfast, leave her tied up, go to his store, and returning to dinner, repeat the castigation, laying the rugged lash on the flesh already raw by repeated blows. He seemed desirous to get the poor girl out of existence.

Thomas Auld taught Fred the meanest side of slavery. After his religious conversion, Auld and two neighbors burst into Fred's Sunday school for slave children, beat them, and threatened Fred with Nat Turner's fate. For nine months Thomas Auld tried to break Fred's spirit through starvation and beatings. Unable to accomplish this, he sent him to Edward Covey, a poor white farm renter, who, in return for the loan of a slave, guaranteed to break his spirit and make him subservient.

The first person whom Douglass hated, so far as we can tell from his autobiographies, was Thomas Auld. For his own father's "crimes" he blamed the system; the only cruelty with which he charged his father was that of whipping his paramour in a jealous rage. But Thomas Auld—with his "Christian hypocrisy, his stinginess, his cruelty, and most of all, his determination to break the spirit"—had taught him to hate. It was a will to survive that allowed Douglass to endure, even resist, Auld. Slaves often had their will to live worked or beaten out of them, and Douglass had known of many broken slaves. His own mother had been "sent to an early grave." But *he* wanted to live and be free. Since Thomas Auld could not be won over, or outwitted, it was either fight or die.

Auld was the first master who had hated him and wanted to break him. When Fred returned from Covey bloodied and beaten,

Thomas Auld refused to take him in and sent him back. Fred's hatred of Thomas Auld seemed to increase with the years. Even after he was free, Fred publicly charged Auld with turning his beloved grandmother out to starve, although she had devoted a lifetime of faithful service to the Anthony family. Auld denied this charge, claiming that it had been the white son of Fred's father who had inherited Douglass's grandmother and "turned her out" to die. Evidently this was true, but Douglass was to include the same long philippic in his third autobiography, *Life and Times,* published twenty-six years after he first leveled the accusation. Not until Thomas Auld was on his deathbed and had sent for Douglass in an attempt to justify himself did Douglass relent.

The sadistic beatings administered by Auld and Covey changed Douglass from the attractive and winning boy his two mistresses had loved, into a resentful, distrustful hater of the slave system and of the whites who had enslaved him. For the next seven years and perhaps longer, he trusted no whites. Even many years later —through the Western extension of slavery, the Supreme Court's Dred Scott decision, the violent mobs—the old hatred would flare up. It finally came to a climax during his close friendship with that most defiant of men, John Brown. In that relationship Douglass was forced to make a decision either to live—or to die in suicidal defiance.

At Tuckahoe, Fred was a city boy on the farm, required to drive oxen, haul logs, and attempt a score of other heavy jobs about which he knew nothing. At first, he did not realize Covey would try to whip him to death if he broke a wagon, or stopped to rest. But he soon found Covey intended to break him under the whip. On the third day, Covey whipped Fred for no reason at all; his blood flowed as the heavy cowhide cut into his flesh, making scars he would bear for the rest of his life. The rough shirt of raw flax kept the wounds open.

Covey purposely ordered him to drive a pair of unbroken oxen to haul lumber, knowing that it was impossible to handle the beasts.

When they ran away and tore down the gate, Covey whipped him again in the fresh wounds. Douglass wrote, ". . . though very severe, it [the whipping] was less so than many which came after it."

Covey demanded more than any man could accomplish, trying deliberately to drive Fred beyond his endurance. During the summer, he worked Fred from dawn to midnight. When he fell exhausted to the ground, Covey whipped him.

> I was somewhat unmanageable at the first, but a few months of this discipline tamed me—in body, soul, and spirit. My natural elasticity was crushed; my intellect languished; the disposition to read departed, the cheerful spark that lingered about my eye died out; the dark night of slavery closed in upon me, and behold a man transformed to a brute!

After six months, on a very hot August day, while feeding wheat to a threshing fan, Fred became ill and fell unconscious. Covey kicked him; Fred tried to get up but was too dizzy to rise. Covey kicked him again. "I again tried and succeeded in standing up, but upon stooping to get the tub with which I was feeding the fan, I again staggered and fell." Covey grabbed a heavy hickory slab and struck "a heavy blow on my head which made a large gash and caused the blood to run freely. . . . This done he ordered me again to rise; but I made no effort to do so, for I had made up my mind it was useless. . . . He could but kill me, and that might put me out of my misery."

This willingness to submit, and seek relief in death, was the lowest point in his life, for his desire for self-preservation, the very core of the human ego, was vanishing. It turned out, however, that his image of himself as a leader was shared by his fellow slaves. While lying in the woods, hiding from Covey, he was rescued by Sandy, a slave hired out to a man named Kemp, Covey's son-in-law. Sandy, who was married to a free Negro woman, took Fred to her home. There he had his first food and sleep in two days. Sandy himself was risking thirty-nine lashes, the penalty for sheltering a runaway slave. He and his wife assiduously cared for Fred, who decided that "although I was beaten by Covey and my master [who had turned him away when Fred fled to him after Covey's floggings], I was loved by the colored people, because they thought I was hated for my knowledge and persecuted because I was feared. I was the only slave in that region who could read or write." No doubt the other slaves were correct; a reading-writing-and-planning slave was a bad slave, and evidently there was something about Douglass, even at this most desperate time in his life, that inspired other blacks to regard him as their leader—just as he had been a few months before in organizing the Sunday school which Thomas Auld demolished.

Sandy had an old head—"a man as famous among the slaves of the neighborhood for his own good nature as for his good sense"— and advised Fred the next morning to "go home with all speed, and to walk up bravely to the house, as though nothing had happened."

Here one is compelled to ponder Douglass's use of the word "home." He had used the word before in promising his master that he would return "home" to Covey. One realizes the desolation he must have felt if his "home" was that of Covey: a home that had been as much a hellhole for Covey's wife and her sister as it had been for Fred. After eight years with Sophie Auld and her son, he had no one to turn to, and no place to go except Covey's, where he would be brutalized. This feeling is despair; literally meaning without hope. In such a situation, defiance certainly is preferable to losing one's will to live. "I had brought my mind to a firm resolve during that Sunday's reflection to obey every order, however unreasonable, if it were possible, and if Mr. Covey should then undertake to beat me *to defend and protect myself to the best of my ability*."

He returned to Covey on Sunday, and on the next day, while he was in the stable feeding the horses, Covey attacked him from the rear, in an attempt to force a slip knot around his legs to string him up for a lashing. "I remembered my pledge to stand up in my own defense." The battle lasted two hours. Fred stood and held him off.

> Whence came the daring spirit necessary to grapple with a man, who eight-and-forty hours before, could with his slightest word have made me tremble like a leaf in a storm, I do not know; at any rate, I was resolved to fight, and what was better still, I actually was hard at it. *The fighting madness had come upon me,* and I found my strong fingers firmly attached to the throat of the tyrant, as heedless of consequences, at the moment, as if we stood as equals before the law. The very color of the man was forgotten. [Emphasis added.]

Also forgotten was his religion, which, according to Douglass, forbade slaves to resist their masters and made nearly all slaves subservient. His defiance was suicidal, but at that moment he preferred death to subservience. His hatred of the oppressor was so strong that it overcame all caution, and in the deepest sense, all desire for self-preservation. He felt only *hatred and the desire to die with his persecutor*.

In the heat of the struggle, Covey yelled for his cousin, Hughes. Fred drove Hughes off. Covey then called two slaves, but they refused to help. In the end, Covey, on his back in the manure where Fred had thrown him, was willing to call off the fight, saying, "Now you scoundrel, to your work. I would not have whipped you half so hard if you had not resisted." "The fact was he had not whipped me at all," Douglass commented. During the final six months of Fred's work, Covey did not try to beat him again. Douglass later wrote:

> This battle was the turning point in my life as a slave! It rekindled in my breast the smouldering embers of liberty. It brought up my Baltimore dreams and revived a sense of my own manhood. *I was a changed man after that fight. I was nothing before—I was a man now.* It recalled to life my crushed self-respect, and my self-confidence, and inspired me with a renewed determination to be a free man. A man without force is without the essential dignity of humanity. Hu-

man nature is so constituted, that it cannot honor a helpless man, though it can pity him, and even this it cannot do long if signs of power do not arise. [Emphasis added.]

Douglass continued to champion physical resistance and outright defiance until slavery was crushed.

Douglass felt that his victory over Covey was just the beginning of his independence. He still was dependent upon Covey and his master for food, shelter, clothes, and even for the permission to live. It would take another ten or eleven years to achieve the kind of independence that is inherent in a self-directed life. In our society, this self-direction is the most highly regarded form of social aggression.

But Douglass's successful stand against Covey was his first expression of a lifelong fierce belief in physical resistance as a last resource. At the end of his account of that fight, he quotes with admiration: "Hereditary bondsmen, know ye not, who would be free themselves must strike the blow?"

In facing the slave breaker at seventeen, Douglass learned *very early* in his life that no one could walk over him *unless he bent his own back;* that there really were no giants except in his childish imagination. This healthy ability to stand up for himself became one of the two traits which insured his survival and his later success.

The other valuable skill he then began to learn was negotiation—first with his owners and later with other powerful whites. As a boy and adolescent, he was a great charmer, a facet of his personality acknowledged in his autobiographies, but completely overlooked by his biographers. In childhood, he was anxious to please and sought to charm both his father-master, Anthony, and his first two mistresses. He actually got along well with his father, who often beat Hester and the others, but never Fred. He was never beaten by his mistresses, nor by Hugh Auld, his master in Baltimore. Fred used his intelligence, his attractive appearance, and his desire to please in order to win over his father and Lucretia (even serenading her!), as well as to ease the danger of a slave's life. Even in adolescence, when he—like any adolescent—became more defiant, Fred argued rationally with Hugh Auld for the privilege of hiring himself out as a skilled worker. He finally gained his point by patient, shrewd negotiation. Thus in his earliest years, a foundation was laid for the successful relationships he later enjoyed with Northern whites and the British.

He completed the assigned year (1834) without further attacks by Covey, Thomas Auld hired him out for the next two years to a landlord named Freeland, who proved to be a "good master" and fed him well. Douglass always gave Freeland a hard day's work. Before long he became proud of his ability to "do as much hard work as some of the older men." In fact, he came to prefer the severe labor in the field to the enervating duties of a house servant.

As a worker who pulled his share of the load, and as a civic leader, Fred earned the respect of the other slaves. Freeland did not interfere with his efforts to start a Sunday school, whose actual purpose was to teach slaves to read. Evenings and Sundays the students gathered at the home of a free Negro, and Douglass succeeded in proselyting forty students, many of whom learned to read.

With this achievement he convinced the slaves that despite their bondage their minds were potentially as able as their masters'. "I hated slavery, slaveholders, and all pertaining to them and I did not fail to inspire others with the same feeling wherever and whenever opportunity was presented." His image of himself as leader and as a future hero of his people was not simply an idle dream. From the age of twelve, when he had read in the *Columbian Orator* the speeches of Pitt, Fox, Sheridan, and others—and at fifteen, when he started his first Sunday school on Thomas Auld's farm—he took the role of leader with the admiring slaves. He, in turn, was impressed by them; "everyone of them [was] manly, generous and brave. . . . It is seldom the lot of anyone to have truer and better friends than were the slaves on this [Freeland's] farm." Here was a new kind of potential leader: one who admired his followers, and identified with their manliness. *It was this capacity for empathy that would eventually invest him with a broad compassion for all oppressed and downtrodden peoples.*

At the start of a second year under Freeland in 1836, Douglass made his first attempt to escape. He was then eighteen. Seeing no hope of returning to Sophia and Hugh Auld in Baltimore, fearing the ever-present possibility of being sold to the lower South, and driven by the vision of himself as a future hero, he decided to try for freedom. The geographical site was most unfavorable for an escape, since Tuckahoe and Easton were located on a peninsula between Chesapeake Bay and a small river. The only escape route lay north, and ran through the town of Easton.

Douglass wrote that he was impelled to escape by the memory of Father Lawson's "solemn words of what I might become in the providence of God"—a prophecy made six or seven years before. "I was verging upon manhood and the prophesies of my childhood were still unfulfilled." There can be no doubt he took seriously this "divine" prophecy made by a man who prayed constantly and saw visions.

He shared his plan with the two Harris brothers, with Sandy, who had protected and fed him after Covey's effort to kill him, and with two other slaves. Douglass wrote a pass for each person in this group, granting them permission to go to Baltimore for Easter. He then signed it with the initials, not of Freeland, but of the powerful landlord Hamilton. The day before they were to run away, Douglass realized he had been betrayed by the prudent Sandy. Later Douglass realized that Sandy may have saved their lives, for, had they tried to escape, they certainly would have been shot—as other slaves had been—or sold south.

Except for Sandy, who had not been arrested by the sheriff, all were tied to horses and dragged over the dusty road to Easton. Along the road, whites jeered at them; some tried to incite the mob to hang or, better, burn them at the stake. (One hundred years later, just prior to the Second World War, such lynchings of Negroes still took place on the Eastern Shore.) Once in Easton, all five slaves were thrown in jail, where they were physically examined by slave traders, who tormented them, saying that their masters intended to sell them off to the lower South. In a few days, all except Douglass were taken home by their masters in time for Easter. Only Douglass remained in prison for another week, expecting to be sold south by Thomas Auld.

Auld, however, had become deeply religious during the two years following his conversion. His new ethics prevented him from sleeping until he had freed Douglass from jail. Auld still feared that if he did not send him away from that area the powerful Hamilton, his father-in-law, would shoot Fred, as he had threatened. Hamilton had said that Douglass would never stop "tampering with" his slaves and "stirring up trouble." Thomas Auld, having made peace with his brother since his own conversion, decided to send Fred back to Hugh and Sophia. He now wanted Fred to learn a trade, and had promised to emancipate him at twenty-five.

Douglass, who had found Thomas Auld as cruel as Covey, was amazed by Auld's desire to save him from Hamilton and other hostile slaveholders. He commented with some chagrin that Thomas Auld had "acted on the whole very generously, considering the nature of my offense."

Upon Fred's return to Baltimore in 1836 at the age of eighteen, after three years spent on the slave farms, he was hired out by Hugh Auld to work in William Gardener's large shipyard on Fell's Point. The shipyards attracted the roughest white carpenters, caulkers, and their apprentices, who used Fred hard, and prevented his learning the trade that Hugh Auld had intended him to acquire. For the first, but not the last, time Douglass met the fierce hatred of working-class whites, who resented slaves because they often were rivals for the same skilled and semiskilled jobs. Soon a group of white apprentices encouraged by white mechanics tried to beat Fred to death. He defended himself, but was one against many. "I came out of it shockingly mangled. I was cut and bruised in sundry places, and my left eye was nearly knocked out of its socket." Hugh Auld complained to the owner, tried to protect Fred, and sought to have the white attackers arrested. But no white man could be prosecuted on a charge by a Negro, and no white witnesses would admit that Fred had been attacked.

In his battered condition, Douglass again found his white family considerate and helpful. Now a man of eighteen, living with Hugh and Sophia, he still was treated as a son.

> Master Hugh . . . was a rough but manly hearted fellow, and at this time his best nature showed itself. The heart of my once kind mistress Sophia was again melted in pity towards me. My puffed-out eye and my scarred and blood-covered face moved the dear lady to tears. She kindly drew a chair by me, and with friendly and consoling words, she took water and washed the blood from my face. . . . No mother's hand could have been more tender than hers. She bound up my head and covered my wounded eye with a lean piece of fresh beef. It was almost compensation for all I suffered, that it occasioned the manifestation once more of the originally characteristic kindness of my mistress. Her affectionate heart was not yet dead, though much hardened by time and circumstances.

Hugh Auld then took Douglass into the shipyard he had formerly owned, but where Auld now had been reduced to foreman. Here Fred soon became an expert caulker, "and in the course of a single year was able to command the highest wages paid to journeymen caulkers in Baltimore." He learned he could work as a caulker alongside white mechanics, provided he had a powerful white protector, the foreman. Earning $1.50 per day, he brought Auld $9.00 each week.

Douglass mentions casually, in just one sentence, that he soon found his own employers, made his own contracts, and collected his own earnings. Each change in his status, however, involved long and careful bargaining with his master. This skill in negotiation had been learned during the two and a half years following his fight with Covey, and was a great personal achievement for an adolescent who just a short time before had proved irreconcilably defiant.

Douglass first asked his owner, Thomas Auld, for the opportunity to select his own job and employers. He was refused. He then asked permission of Hugh Auld, without informing him of Thomas's refusal. Hugh agreed. Douglass had learned to keep trying until his point was won; he had adopted the behavior older Negroes had in mind when they advised, "Don't get mad, get smart." To some degree, it is the age-old recourse of the underdog.

He joined an "improvement society" of free Negro mechanics—a typical middle-class undertaking. It was his first learning experience with free Negroes who subscribed to middle-class goals. Later, in New Bedford, he would find a much stronger and more independent Negro group, which stimulated him to learn the culture and the economic goals of black Yankees.

His contacts with free Negroes in the East Baltimore Improvement Society led to his courtship of Anna Murray, a free black maid. Anna was illiterate, but exceptionally provident; she had saved her wages and acquired decent middle-class furniture, dishes, and clothing. A maid to a prosperous French family, she had learned manners and language. She fell in love with Fred, as many women had, and Douglass loved her. He now had the strongest possible motive for escape: to enable him to marry the woman he loved as a free man, not as chattel. Anna had saved enough money to finance his escape, and urged him to use her nine years' savings for that purpose.

One Saturday evening during the summer of 1838, when Douglass was a man of twenty, he went to a religious camp meeting without first going to Hugh Auld to give him his share of the weekly wages and to ask his permission. Auld became enraged and refused to permit him to arrange his own employment any longer. By now an alcoholic, Auld threatened to whip Douglass for the first time, and they were at the point of blows. Fred finally decided to attempt escape—his first effort since the attempt from Tuckahoe two and a half years before.

The notion that Douglass was impelled to escape by a fierce desire for freedom at all costs—a notion he and some of his biographers advance—simply does not agree with the facts. He was strongly attached to his foster mother, Sophia Auld, as well as to her son, Tommy. He felt at home. Only after the death of Lucretia, and after, as he thought, he had been sent away from Sophia forever, did he make his first attempt to escape. After that attempt failed, he did not try again for two and a half years, despite the fact that he had the free run of Baltimore. Again, the chief reason was that he had a good home with his adoptive mother. Life with Sophia's family, in which he had lived for nearly ten years—from seven to fifteen, and eighteen to twenty—proved far more attractive than the grim possibility of encountering slave hunters and bloodhounds, or of being sold south if he failed.

After his break with Hugh Auld, however, he used the identification papers of a black sailor, and escaped by rail and boat to New York City. There, after days of hiding from slave hunters and Negro informers, he was befriended by a second black sailor, who took him home and introduced him to the free Negro David Ruggles. Ruggles, a remarkably able man, was secretary of the New York Vigilance Committee, and officer of the Underground Railroad. He had made way for more than 600 slaves through New York to freedom in Canada.

David Ruggles hid Douglass until Anna Murray arrived from Baltimore. She and Fred were married by the Reverend J. W. C. Pennington, a slave who had become a Presbyterian minister. Ruggles advised the newlyweds to go to New Bedford, Massachusetts, a large port where Fred might be able to secure work as a caulker. The couple took a steamer to Newport and a stagecoach from there to New Bedford. There, they were hospitably received by a prosperous free Negro, Nathan Johnson, who took them into his home. "Thus, in a fortnight after my flight from Maryland, I was safe in New Bedford—a citizen of the grand old commonwealth of Massachusetts."

He was not, however, a legal citizen, because he was still owned by Thomas Auld, and could be apprehended at any time. Moreover, he was not allowed to work as a caulker. The North, in this sense, proved worse than Baltimore. Douglass had to resign himself to unskilled work for the next three years: sawing lumber, shoveling coal, digging ditches, moving trash, stevedoring, and scrubbing down vessels.

A Quaker whom he had met on the stagecoach from Newport gave him a regular job lifting heavy casks of oil in his oil refinery. Subsequently, he worked as a laborer on two ships, and at the bellows in a foundry. Despite intense heat, he would nail abolitionist newspapers to a post near the bellows and read while pumping the bellows. As on the plantation, he liked and admired his fellow workers and praised their intelligence, sobriety, and "upright" spirit. They were typical black Yankees. In order to conceal his identity from slave hunters who might stalk the shipyards, the Johnsons persuaded him to change his surname from Bailey to Douglass.

Douglass refused to accept the civic segregation which was the rule in New Bedford. He criticized the New Bedford Lyceum for barring Negroes; he left the white Methodist church because it segregated blacks. He eventually found that all other white churches did the same. Disillusioned with white Christianity, he joined the black Zion Methodist church.

Remarkably enough, learning from the black Yankees in abolitionist meetings and fortnightly discussion groups, he was able to alter his speech and his other basic culture. He knew that a skill in standard English—whether it be the Southern or Northern version—was essential to a man who aspired to public recognition and leadership. Douglass already had the advantage of having learned the speech of Sophia and her little son, Tommy. Before that, he had played with Colonel Edward Lloyd's son, and learned the speech of the Maryland upper class. But his main instructors had been Lucretia and Sophia. We know that in any given social class, women are better-spoken than males. The speech of Southern males like those in Tuckahoe was crude and would have been virtually incomprehensible to Yankees. But thanks to Sophia, Tommy, the blacks of New Bedford, and his own quick mind and great desire, Douglass was able to *lecture* successfully in Massachusetts, New York, and Ohio just four years after having escaped slavery. Three years later he enjoyed tremendous success as an orator in England.

Similarly, he learned with incredible rapidity the New England way of life. He and Anna saved their money, kept a typical Yankee home, and worked constantly. Douglass neither drank, nor smoked, nor wasted. Yet he was not an ascetic; unlike Garrison and most of the white abolitionists, he enjoyed the basic pleasures of life, and had great vitality. The photographs of the mature Garrison show a grim face, like that of Savanarola. Photographs of the mature Douglass show a vigorous, confident man, whom admirers dubbed "the lion."

In September of 1838, four months after his arrival in New Bedford, he began to read Garrison's newspaper, the *Liberator*. "My soul was set on fire. Its sympathy for my brethren in bonds—its scathing denunciation of slave holders sent a thrill of joy through my soul, such as I had never felt before!" It was as if his fantasies had come true: here he had a father figure with sympathy for his cause, and who himself was the embodiment of defiant hostility. That first year he started attending the abolitionist meetings of Negroes in the city, and the *Liberator* of March 29, 1839, reports that he spoke at one of those meetings in support of a resolution that condemned slavery and denounced the reactionary African colonization movement. The resolution insisted that Negroes were *"American citizens;* born with natural, inherent and just rights." With such speeches, Douglass gradually took the lead in the Negro abolitionist group. Two years later he heard Garrison speak at a local meeting of a branch of the Massachusetts Anti-Slavery Society. He wrote that Garrison had inspired him. (Near the end of his life, long after his final break with Garrison, he wrote that "no face and form ever impressed me with such sentiments as did those of William Lloyd Garrison." The attraction was mutual.) Douglass spoke at this same meeting, and Garrison wrote in his paper that he had been much impressed by "a slave whose addresses were listened to by large attentive audiences with deep interest."

Douglass felt he had found his personal champion: the first white man to express the anger and hurt Douglass himself felt in the institution of slavery. He took off from work for the first day in three years to accompany Garrison and his group on a boat trip to Nantucket. He was exhilarated when the abolitionists convened a protest meeting on the top deck of the ship after the ship's captain had insisted Negro passengers be segregated. (Douglass saw once more that in segregation the North was as unjust as the South.)

The next day Douglass was asked by William C. Coffin of the Anti-Slavery Society to speak. Douglass spoke of his life as a slave, and so stirred Garrison that he began his own speech by shouting, "Have we been listening to a thing, a piece of property, or to a man?" "A man! A man!" came from 500 voices.

> Then he asked if they would ever allow Douglass to be carried back to slavery, and he received a thunderous "No!" in reply. "Will you succor and protect him as a brother man—a resident of the old Bay State?" was the next question. "Yes!" shouted the audience with such vehemence that the walls and roof of the Athenaeum seemed to shudder.

Douglass was asked to speak again that evening, and the *Anti-Slavery Standard* reported the reaction as follows:

> One recently from the house of bondage spoke with great power. Flinty hearts were pierced, and cold ones melted by his eloquence. Our best pleaders for the slave held their breath for fear of interrupting him. Mr. Garrison said his speech would have done honor to Patrick Henry. It seemed almost miraculous how he had been prepared to tell his story with so much power. In the evening, which was to be the last meeting, he was again called forward, and listened to by a multitude with mingled emotions of admiration, pity and honor. . . .
>
> Then Garrison arose, and burst forth into a more eloquent strain

than I had ever heard before. He eulogized, as he deserved, the fugitive who had just spoken and anathematized the system that could crush to the earth such men.

Fred's boyhood dream had come true. After twenty years of slavery and three years of sawing lumber, digging ditches, and working at a bellows, he had emerged through his own initiative as a hero to both blacks and whites. The "vision" which Father Lawson had revealed to him, his private fantasies of overcoming his father, and his adolescent efforts to organize slave dissension in Sunday schools had brought him at twenty-three to a point of national prominence.

After Nantucket, John A. Collins, general agent of the Massachusetts Anti-Slavery Society, immediately offered him a position as lecturer and agent for the Society with a salary of $450 a year. Douglass doubted he could leap from unskilled work to lecturing so quickly. He agreed to attempt the job for only three months. But with his amazing skill in oratory, his fears were proved groundless. Lecturing alongside Collins, Garrison, and other agents, he achieved immediate success.

Collins had persuaded Garrison to employ Douglass as lecturer and agent because a black man, especially a slave, could be far more effective in denouncing slavery, he said, than a white man. But the abolitionists felt there should be limitations placed upon the slave's role. They wanted Douglass to tell a "straight unvarnished tale" of his personal experiences in slavery, and to leave the discussion of moral, religious, economic, and political issues to them. Nevertheless, within two months Douglass began to attack the very foundations of slavery. He made the most of his oratorical gifts in humorous dramatizations of hypocritical Southern ministers and of his own master, Thomas Auld, who would weep with religious ardor in church but had broken up Fred's Sunday school. He also employed his analytical powers to attack the fallacies in the apologists' defense of slavery. Although Garrison and his colleagues continued to insist that he stick to his experiences as a slave, Douglass refused to yield.

It is difficult today to appreciate the influence of the Southern slave kingdom in 1841. In the South, promoters of slavery held absolute power. Northern mills needed Southern cotton, and the North and Midwest sold mules and supplies to the South's plantations. The abolitionists had no political or economic power in 1841; indeed, they were totally rejected by the vast majority of Northerners.

The absolute ownership of a slave by a slaveholder had been defined arrogantly by the Supreme Court of South Carolina in 1829. The statement outlined a power which would only increase with the advent of the cotton gin.

> The end [of slavery] is the profit of the master, his security, and the public safety. The subject [slave] is one doomed in his own person and his posterity to live without knowledge and without the capacity to make anything his own, and to toil that another may reap the fruits. . . . The power of the master must be absolute to render the submission of the slave perfect. In the actual condition of things it must be so. There is no remedy. This discipline belongs to the state of slavery . . . .

Douglass was well acquainted with this arrogance and did not underestimate the South's capacity to destroy anything which got in its way. He never believed, as did the Eastern abolitionists, that the Southern overlords would yield to moral persuasion.

After his three-month trial period with the Anti-Slavery Society, Douglass was established. Editors continued to praise "his language and manner" and "the grammatical accuracy of his speech," as well as his tremendous power to move an audience both to tears, as well as to laughter at the hypocrisy of masters and preachers. He spoke, the *Boston Courier* reported on May 26, 1842, in a way which highly educated men might well wish to emulate. The writer, who understood Douglass's more profound feelings, wrote

> It was sterner, darker, deeper than [oratory or eloquence]. It was the volcanic outbreak of human nature, long pent up in slavery and at last bursting its imprisonment. *It was the storm of insurrection and I could not but think, as he stalked to and fro on the platform, roused up like a Numidian lion, how that terrible voice of his would ring through the pine glades of the South, in the day of the visitation, calling the insurgents to battle, and striking terror to the hearts of the dismayed and despairing masters.* He reminded me of Toussaint among the plantations of Haiti. . . . He was not [there] as a speaker, performing. He was an insurgent slave, taking hold on the right of speech . . . . One of our editors ventured to cross his path by a rash remark. Better to have run upon a lion. It was fearful, but magnificent to see how magnanimously and lionlike the royal fellow tore him to pieces. . . . [Emphasis added.]

This comment not only helps us understand the "lion" in Douglass, but also strikes close to the heart of his conflict. *The old defiance, arising from a blazing anger at injustice and hypocrisy, still was with him.* It caused him to suffer many beatings in the North, where he was labeled a "bad nigger," just as he had been in the South. It led him to embrace John Brown's idea of violence. The same suicidal defiance which had lashed out against Covey still lashed out at the slave power.

The basis of his anger was hatred. Hatred is the desire to kill or destroy; *the healing of hatred is the process of changing the wish to kill into a desire and an effort to tolerate, to accept, and finally to forgive.* In the life of Douglass, the healing process was initiated by his admiration of Garrison.

When, in 1841, he had sat in the back of a dilapidated hall in New Bedford and listened to Garrison denounce slavery, Douglass had felt, "you are the man—the Moses raised up by God to deliver His modern Israel from bondage." That was "the spontaneous feeling of my heart." As his champion and father figure, Garrison *justified* Fred's hurt and anger against his own father. He once had made Sophia his second mother; he now made Garrison his second father. Beneath the anger he held for his father there always had lingered a far more powerful desire to be accepted and loved by him. Garrison filled this need for approval and praise. The immediate result was a *somewhat irrational overestimation of Garrison*. Years later, when he knew Garrison to be a vain man—an exaggerator, as well as a sponger—he continued to retain the image of Garrison as he first had perceived him. Forty years later, long after Garrison had libeled him and broken off their relationship, Douglass still expressed great admiration for Garrison's work to end slavery.

Garrison, according to his most knowledgeable biographer, John Thomas, was prey to self-deception, suspicion, and uncontrollable jealousy. Born in 1805 in Newburyport, Massachusetts—the site Lloyd Warner chose for his classical study of the Yankee class system—Garrison had been far more deprived as a boy than Douglass. He often had neither home nor food. His father, a Canadian immigrant, was an alcoholic who deserted his wife and two sons, and left them penniless. The boy William had little or no formal education. Living in the working-class area of Newburyport, he aspired to be noticed, and he both envied and admired the prosperous shipowners on Elm Street, whom his mother continually disparaged as godless and snobbish. He was most unhappy with his mother's choices of a career for him; she had first apprenticed him to a shoemaker in Newburyport, and later to another in Baltimore, where she had gone to search for work. Desperate to find him a home, his mother then apprenticed him at the age of thirteen to a cabinet-maker in Haverhill, Massachusetts, but he quickly ran away. His mother finally made the correct choice: she indentured him to a reputable newspaper publisher in Newburyport. In the service of this man, Ephraim Allen, proprietor of the local *Herald,* Garrison worked at printing from the age of fourteen until he was twenty-three.

With a part-time pilot and alcoholic for a father, an embittered religious fanatic for a mother, and an alcoholic brother, Garrison's early life certainly was far more damaging than Douglass's. From childhood, he bore the traits that would shape his personality and career. Like his father, he was irresponsible; he deceived and disappointed several newspaper owners and editors who had trusted him. In one case, after he had agreed to write in support of a political candidate, he took advantage of the space to attack liquor. None of the papers which he edited was successful, and he drifted from one cause to another as employment dictated.

Denied an education and a chance to enter a profession, Garrison identified with popular speakers and leaders such as Daniel Webster, Harrison Otis, and Lyman Beecher. These were spellbinders who inspired awe in Garrison "by the sheer force of their personalities"; but as biographer John Thomas points out, "ironically all three would soon disillusion him by disclosing lack [of the very] moral fiber he credited them with"—a fiber which Garrison himself lacked.

Garrison early showed an inability to keep friends, even friends who sponsored him and gave him money. He fought with and betrayed them all, just as he would eventually betray Douglass. He borrowed money continually, but never repaid from his own pocket. The $600 for his trip to England in 1846 was raised by free Negroes; when stranded in England because the English abolitionists would not help him—just as American whites had refused to—Garrison begged the $200 for his return passage from a Negro minister in London, Dr. Nathaniel Paul.

His moral self-righteousness was insufferable to many. He wrote to an Englishwoman that he had never known fear. "I cannot know fear. I feel that it is impossible for danger to awe me. I tremble at nothing but my own delinquencies as one *who is bound to be perfect even as my heavenly Father is perfect.*" [Emphasis added.] This monomaniacal declaration reveals a penchant for paranoidal exaggeration and a fantasy of godlike perfection that was probably learned from his fanatically religious mother.

In 1831, when he was twenty-six, Garrison found his life's mission—a cause to which he could commit himself. It allowed him to express hostility toward authority ("bad-father") figures, and tilt against the powerful political and religious forces in both the North and South. While in New England, blundering from one newspaper and one cause to another (moribund Federalism, temperance, women's rights), he met Benjamin Lundy of Ohio, who taught him about the conditions of slaves, and asked his cooperation in publishing his occasional paper, the *Genius of Universal Emancipation*. Having nothing else to do, Garrison joined Lundy in Baltimore. He soon discovered that Lundy was working for a movement to colonize slaves as freemen in Haiti or Africa. Garrison supported emancipation in the United States and opposed colonization as being an effort to dispose of the most intelligent, most literate, and most "troublesome" slaves—as indeed it was.

Garrison soon got Lundy and his paper in trouble by writing an attack upon a Newburyport shipowner, one of whose vessels was carrying slaves from Baltimore to New Orleans. Garrison's old hostility toward the wealthy Elm Street groups in his hometown, and all his mother's anathematization of them as infidels and slave traders, swept back over him, and he went far beyond reporting the facts. Garrison accused the shipowner of being a depraved trader in human flesh, and claimed falsely that many slaves had died on his vessel. He was promptly sued for libel, convicted, and, when unable or unwilling to pay a fifty-dollar fine, served seven weeks in a Baltimore jail. His fine was paid by Arthur Tappan, a New York philanthropist, who would later be a positive influence on Garrison. Also in Baltimore at the time was Douglass, an adolescent of thirteen, about to be sent away to work on Thomas Auld's plantation.

In that same year, 1831, Garrison began publishing the *Liberator*. He worked sixteen hours a day and lived in the same small attic room where he printed the paper. The sheer physical work left Garrison little time to write, but he talked as he worked, and managed to gather a coterie of enthusiastic adherents. Strengthened by their admiration and encouragement, he found his identity as an abolitionist leader. With the publication of the *Liberator,* Garrison entered a period of rapid intellectual and moral growth. In his previous newspaper work, he had been paid to please his employers, but had defiantly deceived them. Now he worked sixteen hours a day or longer to please himself. Without funds to publish, and unable to attract white subscribers, he turned to poor blacks, who became his champions. Only fifty whites subscribed to the paper the first year, and only 400 in four years. The *Liberator,* Garrison said, did not belong to whites; "they do not sustain it—but emphatically the people of color—it is their organ."

Although white philanthropists and New England whites in general ignored the *Liberator,* its editorials were reprinted in the leading Northern and Southern white papers, and thereby gained in circulation and influence. Garrison and the American Anti-Slavery Society thus gained visibility before the larger American public in spite of the tiny circulation of their newspaper. So deeply was the *Liberator* feared in the South that it was charged with having caused Nat Turner's rebellion, although the *Liberator* actually bitterly opposed the use of any kind of force.

By the time Douglass escaped from slavery in 1838, the *Liberator* had become the center of a national legal controversy over the freedom of the press. Efforts to suppress it had continued since its inception. One such effort was made by a U.S. senator from South Carolina—always the most reactionary, anti-Negro state with the possible exception of Mississippi. The senator asked Harrison Gray Otis, the Mayor of Boston, to stop the publication of the *Liberator*. Otis, missing the point, answered with an *argumentum ad hominem* against Garrison, whom he found, after investigation, to be "a disgruntled, Ne'er-do-well [whose] paper [was] read almost only by Free Negroes."

But Garrison led this pivotal civil-rights battle for the constitutional freedom of the press to a successful conclusion. In the process, he finally won the attention and cooperation of powerful wealthy Northern businessmen, who, although they benefited from slavery and were not opposed to its perpetuation, *were ready to defend the Yankee freedoms of speech and the press, because they held that the right to dissent was the very foundation on which the nation had been built.*

Garrison's astonishing capacity for growth shown in this battle for freedom of the press—a cause for which he fought cleverly and relentlessly through the thirties and forties—proves that he had far greater strength and strategic skill than his biographer, Thomas, is willing to acknowledge.

By 1841, when Collins persuaded Garrison to add a black man to their group of speakers, however, the *Liberator* had fallen upon very difficult times, and sorely needed recruits. Two equal factions had arisen within the American Anti-Slavery Society. The one led by Garrison opposed any force except moral suasion, rejected the Constitution as favoring slavery, and was in favor of "Disunion." The other faction, led by the wealthy Tappan brothers, one of whom had paid Garrison's fine when he had been convicted of libel in Baltimore, supported the organized church, the Constitution, and "Union." In the end, the issue on which the factions split was the acceptance of women as members, and, especially, as officers. It seems inconceivable that a Society for which women raised most of the money should have excluded women; but, at that time, the subordination of women was the most powerful form of oppression in the land, except that of Negroes.

Two years after Douglass reached New Bedford, in 1840, this issue underwent a trial vote in New York City. Garrison won by a vote of 557 to 451. Neverthless, Lewis Tappan proceeded to call a meeting of the dissenters that included all the ministers present. They immediately formed the American and Foreign Anti-Slavery Society, which supported the existing government, prayers, and political action, and declared that the *admission of women* was "repugnant to the constitution of the Society," and "contrary to the usages of the civilized world." So much for the distortion of the word "civilized" and the nineteenth-century upper-class Yankee view of women. Although this new society was never successful in antislavery work, it took away most of Garrison's prosperous donors. His own society's income dropped from $47,000 annually to $7,000, and never rose above $12,000 during the next ten years.

It was at this time that John A. Collins urged Garrison to take on a Negro speaker, arguing that such a man would be a more persuasive pleader in the cause of the slave. When Douglass appeared at the New Bedford meeting in 1841 claiming to be a fugitive slave and speaking like a "Numidian lion," they at once saw in him the remedy for their badly depleted treasury.

Since Douglass perceived in Garrison the personification of his fantasy of a "good father," he initially overidentified with him. In fact, his association with Garrison began to change his orientation to whites in general. The intimacy of his experiences on the lecture circuit—traveling, living, eating, and sleeping in the same room with four or five white agents—was most effective in abating his fear and hatred of white men. On the road, Douglass encountered white train conductors and passengers who would try to expel him forcibly, captains of lake vessels who denied him passage or meals, and white mobs that broke up their meetings. When Garrison's agents defended him, he was forced to reassess the white stereotype he had based on men like Thomas Auld, Covey, and Hamilton. But Douglass's basic predisposition toward whites actually had been formed in his years with Sophia and her son, Tommy, and before that with Lucretia. The catharsis of his hatred of whites, then, might have been facilitated by an admiration for and identification with Garrison, but the basic desire for good relationships with whites had been established in his early years with his white family.

Even so, this redirection of his ancient anger against white males (his masters) *into constructively aggressive and self-enhancing behavior* ("initiative") *was continually impeded by the white disdain he encountered outside the tiny groups of abolitionists.* And the process of redirecting his anger was not a rapid one. Douglass had been known to fight so hard with his fists to keep from being segregated by the

Eastern Railroad that the superintendent of the railroad ordered trains not to stop at the station where he usually boarded.

On his Western tour with Garrison and others, particularly in Ohio and Indiana, the attacks by mobs were violent and well organized. In Pendleton, Indiana, a mob from Andersonville attacked the white agents as well as Douglass. Hoodlums tore down the speaker's platform, and knocked Garrison to the ground, severely injuring his scalp. Douglass stubbornly tried to fight his way out. He was beaten unconscious and left for dead, his right hand broken. Since the broken bones were not set, his right hand remained crooked the rest of his life. A white woman—again—nursed him in her home. In this case, the nurse was a member of the Society of Friends, which, according to Douglass, was the most unselfish and honest of all abolitionist groups.

At some point during Douglass's many efforts to resist violence, it must have occurred to him that *only he was fighting*. The others were "passively resistant." In fact, their creed prohibited physical violence, whether on behalf of slaves or in self-defense. Douglass tried to learn this behavior. He preached Garrison's three doctrines: exclusive use of moral suasion, rejection of political or other means of defense, and withdrawal from the Union. But he hadn't been called "the lion" frivolously. *His fight with Covey, he always recalled, not only had saved his life, but also had actually renewed his will to survive.* It had saved him from a double death, not only of the body, but also of the spirit. He had chosen, afterward, to defy and fight, rather than to submit to and accept segregation.

His dream of perfect accord with Garrison and the abolitionists faded when he discovered that they, too, were determined to keep him in his place. The real problem was that he moved and grew much faster than anyone had thought possible. In the exhilaration of his growth and his feeling of power over white audiences, he momentarily forgot that the general public hated abolitionists and was suspicious of their tactics. Collins, George Fish, and a hostile woman, Maria Weston Chapman, who had great influence over

Garrison, warned Douglass that if he dealt with basic issues and ideology, no one would believe he was a fugitive slave. Fourteen years later he wrote bitterly in *My Bondage and My Freedom,* "I was generally introduced as 'chattel'—a 'thing'—a piece of southern property—the chairman assuring the audience that it could speak. . . . 'Better have a *little* of the plantation manner of speech than not; 'tis not best that you seem too learned!' "

Douglass continued, nevertheless, to include discussion of those economic and religious factors that supported slavery. Three years later in a pamphlet he answered all "doubting Thomases" who still claimed he really was not a fugitive slave at all, but an educated Negro being used by the abolitionists to impersonate a slave.

The rub was that Douglass had become the greatest orator among them, and soon was to test his power against the leading speakers in England and Ireland. In 1841, when they had started out together, John A. Collins usually introduced Douglass as "a graduate of the peculiar institution"—"with his only diploma written on his back!" But Douglass soon became well read in fields relating to slavery, and actually made a careful study of the literature on the Constitution to determine whether it was, as Garrison claimed, a pact with the Devil which gave the Southern states the hellish power to own and use the bodies of black men, women, and children like so much cattle. After study, Douglass decided the Constitution did *not* so do, and that there was a legal right, guaranteed by the Constitution, to fight for the abolition of slavery. Correct or not, it was the only interpretation which a hopeful moderate could find useful.

This decision meant no "Disunion." It was the seed for Garrison's bitter rejection of Douglass, for it revealed that Douglass had become his own man. Anyone who tried to break him, intimidate him, or silence him now found they had grasped a lion by the tail. As the editor of a Boston area newspaper, the *Hingham Patriot,* wrote in November 1841, "As a speaker he has few equals. It is no declamation—but oratory, power of debate. He has wit, arguments, sarcasm, pathos—*all that first rate men show in their master efforts.* His voice is highly melodious and rich, and his enunciation quite elegant, and yet he has been but two or three years out of the house of bondage." (Emphasis added.) This extraordinary gift, cultivated not by formal education but by drive and intellect, made his position very similar to that of W.E.B. Du Bois later—a man subordinate in caste, but superior in ability.

The fact that Garrison, Stephen S. Foster, Willliam A. White, and the strongly prejudiced Mrs. Chapman were dealing with a man gifted beyond their imagination was shown by his first book. There are few American autobiographies with the dramatic suspense and emotional power of *A Personal Narrative.* Douglass wrote it in less than a year, while lecturing full time. Sometime later, Garrison tried to dissuade Douglass from editing his own newspaper by saying that Douglass spoke more effectively than he wrote. Most others disagreed. Horace Greeley of the *New York Tribune* said, after reading one of Douglass's letters to Garrison, that it contained passages "which, for genuine eloquence, would do honor to any writer of the English language, however eloquent." And Thurlow Weed, editor of the *Albany Evening Journal,* said that the same letter gave Douglass "rank among the most gifted and eloquent men of the age." But Garrison was already becoming jealous of his black protégé.

In 1844, after publishing a pamphlet naming his masters on Maryland's Eastern Shore as well as the places where he had been enslaved, Douglass decided it was best to go to England, since his master then had the information to apprehend him and the power under the Fugitive Slave Law to do so. Worst of all, Garrison and his group opposed any form of purchasing a slave's freedom, including the purchase of one's own freedom. They held that such action implied slavery to be legal—in the eyes of God, apparently, since there was no doubt that it was legal under the laws of the United States. His national reputation established, Douglass would be a rich prize for a slave hunter. With his book, *A Personal Nar-*

rative, just off the press and royalties expected, it seemed to him the strategic moment to go to Britain.

During the four years he had been working for the Society, he had become close friends with six or seven white men. His two best friends in New England were Gerrit Smith and James N. Buffum. On June 21, 1845, Buffum wrote to Smith, a wealthy abolitionist and later a supporter of John Brown, giving Smith the reasons for supporting a European trip by Douglass at that time:

> When they shall see before them a man so gentle and eloquent as Frederick, and learn from his own lips that he is only seven years out of bondage; that he has now the marks of the whip upon his back, which he will carry with him until the day of his death, that he has near and dear relatives that are now pining in bondage; they will realize to a considerable extent, the horrors of the American Slave trade; the effect cannot be otherwise than good.

Gerrit Smith agreed, and became for the rest of Douglass's life his most loyal and trusted friend.

Douglass did not know how long his master might have him hunted, so he could not foresee the length of his stay in Britain. Certainly, however, he would not have enough money to support Anna and their children. He left them the major portion of the royalties from his book, keeping only $350 for his trip. His friends in the Society gave him $250. From England, he sent Anna money earned by lecturing; later, he borrowed more from the Society for his family's care. But Anna, as usual, earned her share and more by shoemaking. Upon Douglass's return after eighteen months, Anna gave him back all the money he had sent from Britain so that he could pay his debts to the Society and others.

The most knowledgeable student of Douglass, Philip S. Foner, reports that before Douglass left for England, the great abolitionist senator from Massachusetts, Charles Sumner, seeking to prepare Douglass for the unknown world he was about to enter, advised, "Be yourself! Be yourself, and you will succeed." Foner adds that not even Sumner, who had the highest opinion of Douglass's ability, "dreamed that his success would reach such heights. His European visit gave Douglass an international reputation. He returned to the States a world figure, a mighty power for freedom."

Douglass went to England during the most triumphant phase of his life. He was only twenty-seven years old, yet the reputation he had earned with his first book preceded him to England. He still had all his youthful energy, hope, and vigor. The tour was a great success. He landed in Liverpool, having been insulted and menaced on the voyage by several American slaveholders, who were eventually stopped by the captain and threatened with irons. With his friend, Buffum, he then went to Dublin, where his audiences were far larger than in America. After five successful weeks in Dublin, he went to Cork, where he addressed crowded audiences at each of his eleven appearances—according to the Cork newspaper, many of his listeners were of the "suffering poor." After visiting Belfast, he returned to Liverpool and Birmingham, the heart of the English industrial slums. In Birmingham, he addressed 11,000 at a temperance convention; Douglass neither drank nor smoked nor cursed—he was, in fact, a black puritan. After having been abroad for four months, and having returned to Belfast on December 19, 1845, to make another speech, he was praised by the correspondent of the *London Inquirer:* "He is, in truth, a wonderful man." A public breakfast, presided over by a member of Parliament, honored him. Foner writes, "The four months Douglass spent in Ireland were the happiest he had ever known—the complete lack of anti-Negro prejudice, the open door everywhere. . . ." Douglass wrote Garrison from Belfast on January 1, 1846:

> The warm and generous cooperation extended to me—the prompt and liberal manner with which the press has rendered me its aid—the glorious enthusiasm with which thousands have flocked to hear the cruel wrongs of my down-trodden and long enslaved countrymen—the kind hospitality constantly proffered to me by persons of the highest rank in society and the entire absence of everything that looked like prejudice against me on account of the color of my skin—

contrasting so strongly with my long and bitter experience in the
United States, that I look with wonder and amazement on the tran-
sition.

After more than fifty lectures, Douglass moved on to Scotland.
There, he was drawn into a battle waged by American and English
abolitionists to force the Free church of Scotland to return a sum
of £3,000 that American slaveholders had donated to build churches
in Scotland. The committee which had raised the funds defended
the slaveholders as "respectable, useful, honored Christians, living
under the power of the truth . . . and serving God in the gospel
of His Son." The great majority of Free church members in Scotland rejected this view of slaveholders and would not countenance
their donations. Douglass addressed this issue, denouncing the use
of money gained from the toil and the blood of slaves.

While there, he was shown a letter which Richard D. Webb,
the Irish abolitionist, had received from Maria Weston Chapman
of the Massachusetts Anti-Slavery Society. In the letter, Chapman
warned Webb that Douglass, being poor and needing money for
his trip and family care, might be "bought off," as she wrote, by
the anti-Garrison wing of the English antislavery movement.
Douglass's friend and fellow traveler, Buffum, she wrote, might not
be susceptible because he was independently wealthy—and white.

Douglass regularly met insults like these from Americans, including abolitionists. The "no niggers allowed" warnings, reducing
him and all colored men and women in America to subhumans,
were insults Douglass would confront all his life. But his welcome
in Britain as a man like any other, and the tremendous burden of
self-contempt which it lifted from his shoulders, emboldened him
to write Maria Chapman a letter that she had not expected. It was
not a defiant statement, but a mature expression of his increasing
independence, and of a determination to direct and control his own
actions. "If you wish to drive me from the Anti-Slavery Society,"
Douglass wrote her, "put me under overseership and the work is

done. Set someone to watch over me for evil and let them be so simple-minded as to inform me of their office, and the last blow is struck."

During that time, Douglass was writing Garrison long, intimate, and appreciative letters, and was looking forward eagerly to Garrison's visit to England. Nevertheless, having thrown off the chains of slavery that had shackled him for twenty-one years, he was not prepared to accept a missionary "lady's" treatment of him as an irresponsible child. In this, Maria Chapman was not unique among white missionaries. General Samuel Chapman Armstrong of Hawaii, founder of the Hampton Institute, for instance, wrote in his description of the "proper" education for "weaker" and "inferior" people that they could not be expected to attain the same moral or intellectual level as whites. Such doctrine might have been swallowed whole—along with all the subservience to whites which it entailed—by the poverty-stricken Booker T. Washington, but not by Douglass.

Douglass soon met the full impact and fury of the irrational dogmatism of the general American Anti-Slavery Society when he accepted the papers that purchased his freedom. They had been obtained from his unwitting master by two English Quaker women, Miss Ellen Richardson and her sister-in-law, Mrs. Henry Richardson, who had collected the money from Douglass's English friends and admirers. Douglass, after less than six years with the Garrisonians, had already begun to perceive that several of their basic tenets—their insistence that slaveholders could be converted by moral suasion, that the free states should secede from the Union, and that abolitionists should in no way recognize the legal, economic, and political realities of the slave system—were naïve and foolish. Their objections to the manner in which his freedom had been bought, and their indignation at his having sanctioned that manner, contributed to his dissociation from the Eastern branch of the Society. He referred to them sarcastically, pointing out that they opposed the purchase of his freedom even though that freedom allowed him to return home to his wife and sons: "My uncompromising anti-slavery friends . . . were not pleased. . . . They thought it a violation of anti-slavery principles . . . and a wasteful expenditure of money."

Douglass was learning that much of the Society's dogma and indignation were, in the end, only words which would never free a single slave, nor protect him from the slave hunter and the Fugitive Slave Law. He remembered the case of another fugitive slave, George Latimer. In 1842, Massachusetts Chief Justice Lemuel Shaw had refused him a trial by jury and a writ of *habeas corpus*. The law had proved steadfast even though the people of Boston had rallied to the slave's cause and Whittier had been prompted to write his celebrated defiance of the South:

> No slave hunt in our borders,
> . . . .
> No fetters in the Bay State
> no slave upon our land

The only recourse for Latimer's supporters had been to pay $400 to buy his freedom. "Around this event, the Abolitionists organized a series of celebrations with Latimer as the central figure." Douglass had spoken at that earlier meeting and the *Salem Register* had reported, "The most wonderful performance of the evening was the address by Frederick Douglass, himself a [runaway] slave." Douglass thus had a precedent in allowing the Richardson sisters to purchase his freedom.

After speaking in Scotland, Douglass went to London in May 1846, and within four days had spoken at an antislavery meeting, a peace meeting, a woman suffrage meeting, and a temperance meeting. On the fifth night, he addressed an audience of 3,500 for nearly three hours. During one year's stay in England, he gave hundreds of speeches, earning enough money to support himself and his family in Massachusetts. In the meantime, the English abolitionists offered to bring his wife and children to England, and to support them there permanently, but Douglass declined, saying that he was determined to spend his life in America working for the emancipation of the slaves.

During the summer of 1846, Garrison also went to Britain, upon the invitation of the Glasgow Emancipation Society. His expenses were paid by free northern Negroes. He organized an "anti-Slavery League for All England" to cooperate with and financially aid his American Anti-Slavery Society, but received little or no money from the British. Douglass traveled and spoke with Garrison, leaving him in London to return and speak in northern England and Scotland. Garrison, however, gave up and returned to America, borrowing money, as we have said, from a Negro clergyman for his return passage. Douglass wished to return with him, but upon the insistence of both Garrison and George Thompson, head of the English abolitionists, he agreed to work in Britain another six months. Finally, in March 1847, he was given a public farewell in London by 1,400 admirers, and returned a free man with the offer—from Mary Howitt and English supporters—of a subsidy to start his own newspaper in America.

In Britain his boyhood fantasies had materialized, for he had become a hero of the British, and was admired by many of their great men: Disraeli, Bright, Cobden, Thomas Clarkson, Peel, Daniel O'Connell, Lord Brougham, and George Thompson. But, as nearly always was true in his life, a canker nettled the heart of his triumph. The Cunard Line refused to allow him to board one of its vessels unless he would give up his reservation for a stateroom. Homesick, Douglass had to agree, but the *London Times* and the British press in general ran editorials condemning Cunard. Samuel Cunard himself immediately wrote a public letter to the *Times*, apologizing for the insult and promising that "nothing of the kind will again take place in the steamships with which I am connected." (Eighty years later, the heiress Nancy Cunard became a leading patron of Negro-American art and literature, and a courageous speaker against racial discrimination.)

LEADERSHIP, LOVE, AND AGGRESSION

. . .

When Douglass made his triumphant return to America, he was received in his hometown of Lynn, Massachusetts, with a public welcome by white friends, the Negro people of Boston, Negroes of New York City and New Bedford, and, finally, his fellow workers in the American Anti-Slavery Society. Soon after, Mary Howitt renewed her offer to support him in founding his own abolitionist newspaper. Douglass accepted with enthusiasm. He learned, to his amazement, that Garrison, Wendell Phillips, and the Anti-Slavery Society in general strongly objected to having him edit his own paper. Surprisingly, Douglass deferred. He still felt emotionally dependent upon Garrison's good opinion, and was not yet quite ready to assert his independence. He therefore returned to his previous position as a subordinate to Garrison, a status which the Eastern abolitionists regarded as proper and necessary.

In August he set out with Garrison on a long and difficult lecture tour into Pennsylvania, northern Ohio, and Indiana. Despite the success of his speeches, Douglass often had occasion to contrast his treatment there with his reception in Britain. On a train to Harrisburg, for example, he was ordered out of the car, and dragged from his seat. On another occasion, when he was to speak in the state capital, rioters broke up the meeting with stones, garbage, and rotten eggs, shouting, "Out with the damned nigger!" He was often refused meals, and would barely eat for days. In New Brighton, Pennsylvania, as in most places, no church would allow abolitionists to meet in their buildings. But the tour had its gratifying moments, too. Negroes greeted him with a band in Pittsburgh and held five large meetings. Garrison and Douglass were enthusiastically received in the Western Reserve, at Oberlin College, and in Salem, Ohio, where they met 5,000 adherents. In Cleveland, they worked until they both fell ill—Douglass with tonsillitis and Garrison with pneumonia—and they had to remain there for several months.

Although Douglass wanted to stay with Garrison until he had

recovered, Garrison urged him to fulfill their engagements in northern New York. Foner writes:

> Worried and depressed, Douglass left for Buffalo. A week later he was disturbed to learn that Garrison's condition was critical. He kept reproaching himself for leaving at all. Half-heartedly he went through his talks in Buffalo, Rochester, and Syracuse, but his mind was troubled.

On October 8, 1847, Samuel J. May of Syracuse wrote Garrison:

> Frederick Douglass was very much troubled that he did not get any tidings from you when he reached Syracuse on the 24th of September. He left you reluctantly, yet thinking that you would follow in a day or two; and as he did not get any word from you at Waterloo, nor at Auburn, he was almost sure he should meet you at my house. His countenance fell, and his heart failed him, when he found me likewise in sad suspense about you. Not until he arrived at West Winfield did he get any relief, and then through the *Liberator* of the 23d.

But Garrison apparently did not believe May's report, for he wrote his wife that Douglass had "not written a single line to me or to anyone else in this place, inquiring after my health, since he left me on a bed of illness." He and Douglass never again shared a lecture platform as friends.

Thereafter, Garrison always displayed strangely dependent but hostile behavior toward Douglass. His bitterness and vindictiveness toward his former protégé during the following thirty years must be attributed to an old unresolved conflict of his early years. That conflict was between (1) *his desire for the love of a man,* and (2) *his early distrust of men caused by his father's desertion. Since boyhood Garrison childishly had watched every male for signs of desertion. His irrational defense was to desert first.*

The brilliant success of Douglass in England in contrast with Garrison's own failure there had already aroused Garrison's fears of being deserted. Moreover, Douglass's plan to start his own newspaper in competition with Garrison's *Liberator* was interpreted by Garrison as bold desertion. Garrison's anxiety was well founded: more than 75% of all subscribers to the *Liberator* were Negroes, and Garrison foresaw that many would turn to the newspaper edited by Douglass.

To further the estrangement, Douglass was beginning to throw off his myopic overestimation of Garrison, which had lasted six years. He still admired Garrison, but he was not willing to remain subservient to him or to anyone. Like all protégés worth their salt, he had to grow up and assert his own rightful place in the world.

Owing to Garrison's pacifism, Douglass was growing closer to Gerrit Smith and the northwestern New York abolitionists who favored political action, the economic rehabilitation of slaves, and even physical resistance to the Fugitive Slave Law. To be nearer to Gerrit Smith and the western Society, Douglass already had moved his home from Lynn, Massachusetts, to Rochester, New York. No doubt he had decided to print his paper among abolitionists more aggressive than Garrison. Gerrit Smith encouraged him and aided him financially. A wealthy man, Smith was prepared to contribute much of his wealth to large-scale rehabilitation of former slaves. To start with, he bought 150,000 acres of wilderness in the northern Appalachians and offered to give parcels to Northern blacks who were willing to clear the land. But few Negroes wanted to live on the barren soil. At one point, John Brown cleared a small tract in order to teach blacks how to survive in the wilderness; but even the indomitable Brown could not make a living on the rocks. Gerrit Smith did not give up, however. For more than twenty years, he proved an unselfish and courageous benefactor to Northern Negroes, the Underground Railroad, and Douglass, his closest friend.

When Douglass announced at the 1851 annual meeting of Garrison's American Anti-Slavery Society that he had decided to support political action against slavery, Garrison accused him of "roguery," and moved to drop the *North Star*, Douglass's paper, from the Society's list of approved publications. Douglass responded not with defiance or defense, but with the statement that he still held Garrison in "veneration only inferior in degree to that we owe to our conscience and to our God." Such was his over-idealization of his first "good father." Garrison replied by accusing Douglass of having been bought with Gerrit Smith's money. Every attack he made upon Douglass was a vicious and personal insult—the rage of a deserted child.

The next year at their annual meeting, the Garrisonians listed their "reasons" for treating Douglass, now the leading antislavery figure in America, as an enemy. The next year they portrayed Douglass as an *ally of proslavery* forces, and Garrison reprinted parts of Douglass's *North Star* editorials in the *Liberator*'s column that dealt with "enemies of the slave." Finally, Garrison went to the extreme of sexual slander, attributing the change in Douglass to the influence of an English woman, Julia Griffiths, who had devoted herself to keeping the *North Star* financially solvent, obtaining subsidies, and finding subscribers. Anna Douglass, always a strong and courageous woman, denied the charge. But Garrison, like his mother in her fire-and-damnation attacks upon her husband and other son, vented his hatred on Douglass, calling him a tool of Julia Griffiths and implying that they were sexually intimate.

In 1853, he was still reviling Douglass in editorials and letters. Harriet Beecher Stowe finally tried to reason with him. She interviewed Douglass, and later presented Garrison with her findings.

Cabin, Dec. 19 [1853]

Mr. Garrison
Dear Sir:

After seeing you, I enjoyed the pleasure of a personal interview with Mr. Douglass & I feel bound in justice to say that the impression was far more satisfactory, than I had anticipated . . . he did not seem to me malignant or revengeful. . . . I was much gratified with the growth & development both of his mind & heart. I am satisfied that his change of sentiments was not a mere political one but a genuine growth of his own conviction. A vigorous reflective mind like his cast among those holding new sentiments is naturally led to modified views.

At all events, he holds no opinion which he cannot defend, with a variety & richness of thought & expression & an aptness of illustration which shows it to be a growth from the soil of his own mind with a living root & not a twig broken off other men's thoughts & stuck down to subserve a temporary purpose.

His plans for the elevation of his own race, are manly, sensible, comprehensive, he has evidently observed carefully & thought deeply & will I trust act efficiently.

You speak of him as an aspostate—I cannot but regard this language as unjustly severe—Why is he any more to be called an apostate for having spoken ill tempered things of former friends than they for having spoken severely and cruelly as they have of him?— Where is this work of excommunication to end—Is there but one true anti-slavery church and all others infidels?—Who shall declare which it is.

I feel bound to remonstrate with this—for the same reason that I do with slavery—because I think it an injustice. I must say still further, that if the first allusion to his family concerns was unfortunate this last one is more unjustifiable still—I am utterly surprised at it— as a friend to you, & to him I view it with the deepest concern & regret. . . . I must indulge the hope you will reason at some future time to alter your opinion & that what you *now cast aside as worthless shall yet appear to be a treasure.* . . .

Very truly your friend,
H. B. Stowe

Garrison met Douglass at various antislavery functions but refused to speak to him, still regarding him as one of his "malignant enemies," and as being "utterly unscrupulous in carrying out his own designs." Characteristically, Garrison rejected an invitation to attend a celebration in Syracuse in October 1860. After indicating that he was in poor health and had been advised by his doctor not to travel, he wrote:

But, were I "in speaking order," the fact that Frederick Douglass is to be present at the celebration, and to participate therein, would powerfully repeal me from attending. I regard him as thoroughly base and selfish, and I know that his hostility to the American Anti-Slavery Society and its leading advocates is unmitigated and unceasing. . . . In fact, he reveals himself more and more to me as destitute of every principle of honor, ungrateful to the last degree, and malevolent in spirit. He is not worthy of respect, confidence, or countenance.

It was clear by this time that Garrison had fallen into a paranoid hatred of Douglass. His insane antagonism to Douglass smacked of that same cancer he found in Southern slaveholders, racial hatred. The maniacal excess to which Garrison's contempt and hatred drove him was demonstrated in his claim that Douglass and Julia Griffiths were sexually intimate. That claim was typical of the age-old American image of the Negro as always and everywhere innately sexual. As soon as Garrison began to see Douglass as a "deserter" and "traitor," the first feeling that came to him was obviously, "What could I expect of a nigger! He has the morality of a nigger slave." To Garrison, Douglass suddenly became black, primitive, bestial, and, most of all, sexually degenerate (in fact, he led an exemplary married life for forty-three years). Garrison's fear and anger affixed themselves to this culturally acknowledged image of the "savage Negro." His deeply seated racial prejudice, then, took that image, and from it nursed a hatred that would last the rest of his life.

Is it really possible that Garrison's jealousy and suspicion of Douglass bordered upon paranoia? The two men had traveled and lectured together in Britain and the United States. They had been like father and son. On lecture tours, Garrison, older and weakening under the hard schedule, had come to depend more and more upon his younger, dutiful "son." His distrust developed suddenly, after Douglass had failed to write him from Buffalo. He feared that his *protégé* had deserted him. This behavior is similar to Freud's well-known example of paranoia: The jealous and "persecuted" husband who tortured himself with the false notion that his wife was unfaithful. Where did these unmerited suspicions arise, and why? Freud discovered that they stemmed from the paranoiac's own wish to be unfaithful to his wife. *What he recognized in his own heart he attributed tenfold to his wife;* "the enmity which the persecuted paranoiac sees in others is *the reflection of his own hostile impulses against them* . . . we know that, with the paranoiac, it is precisely the most loved person of *his own sex* who becomes his 'persecutor.' . . ." (Emphasis added.)

It was John Brown's rebellious spirit that initially attracted Douglass. There is no question that there is something insane in defying overwhelming power—that such defiance flies in the face of reality. Nevertheless, there were times when Douglass and John Brown each felt and acted with such defiance.

Defiance, in its old sense of the French *défier,* implies the *unmasking* of a deceiver, of a hypocrite (e.g., the falsehearted knight). John Brown, like Garrison's mother, saw hypocrites, deceivers, and the spawn of Satan everywhere, and believed they should all be killed. In Kansas he killed women and children as well as male slavers. There is no doubt that Brown had many insane episodes, that in his paranoiac fantasies he was both the military conqueror and the vengeful Old Testament God in whose person he spoke, acted, and killed.

Since childhood, Douglass had nurtured a fantasy of rebellion and leadership, a desire to unmask the deceiver and hypocrite—his father—and to avenge himself and his people. Fortunately, his hatred had been softened and transformed, and had taken the form of verbal aggression. Where whites were concerned, his sense of reality increasingly mastered his fantasy of revenge. He found he could make loyal white friends in Britain and America. He felt closer, for example, to Gerrit Smith than to anyone except perhaps his wife and children.

Douglass met John Brown the very year he returned from England, in 1847. Following the advice of leading free Negroes who were interested in Brown's plan to "run off" slaves by establishing armed groups in the Allegheny Mountains, he visited Brown at his home in Springfield, Massachusetts. Brown tried to convince him that slaveholders "had forfeited their right to live," and that the friends of slaves should use force to free them. Douglass carefully pointed out the unsuitability of the site Brown had chosen for the uprising, and the certainty of his defeat. Nevertheless, Brown's conviction that slavery would be ended only by force made a deep impression upon Douglass, and he became even more alienated from Garrison.

A year after his visit to Brown, Douglass wrote in his *North Star* that slaveholders had

> no rights more than any other thief or pirate. They have forfeited even the right to live, and if the slave should put every one of them to the sword tomorrow, who dare pronounce the penalty disproportionate to the crime, or say that the criminals deserved less than death at the hands of their long-abused chattels?

Less than a year later he said in Faneuil Hall, Boston:

> I should welcome the intelligence tomorrow, should it come, that the slaves had risen in the South, and that the sable arms which had been engaged in beautifying and adorning the South, were engaged in spreading death and devastation.

In defense of his new position, he alluded to the precedents of the French and American revolutions. Clearly, he still vengefully remembered his own beatings, as well as the even more brutal whippings of his Aunt Hester and Nellie, a beautiful octoroon. Although he was no paranoiac like Brown, those beatings had taught him that slavery depended upon physical force and subjugation; he agreed with Brown that it would end only by force. Although Douglass had never killed or attacked anyone, and had never fought except in self-defense, the old anger and hate still stirred within him.

Furthermore, the political power of the South was increasing. Now Douglass was firmly convinced that the economic and political death grip of legalized slavery could be broken only by a war between the North and the South. It was a horrifying prospect of slaughter; one he probably never imagined—even with his mind's eye—for, unlike Brown, he was a compassionate man. He could never murder as Brown had—and he never did. Douglass might have found it easier to close his mind to the 30 million Africans who had died in the charnel houses which the slave ships became. Logically, violence seemed the only way to freedom. The Garrisonians had tried peaceful "moral suasion," and the radical abolitionists and Gerrit Smith had either helped slaves escape to Canada or tried to resettle them in the Pennsylvania mountains. But each year the number freed or resettled was smaller than the number of new slaves born. In the meantime, the South was increasing in political power, the North yielded more and more, and the slave hunters were free to roam the North recapturing escaped slaves.

Douglass was forced to face reality. Neither he nor Gerrit Smith nor Garrison was a Jack the Giant Killer. They might lecture and agitate forever, but no appeal to the conscience of slaveholders and no radical political conventions could ever attract enough followers and gain enough power to break the hold of the slave states.

Within a few years, when the drums of war called the Northern boys to throw themselves upon the deadly Southern artillery to the tune of "John Brown's body . . ." and when the Southern boys charged the Northern breastworks at Gettysburg in the bloodiest battle in American history, the inevitable cost in human blood that Lincoln had predicted was finally "paid." But to whom, and by whom? By armies of naïve boys—ignorant of the real economic causes at issue, and terrified by the carnage of battle. Douglass had his three sons enlist, and himself offered to raise Negro troops. But nowhere did he mention his feelings about the human slaughter-house into which slavery had driven the youth of America.

In sharp contrast to his call for violence was his concurrent and ongoing study of the Constitution and its origins. Encouraged by Gerrit Smith and Lewis Tappan, he spent two years reading constitutional law, political philosophy, and history in order to determine the contextual meaning of the Constitution. Finally, he decided that the Constitution "if strictly construed according to its reading [is] not a pro-slavery instrument." Once more, as in his opposition to pure moral suasion and to disunion from the South, he had broken with Garrison.

In the next ten years, according to Foner, Douglass "became a leading champion of militant Abolitionism, and the greatest organizer and agitator for political Abolitionism during the ten crucial years preceding the Civil War. . . ." Foner holds that the editorials, speeches, and letters he produced in this period "stamp him as one of the greatest minds of his time, a master strategist and tactician, and a people's leader of superb statesmanship." Allowing for Foner's partisan exaggeration of Douglass's political capabilities, it cannot be denied that Douglass's editorials and speeches on slavery now had no superior except those of Lincoln himself.* The strengths behind his rhetoric and behind the man himself, however, were a moral power and an independent spirit. The first quality he had learned from his grandmother; the second he had fought for and won on his own. It is remarkable that a slave with no formal education, with no mother or father to rear him, could have developed a character beyond reproach, and an independence worthy of the cognomen "the Lion."

Yet he remained inclined to feelings of suicidal defiance; and these feelings were constantly restimulated by John Brown's visits to his Rochester home. In the defiant and self-destructive Brown, Douglass saw a man he could admire and follow. But this identification held no good for him, personally.

Brown had a conspiratorial mania, and worked in secrecy with only a few Negro abolitionist confidants. In 1847, he was unknown, had accomplished nothing in the arena of public affairs, but des-

---

*Douglass actually was a poor politician until after the Civil War. He not only spoke against Lincoln and the Republicans in 1860, but he supported the minuscule Liberty Party.

perately wished to be a military leader. On the other hand, Douglass had become the best-known reformer in America. Brown sought Douglass's support to authenticate his own mad crusade. Douglass was vulnerable. In Brown he must have seen a kind of mirror image of himself.

To his backers, John Brown did not appear paranoid. Distinguished New England supporters, such as Thomas Wentworth Higginson, Samuel Gridley Howe, Gerrit Smith, George L. Stearns, Ralph Waldo Emerson, Henry David Thoreau, and Theodore Parker were well aware of his militant plans for slave raids, and even financed his bloody campaign in Kansas. To them, as to Douglass, Brown seemed a pious, responsible, self-sacrificing man of God, who hated slavery and was willing to die to abolish it. They failed to notice his arrogance in assuming the power of life and death over his sons; and they ignored his military and "head-of-state" obsessions. Brown's manias led him to establish military hierarchies, designating himself as commander—or "Captain," as he came to be known—and drawing up a constitution for a new "state." An inveterate inclination to suspicion led him to conceal from Douglass and his closest supporters his true plans for an insurrectionary attack upon a United States arsenal and the establishment of a new free state of which he would be the head. Most consuming was his religious mania, in which he saw himself as the avenging God. These fantasies, most of which were paranoidal, were the driving force beneath his behavior, but Douglass and many others thought of him simply as a crusader and reformer. It was not the first, nor would it be the last, time that paranoiacs led the sane, and headed armies or nations, including the United States.

Twenty-five years after Brown's activities in "bloody Kansas," Douglass still accepted as justification for the murders Brown's higher "law" of a vengeful God.

> The horrors wrought by his iron hand cannot be contemplated without a shudder, but it is the shudder which one feels at the execution of a murderer. The amputation of a limb is a severe trial

to feeling, but necessity is a full justification of it to reason. To call out a murderer at midnight, and without note of warning, judge or jury, run him through with a sword, was a terrible remedy for a terrible malady.

Brown's killings, then, became "moral" murders intended to punish the slave-staters from Missouri who had burned the farmhouses and towns of free-staters and killed their men, women, and children.

There is no doubt that Douglass still harbored his old hatred of slaveholders, a hatred which corresponded to Brown's mania. Although when he first heard Brown's plan in 1847 he prudently pointed out its suicidal aspects, thereafter Douglass allowed his own fantasies to take over. For the next twelve years, until he learned of Brown's secret scheme to attack the United States arsenal, Douglass encouraged and assisted Brown's fund-raising projects and military programs.

Actually, Douglass was a highly *moral* individual—he could not kill, wish as he might. And by the time, twelve years later, that Brown urged him to take up arms against the United States Marines, he had mastered a long-lived fantasy of physical revenge against his father, and had taken up the sword of rhetoric. He had already decided that he was in the battle against slavery to win, and not to furnish victims to a senseless holocaust.

During those intervening twelve years, he endorsed the new Free-Soil Party and its candidates—Martin Van Buren and Charles Francis Adams—because, Foner claims incorrectly, he "understood this was the beginning of a great movement which would finally split the Democrats, destroy the Whig Party, and create a new political antislavery movement with a mass following." In fact, Douglass did not foresee the emergence of the Republican Party, did not accept it when it was formed, and did not ride the winning tide of its rapid and powerful rush to victory and the Presidency. As usual, he supported losers. Van Buren did not carry a single state. When Gerrit Smith and others formed their small antislavery group in 1852, Douglass enthusiastically followed them. But a few months later, he renewed his support for the Free-Soil Party (with which the Liberty Party had merged) because it was much larger, and could, he hoped, be persuaded to take a strong antislavery position. At the Free-Soil Party's convention in August 1852, Douglass, nominated by Lewis Tappan, was elected a secretary by acclamation. Cries went up for him to speak, and he called for a party "identified with eternal principles." He wanted to exterminate slavery in New Orleans as well as in the West. "Slavery is a system, not only wrong, but is of a lawless character, and cannot be Christianized or legalized." In London, the *Anti-Slavery Reporter* regarded his election as evidence "of the advance of anti-slavery sentiment in the United States."

In supporting the Free-Soil Party, however, Douglass again missed the boat politically. Not only were their candidates, John P. Hale and George W. Julian, defeated, but Gerrit Smith, his closest friend, was nominated for Congress and won. Elated, Douglass changed allegiance again and predicted Smith's group could carry New York State "for freedom" in 1856. But by that year, he was supporting the Republican Party, because he felt its newly gained power might be used against slavery. His delight in Gerrit Smith's election to Congress was soon over when Smith resigned after only eight months in office. Smith, like Douglass and Lewis Tappan, was a reformer, and was not geared to political office-holding. None of them liked dickering and compromise, and they were not good at it. Douglass himself never held an elective office, although men of much less ability—white and black—were winning elections to Congress after the war.

In both 1854 and 1855, Douglass attended the conventions of the small group of "true" Liberty party men because they alone called for the abolition of slavery. But in 1854, only thirty persons were present at the convention. The next year, in Boston, he was appointed to the Business Committee, but the group could not agree even to designate a slate for national office. In 1857, the little group dissolved, and a year later Douglass worked enthusiastically in Gerrit Smith's campaign for governor of New York on the Radical Abolitionists' ticket. This time Smith received a very small vote: Negro voters had turned to the Republican Party.

During these years, John Brown wrote to Douglass about the guerrilla warfare and the pitched battles he was waging in Kansas, and his need for arms and money to free slaves in Virginia and Maryland. In Kansas, Brown's homicidal military mania and his paranoid identification with the God of vengeance broke into a full psychosis. His own half-brother wrote:

> Since the trouble growing out of the settlement of the Kansas Territory, I have observed a marked change in brother John. Previous to this, he devoted himself entirely to business; but since these troubles he has abandoned all business, and has become wholly absorbed by the subject of slavery. He had property left him by his father, and of which I had the agency. He has never taken a dollar of it for the benefit of his family, but has called for a portion of it to be expended in what he called the Service. After his return to Kansas he called on me, and I urged him to go home to his family and attend to his private affairs; that *I feared his course would prove his destruction and that of his boy.* . . . He replied that he was sorry that I did not sympathize with him; that he knew that he was in the line of duty, and *he must pursue it, though it should destroy him and his family.* He stated to me that he was satisfied that he was a chosen instrument in the hands of God to war against slavery. From his manner and from his conversation at this time, *I had no doubt he had become insane upon the subject of slavery,* and gave him to understand that this was my opinion of him! [Emphasis added.]

The brother had based his conclusions on firsthand observations of Brown's manner, countenance, and speech. About the same time, in Springfield, Kansas, Brown confided to his landlord—a strong antislavery man—his plans to strike in Virginia and other Southern states. The man wrote:

> I did my best to convince him that the probabilities were that all would be killed. He said that, as for himself, he was willing to give his life for the slaves. He told me repeatedly, while talking, that he

believed he was an instrument in the hands of God through which slavery would be abolished. I said to him: "You and your handful of men cannot cope with the whole South."

Even Brown's Radical Abolitionist supporters in the East refused—after hearing his plans, and seeing "the manifest hopelessness of undertaking anything so vast with such slender means"—to give him $500. He tried to raise the money himself. But he failed. Brown's behavior clearly did not inspire confidence, and he commented bitterly that people who received him privately did not wish to be seen with him in public.

His wife and daughter had similar doubts. But to all, Brown's answer was the same. It was the same answer he had given his wife when she had questioned him about the murders he had planned and ordered in the Swamp of the Swan in Kansas:

> Brown: ". . . in doing so I believe I was doing God's service."
> My wife spoke and said, "Then Captain, you think that God uses you as an instrument in his hands to kill men?"
> Brown replied, "I think He has used me as an instrument to kill men; and if I live, I think He will use me as an instrument to kill a good many more."

One may assume, then, that Brown suffered from a homicidal mania with a military and religious symbolism.

During twelve years Brown had visited Douglass many times in Rochester, lived with him for weeks while writing to Douglass's friends for aid, and made detailed plans for slave raids in the Maryland and Virginia mountains. Under his influence, Douglass had moved completely away from Garrison's nonpolitical, nonviolent program. Not only did he use his home as a hideout for runaway slaves—at one time he hid twelve slaves until he could arrange their escape to Canada—but also he was an active conspirator with Brown: advising him, raising money, and making contacts for him with wealthy Radical Abolitionists. In Douglass's home, Brown drew up a constitution for the free state that he planned to form out of conquered areas.

Conferring with Douglass and other Negro leaders in 1858, Brown sought men and funds for a strike later that year. But he was thwarted by the treachery of Hugh Forbes, an Englishman who had promised to drill Brown's recruits and to recruit additional army officers, but instead only bilked Brown and his sponsors out of their money. Thinking that Forbes had betrayed them, Brown's Radical Abolitionist supporters sent Brown to Kansas, and promised him new funds in the spring for his raids in Virginia.

About a year later, in April 1859, Brown visited Douglass in Rochester, but carefully refrained from telling him he now planned to attack the United States arsenal at Harpers Ferry—that it was no longer a matter of running off slaves, but of insurrection against the United States Government. Three months later, Brown rented a farm near Harpers Ferry where he planned to station his men and to store arms. He had collected twenty-one men, most of them white, and in August he finally revealed to Douglass his plan to take the United States arsenal.

The meeting took place on the night of August 20, in a stone quarry near Chambersburg. Brown, his lieutenant Kagi, Douglass and Green were present. It was in the old quarry that Douglass for the first time learned of Brown's plan to seize Harpers Ferry, capture the leading citizens and hold them as hostages while his band rounded up the slaves in the surrounding areas. Brown was dismayed by the emphatic disapproval registered in Douglass's reaction to his plan. Douglass assured Brown that he was still prepared to join with him in carrying out the original plan of running the slaves through the Alleghenies, but the raid on Harpers Ferry was an attack on the national government and was doomed to failure.

Less than two months later, on the night of October 16, 1859, Brown and his tiny party struck, taking the United States arsenal and the bridges to the town. The next night, Robert E. Lee, commanding a company of United States Marines, moved in; the following morning he retook the arsenal and captured Brown. Forty-five days later, Brown was hanged at Charles Town.

Douglass was lecturing on "Self-Made Men" to a capacity audience in Philadelphia's National Hall when Brown was captured. He was told that letters implicating him in the attack had been found in Brown's possession. Realizing that his own life was in immediate danger, he left at once for Rochester. In New York he wired a telegraph operator in Rochester to tell his son, Lewis Douglass, to hide his papers. Another telegraph operator, in Philadelphia, an admirer of Douglass, had given him time to escape Philadelphia by delaying—for three hours—delivery of the sheriff's orders for his arrest. In the *New York Herald* Douglass read that Brown's alleged confession had implicated Douglass, Gerrit Smith, Joshua Reed Giddings, and other abolitionists; and that the Governor of Virginia had requisitioned his and Smith's extradition from the Governor of New York. The bloodhounds were already on his trail, and the outraged Virginian slaveholders wanted to execute him along with Brown.

Although he was willing to resist federal marshals seeking to arrest him, Douglass's friends in Rochester convinced him that his only chance for safety lay in Canada. He took their advice, and wisely so, for already he had been charged in Virginia with "murder, robbery, and inciting to servile insurrection." The Governor of Virginia had arranged for the United States Attorney, other federal officers, and two detectives from Virginia to arrive in Rochester on October 25 to arrest Douglass.

In his own defense, Douglass wrote an ironic letter to the *Rochester Democrat* saying that he had never agreed to the attack on the arsenal, had refused to join it, and that it was not fear for his own life which had prevented him from joining Brown, but the very nature of his own involvement in the fight against slavery. He wrote, "The tools to those who can use them . . ." meaning that for eighteen years he had publicly fought slavery by writing, speaking, and organizing, and not—he might have added—by hopeless attempts at insurrection that were so poorly prepared and executed that one company of Marines could suppress it quickly! Douglass was not a masochist; he liked to win. A penniless slave who had risen to world prominence, he had been winning now for eighteen years. True, he wanted war against the slave power, but he wanted a war waged by the United States Government. It was clear he would not join Brown in a war against that very government. As he said years afterward, "It is gallant to go forth single-handed, but is it wise?"

In refusing to attack the United States arsenal with Brown, Douglass finally turned his back on his fantasy of revenge against his "bad father," his master. His writings, however, also summon up an image of a good father, who had spoken to him "in soft caressing tones," and had called him his "little Indian boy." In actual fact, Douglass's father had two real personae: the master and the father. The split image arose from the double role his father played. The "bad father" was an image of the master who enslaved, "imbruted," and tyrannized him and his fellow slaves.

To Douglass, Brown at first seemed a "good father" who admired and praised his "son." But Brown also rekindled Douglass's old fantasy of overcoming the master, of being avenged. The dream of leading his people out of bondage through violence was the other side of Douglass's fantasy of revenge upon his "bad father." As with most fantasies of family revenge, it was a bloody one. This longing for revolt against the master was answered in Brown's plan of revenge upon the South, but it clearly led to death! And death was not part of Douglass's childhood dream. He was to be victorious and triumphant, and to lead his people to freedom himself.

Brown—who, like the father-master of Douglass, had psychotic episodes in which he saw and talked to devils and demons—saw in Douglass an enthusiastic admirer and a fifth son. As he had done with his own four sons, Brown tried to use Douglass, even if it meant he must die, as they had, in support of Brown's fantasies. He brought great pressure on Douglass to join him on a suicidal mission, and he persuaded the leading free Negroes in Pennsylvania to try to bribe Douglass by offering to support his wife and children if he were killed. They—the Philadelphia Negroes—of course, were not going! In other words, Douglass was to be a bought sacrifice: a pigeon. But Douglass suddenly grew wary of Brown's suicidal fantasies, and refused.

On November 12 of that year, in accordance with plans completed months before, Douglass sailed for England on a lecture tour. The five-month tour, in which Douglass included speeches on John Brown's purpose and exploits, inspired the English commoners. Foner suggests that Douglass's speeches led the English, a year or two later, to favor the Union cause; the English antislavery forces were thus greatly strengthened, and they then worked more effectively against their own government in behalf of the Union cause.

The death of his younger daughter, Annie, "the light and life of my house," brought Douglass home at once, and changed his life. He believed that Annie, who had loved John Brown, had died of grief over the old man's horrible death, and the almost simultaneous loss of her father, who had fled to England. Whatever the cause, she was dead. Douglass felt that if he had not been involved with Brown, and had remained with her, he probably could have saved her. Life is a hard teacher, but it ends by disabusing us of our childish fantasies. After his daughter's death, for which he blamed himself, Douglass was truly rid of his penchant for defiant fantasies.

Fantasies are mere phantoms and are bound to be punctured by reality. The fantasy of revenge against the father is the oldest and the last to go, but someday even it must be abandoned, or it will lead to self-destruction. Douglass had confronted that prospect when asked to join in a doomed insurrection against the United States Government. He had refused Brown. In so doing, Douglass became his own man. He needed no "good" father figures any longer. A few months later he looked upon the new President, Lincoln, objectively—not as a "good father." And, when Lincoln said in his First Inaugural Address that he would support the Fugitive Slave Law and would *not* oppose slavery in any state where it already existed, Douglass did not perceive him as a "bad father." He was becoming a realist—able to deal with Lincoln and four later Presidents without either excessive admiration or suspicion. The prerequisites for adulthood are (1) *emotional independence,* and (2) *the ability to face reality;* Douglass now met both tests.

But not in politics. In the Presidential election of 1860 he remained loyal to his friend Gerrit Smith to the end. In the month before Lincoln was elected, Douglass wrote in his paper that 10,000 votes for Smith would do more to abolish slavery than 2 million for Lincoln! Asked later what abolitionists had gained by the election of Lincoln, he replied:

> Not much, in itself considered, but very much when viewed in the light of its relations and bearings. For fifty years the country has taken the law from the lips of an exacting, haughty and imperious slave oligarchy. The masters of slaves have been masters of the Republic. Their authority was almost undisputed, and their power irresistible. They were the President makers of the Republic, and no aspirant dared to hope for success against their frown. Lincoln's election has vitiated their authority, and broken their power. It has taught the North its strength, and shown the South its weakness.

He now felt it his duty, and that of the abolitionists, to act as watchdogs of the new administration; to prevent capitulation to the slave states' threats of secession and war if the North did not comply with those states' increasingly punitive demands. Foner writes:

> It was no simple task, however, to revive the old spirit of the antislavery movement in the weeks following Lincoln's election. As threats of secession of the southern states mounted, northern conservatives tried to convince the slaveholders that they had nothing to fear from remaining in the Union. Personal liberty laws to prevent the return of fugitive slaves were repealed, resolutions condemning the Abolitionists were adopted by the Union-Saving gatherings, and paid hoodlums were hired to disrupt antislavery meetings. Northern newspapers fanned the flames of hysteria, calling for demonstrations wherever Abolitionists gathered.
>
> Douglass was once again the special target for attack. At a meet-

ing in Boston on December 3, 1860, to commemorate the anniversary of John Brown's execution, ruffians, hired by merchants engaged in the southern trade, invaded the hall, disrupted the proceedings, and singled out Douglass for attack. Fighting "like a trained pugilist," the Negro Abolitionist was thrown "down the staircase to the floor of the hall."

The meeting was adjourned to a church on Joy Street. As the audience poured into the street, Negroes were seized, knocked down, trampled upon, and a number seriously injured. "The mob was howling with rage," Douglass recalled years later. "Boston wanted a victim to appease the wrath of the south already bent upon the destruction of the Union."

But even major concessions made by Northern legislatures and city councils to allow slave-hunting in their areas—not to mention other, more humiliating, demands—did not satisfy the South, which was preparing for war. When South Carolina attacked Fort Sumter and Lincoln was forced to declare war, Douglass threw himself into the work of protecting the interests of slaves, urging Lincoln to emancipate them and induct them into the Union forces. Douglass had become the acknowledged leader of his people, and was so recognized by Lincoln, who was reported to have said in 1864, ". . . considering the conditions from which he had arisen and the obstacles he had overcome, and the position to which he had attained,— he regarded him as one of the most meritorious men, if not the most meritorious man in the United States. . . ." I cannot recall higher praise from Lincoln for anyone else.*

Douglass's identity was now firmly established, and his basic emotional conflicts were solved. Such conflicts are not solved quickly or easily. Often they are never mastered. Being an extremely complex

---

*At the second inaugural reception, Douglass was seized by two policemen. No Negroes could attend the reception, he was told. He was still hearing "No niggers here," as he had all his life. When Douglass finally got word to Lincoln and was allowed to enter, Lincoln said to those around him, "Here comes my friend Douglass."

man in the most difficult of environments, Douglass was not unusual in requiring forty years to resolve them.

To look at the photograph of Douglass taken soon after his
escape from slavery—when he felt and looked like a hunted animal—is to realize the depth of his fear and hatred of white people.
Except for his white family—especially his white "mother," Sophia,
his half-sister, Lucretia, and the two boys Tommy Auld and Daniel
Lloyd—whites had treated him with less regard than their cattle.
His second master, Thomas Auld, had the slave driver Covey beat
him mercilessly; slaveholders and poor whites around Easton tried
to murder him, as did white apprentices and caulkers in Baltimore
shipyards.

Yet Douglass learned to give up his hatred and transmute his
anger into productive social, civic, and political initiative. As Weissman observes, Douglass, in writings as well as in action, showed
himself more a man of love than of hate. He was admired generally
for constant and unselfish work on behalf of women, the Irish, the
Chinese in California, British seamen, and American slaves. His
mission, he said, was "to stand up for the downtrodden, to open
my mouth for the dumb, to remember those in bonds as bound
with them." How does one reconcile his love of mankind—what
Martin Luther King, Jr., called "agape"—with his suppressed hatred
of his father and a conscious vengefulness against all slaveholders?

Is it possible that Christianity, taught him in boyhood by Father Lawson in Baltimore, or Garrison's Christian faith, or his
friendships with the great O'Connell in Ireland and Bishop Wilberforce in England deeply influenced his character? Possible, but not
likely, especially since he had explicitly rejected formal religion and
the church many times.

Compassion and humanitarianism as strongly developed as his
must have derived from the *guilt* his hatred had rooted in him. The
turning of hatred into its opposite—compassion and mercy—is a
process well known to psychologists. Children at the age of two or
three, for instance, are likely to be cruel to both animals and sib-

lings; but eventually they *learn* to become kind and even merciful. This *reaction toward the opposite* takes place as the child's conscience begins to form. Conscience, itself, arises from a *feeling of guilt* instilled by the parents. If the child is cruel to his dog or his siblings, he is made to feel guilty by verbal disapproval or by physical punishment. Thus, guilt is established as a *barrier to future malevolence*. The explanation, then, for a "reaction to inhibit," which replaces a feeling (hate) by its opposite (compassion), is that the original feeling—hate or cruelty in this case—is stopped or *repressed by guilt,* and the socially approved, opposite feeling (mercy or compassion) replaces it. Such was Douglass's reaction to his guilt: compassion.

But what was *the origin of his guilt?* What made him feel guilty? It seems evident it was not religion. The answer must be that he had been treated as a son by Lucretia, his white half-sister, and by Sophia Auld, his sociological mother. From the ages of seven to fifteen he had been reared by Sophia Auld and loved by her as her own son. It seems extraordinary that his biographers have ignored so central a fact in his emotional life and identity development. His life in Sophia's home and their strong mutual affection were one of the two most formative influences in his life. From age six for the rest of his life, except for the three years in Tuckahoe, he was closer to his white relatives than to his black (see Preston, *Young Frederick Douglass*). And yet he hated all other Southern whites—and most Northern. The *guilt* he experienced in hating whites sprang from (1) the desire for revenge against his *father* and (2) *the love and trust of whites he had learned from Sophia, who had trusted him. Sophia had loved him as she did her own son, Tommy;* she had nursed him when he was ill, and—even when he was a man of twenty—had cared for the wounds inflicted by whites. Whereas his relationships with men were often ambivalent because he both loved and hated his father, those with women were uniformly strong, trusting, and lasting. In early life, Douglass had exhibited the same (1) love for women and (2) suspicion and hatred toward men. But sometime in the seven years following his escape—either when he

met Garrison or when he was regaled, praised, and loved by Englishwomen, and lionized by English statesmen and abolitionists—
his hatred of whites made him feel deeply hypocritical and became too
heavy a burden to bear. With both the Garrisonians and the English, his guilt and shame over his own hatred for the very white
people who were admiring and celebrating him drove Douglass to
the reaction opposite to hate: compassion. That is to say, *his strongly
developed capacity for compassion was linked to his guilt from a hidden,
powerful hatred.* When he first found that Garrison and many other
whites actually admired and loved him, his defenses against them
(and against his own guilt) broke down. He was then driven, as it
were, to compensatory behavior, or *atonement for his hatred.* In simple language, he was like the "captain of industry" who becomes
wealthy by exploiting others, and then becomes a lavish donor to
good causes in order to expiate himself. *In the case of Douglass, however, this emotional reaction was unconscious, and his compassion became
as powerful as his hatred had been.* Some of the anger against whites
remained, but it was selectively directed against slaveholders, and
other exploiters (of women, Irish, Chinese immigrants, American
Indians).

The love and trust invested in him by Sophia, Lucretia, and his
grandmother saved Douglass from the kind of paranoidal hatred
exhibited by Brown and Garrison. *For he had learned from Sophia
and Lucretia that all whites did not hate or exploit blacks; some trusted
and loved them.* Since he had spent nearly all his first twenty-one
years in this enviornment, he had acquired a solid foundation for
good relationships with well-disposed whites. In his last autobiography, incredibly, he names *fifty-two white friends or benefactors*—
evidence enough of an excess in the drive (hatred) to which these
friendships were a *reaction.*

For the person like Douglass who wishes to rise in the world, the
handling of his own aggression becomes pivotal. Douglass channeled his aggression in an attempt to break out of the hopeless

night of a color caste system—to rise from a day laborer's lifelong status in New Bedford to that of author and lecturer. To do this, he had to learn a new sense of identity.

In a work published more than twenty years ago, *Psychology of the Child in the Middle Class,* I examined the psychology of social mobility, as well as the learning of a new culture which it entails. I pointed out that the upward-mobile individual, like Douglass, identifies with the culture of a superordinate group. He strives to adopt the characteristics of this group because he admires it and considers it superior to his own birth-culture. This process of taking into oneself, or learning, the values, skills, behavior, and identity of a higher status-group is basic to all upward mobility—it is a process of acculturation (learning a second or later culture). Although the drive to acculturate may be spurred by personal, idiosyncratic forces—as it was by Douglass's wish to overcome his father—it surpasses these initially destructive feelings, and graduates to the learning of a new culture (for Douglass, the American culture), *within which a person can exercise his special competencies and initiatives more fruitfully than in his old culture.*

Douglass would not have agreed with those "Black Power" extremists during the late 1960s who rejected Euro-American culture in general, as well as rejecting Negroes who had been conditioned and educated to compete in that culture. In this sense, Douglass was above all a realist; as his lectures on the Icelandic sagas and Greek and Roman civilization show, he absorbed as much as he could of European culture. To compete in an overwhelmingly white society, he felt he had to know even more about white culture than the average American white. He was for *integration, amalgamation,* and *acculturation.* For that reason, he opposed "all-Negro" schools and colleges; he fought segregation in white churches as early as 1838, exclusion of black men from the armed services in 1861, and discrimination against and segregation of Negro soldiers after they once were enlisted. *He wanted no separatistic black nationalism. He wanted inclusion,* as defined by the Declaration of Independence and, he believed, as insured by the Constitution. He was one of the first great nonracist, nonsexist leaders of the Western world.

Foner writes that when Douglass was bitterly criticized for marrying his white abolitionist secretary after the death of Anna, his black wife of forty-three years, "he would laughingly remark that it proved that he was quite impartial—his first wife 'was the color of my mother, and the second the color of my father.'" The reply had some of his defiance of white taboos, for I doubt it was "a good laugh"; but it also showed that he had a kind of double color-consciousness. How did his various identities fuse?

The concept of social identity was first developed by George Herbert Mead of the University of Chicago. Many years later, Erik H. Erikson revived the concept, added a new "developmental-stages" dimension, and called the result "ego-identity." In Mead's concept of identity, the chief point is that one's sense of "oneness" is learned by imitating the behavior of "significant others" in one's early family. Erikson's concept of identity is only one developmental stage in a series of eight which, optimally, the individual will master in exact order, namely, trust, autonomy, initiative, industry, *identity*, intimacy, generativity, and integrity.

Erikson's earliest definition of identity seems still the best: "the sum total of all previous identifications"; and these include, of course, identifications with mother, father, siblings, other members of the family, peers, teachers, and others whom the individual *fears*, *respects*, or *admires*.

If a stage-conflict is not mastered at the appropriate age, it will remain an unresolved conflict during later stages, and the likelihood that the individual will ever solve that conflict is poor. For instance: Trust is learned in the earliest stage of nursing and weaning, through the child's relationship with the mother. A child who has a painful, unhappy nursing (oral) stage is thought likely to become distrustful of life itself, and probably of women. When he fails to receive enough milk or fondling, he feels the environment itself is threatening. He expects the worst of life and of people.

In the case of Douglass, unfortunately, it is impossible to examine data on his early training (weaning, toilet-training, and masturbation-training) because we have no such information. But we do know that he went through an early period of distrust, owing to the disappearance of his mother at his birth and her return only four or five times before her death. Dr. Weissman points out that when, at the age of twenty-five, he began writing *A Personal Narrative,* this old sense of loss returned, and distorted his depiction of his whole early life. Fortunately, at the same time that he lost his mother, he gained a grandmother whose care and love reassured him. Thus, the loss of his mother did little serious damage. Douglass learned his basic social identities from his black grandmother. She taught him to be a male—a charming "little man"—and he effectively used this training to delight his mistress Lucretia, by singing under her window at the age of six to win bread, care, and love! His grandmother also taught him ambition, the kind she herself had, for by hard work, skill, and determination, she had become the most influential slave on the Tuckahoe plantation. She instilled Fred with a strict conscience, too, and it endured throughout his life.

Since we have no data on his sexual training, fantasies, or acts, and no comments by Douglass himself—who was at least Victorian, if not puritanical, in verbal references to sexual life—we can only conclude that his sexual identity was relatively unconflicted. His great popularity with women of both races offers the best evidence of his affection for them and his sexual vitality.

One could continue in this fashion, using Erikson's ego-developmental stages in an attempt to understand Douglass. But in the absence of observational data, any interpretation is mere surmise. It would be more profitable, perhaps, to discuss that category of identity-manifestations that is in abundant evidence, namely, his *social* identity.

As already stated, Mead pointed out that one's earliest sense of who one is and where one belongs is learned in the family. This complex communication between the young child and his "significant others" in the family (or school) is not yet fully understood, but, as John Dollard and Neal Miller have found by experimental research, *a child imitates most successfully those models who have the highest prestige in his eyes.* This seems an adequate explanation of young Fred's identification *in part*—and only in part—with the culture of his white family and in-laws. When he was sent to Baltimore at eight to live with Sophia and Tommy, his sense of color identity became conflicted. Before that time he had learned from his grandmother, his aunts, and the slaves around him to think of himself as a slave and a "nigger." But he found that Sophia loved him and cared for him the way she did her son; and he was no "nigger" to little Tommy. Identifying with them because he admired them, he learned their way of speaking, and their prized skills of reading and writing. He also developed an appetite for the kind of freedom and self-determination that came naturally to them. In addition to these social motivations, there can be no doubt that his "family-romance fantasy"* included Sophia; that his imagined *role* in the fantasy as well as his competition with Tommy and Hugh Auld for Sophia's attention were powerful motives underlying his irrepressible efforts to learn to read and write.

The two most powerful agents, then, of Douglass's early socialization were his grandmother and Sophia. During his adolescence, free Baltimore Negroes taught him the skills of public speaking and organizing. This they accomplished through their civic and self-improvement associations, in which he was the only slave accepted. From them he learned new goals; and among them he met his future wife, Anna Murray. In New Bedford, too, free Negroes taught him their Yankee values, especially thrift. They also intro-

---

* Freud's term for the fantasy underlying the attachment of daughter to father and son to mother.

duced him to the Massachussetts Anti-Slavery Society, and provided him with a discussion group as well as a platform. In giving him these opportunities, they changed his social concept of himself and his sense of place in the world. At a crucial time in his life, Douglass adopted two identity-models within this group: Nathan Johnson, with whom he lived in New Bedford, and David Ruggles, the brilliant New York Negro—an officer of the Underground Railroad and, later, the head of the National Reformed Convention of the Colored People—who sheltered Douglass in New York. Then a fugitive slave, seeking a way to make a living and to be heard, he found in David Ruggles proof that the leadership role was open to Negroes, and that in the North one's efforts to free slaves led not to the gallows, as in the South, but to acceptance, at least by abolitionists, and, perhaps, even to acclaim.

He identified with white abolitionists. They were openly fighting the same kind of battle he had fought secretly on the plantation. They professed the same hatred of slavery and of slaveholders; they suffered the same rejection and violence which he had suffered. Their meetings were broken up by angry mobs as his Sunday-school meetings had been. The abolitionist United States senator Charles Sumner was even caned at his desk in the Senate, as a slave might have been. Seeing these abolitionists stand up bravely to defend their unpopular views, he was inspired to rechannel his hatred (for the oppressors) and sympathy (for the oppressed) into a movement of broader national and international scope. And instead of having to depend upon deception, or his own two fists, he now could fight the slave system openly, using his oratorical, intellectual, and literary talents.

His identity became, therefore, a fusion of what he had incorporated from "emotionally and socially significant" blacks *and* whites. His grandmother was his model in his very early years, but after age six his consciousness of being a white man's son and the adopted son of a living white mother remained with him, and contributed to his ambition to be "up and above." But, as in the personality of

Du Bois, this sense of divided racial identity led to emotional conflict. At times, thinking of his father, he rebelled against his white identity; at other times, thinking of Sophia and Lucretia, he accepted it.

Those scholars who hold that his racial identity was always firmly Negro will object to this view of Douglass. Clearly, their opinion is unsound, for he always claimed his right to his white family; he even visited Lucretia's daughter, Amanda (his niece), many years after he was free, and also visited his former master Thomas Auld. In his last book he boasted that he had been received in the living room of the daughter of Colonel Lloyd, his "old master's" employer.

> She [Colonel Lloyd's daughter] is now seventy-four years of age but marvelously well preserved. She invited me to a seat by her side, introduced me to her grandchildren and conversed with me as freely and with as little embarrassment as if I had been an old acquaintance and occupied an equal station with the most aristocratic of the Caucasian race.

His pride in his connections with "the Caucasian race" is clear, and it extended to more than just his friendships with eminent whites—as stated earlier, he listed, in his last autobiography, the names of fifty-two of the most eminent white men in the North as his friends and/or benefactors. He also listed the names of equally wealthy and prominent Northern white women who had been his friends or co-workers in the abolitionist and women's movements. But his visit to the Lloyds' mansion, where he drank wine with the son of the then Colonel Edward Lloyd, was important in a different way. First, he regarded it as a kind of family homecoming. He was proud that he had returned on a United States Reserve cutter, accompanied by a white friend, the United States collector of revenue for Baltimore; but it was also clear that he felt attached to these people. He said that for years he had yearned to visit his original home. What he longed for, of course, were the dead Lucretia and his father. In this long account he never mentions *either* his black grandmother or his own mother, although he was visiting the plantations where they had been born and died.

Studying Douglass's observations on his return to his childhood "home" sixty years later, one feels that here is a man of two origins and two ethnic identities. The fact is that he had a type of "racial" consciousness typical—until forty years ago—of most Negro leaders and professional men who were the sons or grandsons of well-to-to white men. (Today there are very few Negro leaders or professional men who had white fathers.) Douglass reflects on this triumphal return to his "old master's" and to Governor Lloyd's plantations; and he underscores the irony by making the point that local whites asked him to speak in the very town, Easton, where, after his failed attempt to escape many years before, he had been dragged by horses and jailed. *I take this story to be an assertion that it was his own initiative and brains that had prompted his reception by the oldest white upper-class family in eastern Maryland,* by the daughter and grandson of the "great" landholder, slaveholder, and governor for whom his own white master-father had worked as a steward. *As a self-made man, he had won their attention as well as their respect.*

In his story of success, Douglass is like millions of self-made Americans who ultimately identify with the powerful. The strong "identification with the aggressor" that they share is far more civilized than that of the great German Martin Luther, who defended the German princes' massacre of the very peasants and miners from whose ranks he had sprung and whose revolt he himself had incited. Luther and his Reformation shook the Western world, but he was not the man Douglass was. We know of no acts of cruelty by Douglass—only acts of compassion. As Weissman puts it, he was indeed "passionate and indignant, but more a man of love than of hate." That was the mark of his greatness.

DOUBLE ETHNIC IDENTITY—A POSTSCRIPT

Freud's own self-analysis sheds much light upon the emotional processes underlying the identity of a man of two cultures, and so serves to elucidate Douglass's dilemma. In Freud's case, the two cultures were Jewish and Christian. Freud was born into a lower-middle-class Jewish family, but through the highest academic attainment and later distinction as a physician and professor, he rose into the Viennese Jewish upper middle class. But not into the Christian class system, from which he always was excluded in Vienna.

Nineteenth-century Vienna, during the time of Freud's youth and early manhood, was a strongly anti-Semitic city. In her biography of Freud, Helen W. Puner writes that Jews "were looked upon as aliens, they were snubbed and humiliated. . . . The Jews of Vienna were a group set aside and rejected by the other ninety percent of the population." Freud's father first lived in a ghetto that was "not quite a slum" and later moved to an apartment in "another dreary Jewish quarter one step removed from a slum," Puner writes.

Freud himself refers to the anti-Semitic feelings and attacks directed against him by his schoolmates in Vienna. In his self-analysis reported in *The Interpretation of Dreams,* Freud writes that in reading of the Punic War, his sympathies were not with beleaguered Rome but with Hannibal, whom he describes as "the Semitic commander." To quote Freud:

> Moreover, when I finally came to realize the consequences of belonging to an alien race, and was forced by the anti-Semitic feeling among my class-mates to take a definite stand, the figure of the Semitic commander [Hannibal] assumed still greater proportions in my imagination. Hannibal and Rome symbolized, in my youthful eyes, the struggle between the tenacity of the Jews and the organization of the Catholic Church. The significance for our emotional life which the anti-Semitic movement has since assumed helped fix the thoughts and impressions of those earlier days.

Freud also played with wooden soliders representing Napoleon's generals. His favorite was one he labeled "Massena (as a Jew Menasse)" under the incorrect impression that Massena was a Jew. Freud's great interest in generals and in war, during his adolescence, certainly was related to his hostility toward anti-Semites; this hostility was probably an effort to defend his sense of worth, of self-esteem, against the derogation he met from the anti-Semites.

As is well known, we are not left in the dark by Freud concerning his youthful indignation and hostility against those Jews who accepted anti-Semitic attacks without making a counterattack. For he has written, in a passage immediately following that on Hannibal quoted above, that he looked down upon his own father for his subservience to anti-Semites.

> I might have been ten or twelve years old when my father began to take me with him on his walks, and in his conversation to reveal his views on the things of this world. Thus it was that he once told me the following incident, in order to show me that I had been born into happier times than he: "When I was a young man, I was walking one Saturday along the street in the village where you were born; I was well-dressed, with a new fur cap on my head. Up comes a Christian, who knocks my cap into the mud, and shouts, 'Jew get off the pavement!' " "And what did you do?" "I went into the street and picked up the cap," he calmly replied. That did not seem heroic on the part of the big, strong man who was leading me, a little fellow, by the hand. I contrasted this situation, which did not please me, with another, more in harmony with my sentiments—the scene in which Hannibal's father, Hamilcar Barcas, made his son swear before the household altar to take vengeance on the Romans. Ever since then Hannibal has had a place in my phantasies.

We know something of the manner Freud used to work out his hostility toward anti-Semites. The resolution of this hostility began when he first decided to be a statesman, rather than a general—that is, to fight *within* the law and by the law, rather than by violence. Thus Freud learned in late adolescence to be against the mob-aggressors. Also, he learned from the Jewish scholarly tradition to regard intellectual superiority as the only real power. In the end, he identified with this tradition, and he added to this training a fierce personal exaltation of the power of the mind in comprehending (but not in overcoming) the violence and anarchy of the world. He enthroned "the spirit of individuation and reason," as Erikson has written, and his "crowning value" was "the primacy of the intellect." From the beginning, he had led his classes in the gymnasium and medical school. As Erikson would say, he had developed "a dominant faculty"—intellect.

Erikson has pointed out that there is a strong pressure by the Jewish middle-class family, in defense against the dominant group's criticism, to make their son "a nice little boy, in spite of his being Jewish." This is a defense against the charges of aggressiveness, foreignness, et cetera. But Freud was never "a nice little Jewish boy." One cannot fully agree, however, with Puner, who writes: "He became, as he was subjected to anti-Semitism in school, as scornful of the turncoats who sought to appease their oppressors by becoming indistinguishable from them, as he was of the oppressors, themselves. . . . Independence and pride . . . held him firmly away from the path of assimilation—attractive as that path might appear." But, as Ernest Jones later pointed out, he never liked Vienna, where Jews were shunted into ghettos, and he always desired to live in England, where the ethnic and social-class barriers against Jews were minimal. Perhaps here we see the typical problem of group identity which remains to some degree unsolved in so-called ethnic and minority groups. How far may one identify with the "aggressor" without losing his sense of autonomy and self-esteem? Only so far, Freud and Douglass believed, as did not make him feel he had no people of his own.

3

The Intellectual as Leader: The Lonely Warrior, W.E.B. Du Bois

William Edward Burghardt Du Bois was the most knowledgeable American empirical sociologist of his time; he was a distinguished essayist and the leading historian of the American slave trade. He lived from 1868 to 1963, nearly one hundred years. Born and schooled in Great Barrington, Massachusetts, he received his higher education at Fisk and Harvard universities and the University of Berlin. His book on the suppression of the slave trade to the United States was published by Harvard University as the first volume in the Harvard Historical Series. He spent fifteen years in Negro colleges as professor and researcher, and twenty-four years with the National Association for the Advancement of Colored People (NAACP) as editor of the successful activist magazine which he founded, the *Crisis*.

This is an effort to understand his personality, his deeply defended conflicts, and the sources of that indomitable strength which he later developed. It is a history of a long embattled journey from his childhood shame and his confusion about his identity to his increasing self-assertion and independence, and finally to his mature identity as an eminent social scientist, gifted essayist, and incorruptible leader of the Negro middle class, their beau ideal.

We shall begin with the impact on his personality of his father's desertion and his mother's disgrace, which forced him to depend largely upon charity during both childhood and adolescence. We shall seek to learn how, after the fear and shame of his early days, he began to develop Tamburlainian ambitions and how he worked for seventy years to achieve these goals. In this endeavor, we shall have to deal not simply with those external attacks launched against him by the American race system, but also with his own internal conflicts. One of these inner conflicts caused him, unlike his contemporary Booker T. Washington, persistently to alienate wealthy or powerful whites who could have helped him attain his goals, and finally drove him to end his life disgraced in their eyes as well as in those of the Negro middle class, as a member of the Communist Party.

Born just five years after the Emancipation Proclamation, in the same year American Negroes got the vote and President Andrew Johnson was impeached, Du Bois lived through nearly a century of the greatest industrial expansion in American history, bloody world wars, and the increasing subordination, segregation, and disfranchisement of American Negroes. Unfortunately, he died just before the federal Civil Rights Act of 1964 and the tremendously effective Voting Rights Act of 1965, which were the crowning successes of his great admirer Martin Luther King, Jr.

In his first autobiographical account, published in *Darkwater* when he was fifty-two, Du Bois offers a highly romanticized and doctored account of his forebears and of his first sixteen years in Great Barrington. He claims his "people were part of a great clan" descended from Tom Burghardt, a slave, who had come to America with his Dutch captor 200 years before Du Bois's birth. His ancestors on the Du Bois side, he claimed, could be traced even earlier—to the era of Louis XIV. Then Du Bois skips "three or four generations" to his great-grandfather, Dr. James Du Bois. But in his next two autobiographies, written twenty and thirty-eight years later, he admitted that he had no records to support these genealogies, and that he no longer accepted the genealogy claimed by the white Du Boises, who maintained that they were descended from French nobility.

His fantasies about his forebears were not as misleading, however, as his embellished account of a happy early life in Great Barrington, his failure to mention the rented rooms in a slum by the railroad tracks in which he and his mother were forced to live, and the racial rejection he encountered in the school he attended until he was sixteen. Instead, he pictures his childhood as idyllic and the racial environment as nondiscriminatory.) In *Dusk of Dawn*, published when he was seventy-two, he recants, admitting that after the age of eleven, owing to the rejection he had met, he withdrew from association with whites. In the *Autobiography* he completed after he was ninety, he changed his stories about his genealogy even more.

The real facts about his early life are these. (On his mother's side, Du Bois's grandparents, the Burghardts, had been respectable small landowners.) (Both his maternal and paternal grandfathers owned their homes; his paternal grandfather read Shakespeare. But their sons and grandsons sold or lost their real estate, and had to go to work for whites as waiters, laborers, or barbers in Massachusetts and Connecticut.) His own mother had lost status more rapidly than any of them because she had borne an illegitimate son, Idelbert, by her first cousin. She later bore Du Bois by Alfred Du Bois, a middle-aged ne'er-do-well, who deserted them a few months after the child's birth. (In *Dusk of Dawn*, Du Bois tells a different story, saying his father died during his infancy.) (Du Bois and his mother then were placed in that most difficult and painful of all social positions—downward social mobility.) Their middle-class status and respectability quietly deteriorated.

(The truth is that Du Bois grew up sensitive and defensive about the possibility of his illegitimate birth, his father's desertion, and his mother's poverty.) (In *Darkwater*, written at the height of his popularity as a Negro leader, he went to great lengths to claim the authenticity of a long family history; he described tracing his mother's people, the Burghardts, to an unidentified West African "Tom" who lived in 1730; and he follows this history forward through more than five generations in America.) (Du Bois also claimed to have traced the ancestry of his father—whom he never saw—from the early 1600s through more than seven generations to his father's father, Alexander Du Bois, born in 1803.) Students of kinship systems know that it is difficult enough to authenticate descent in one direct line through more than three or four generations; and it is nigh impossible where collateral lines are considered over seven generations.

Although most of Du Bois's written accounts of his childhood and adolescence consist of defensive fantasies, the facts do break through at times. He later remembers, for instance, that his mother worked as a domestic and that they lived in rented rooms where they could not pay the rent. To subsist, his mother had to depend upon gifts from charitable whites, and from his illegitimate half-brother, Idelbert, who lived and worked as a waiter in another town: "the little family of my mother and myself must often have been near the edge of poverty. . . . Our landlord, Mrs. Cass, received no rent, I am sure, for long intervals. I think the rent was four dollars a month." The debt finally was written off as a gift when his mother died and he left for college. But before that time, and while his mother was still doing day work as a domestic, they had to move down beside the railroad tracks "right next to the station."

> We lived with a poor white family, kindly, but the wife was near insanity. . . . Soon after, my worrying mother had a paralytic stroke from which she never entirely recovered . . . she was always lame in her left leg, with a withered hand. . . . Sometimes mother went out for a day's work. . . . I always went to bring her home at night. . . .

What kinds of adjustment were available to a very intelligent and ambitious individual like Du Bois who never knew his father in childhood or in adolescence; nor was sure whether his mother had ever really married his father? What recourse does one have if one is able and ambitious, highly sensitive about the color of his skin, and driven to prove—more than anything else in his life—that he is the moral and intellectual equal of any white man despite the fact that whites think him, and he suspects himself to be, "illegitimate"—a "common darky" or a "coon," as most Yankees would call a Negro in that part of Massachusetts?

What can one do if, in school, one surpasses whites in intelligence as well as in aspirations, but is obliged to depend upon the charity of a white woman for schoolbooks, live in a rented room beside the railroad tracks with a poor white madwoman, and move from shack to shack with a crippled, husbandless, penniless mother who does day's work as a servant? What does one do with the inevitable discovery in high school that one is regarded with condescension, if not contempt, despite one's excellence in Latin, Greek, and algebra—and despite all attempts to be the perfect little gentleman with teachers and with the all-powerful whites? How does one swallow insults and humiliation, for instance, if a white girl deliberately turns her back simply because, in a classroom game, one tried to exchange cards with her, as had all the other students?

In short, as a child and an adolescent, how did the fatherless William Edward Burghardt Du Bois resolve his personal struggle for survival in a white world? What kind of man did he become in order to deal with incessant attacks upon his self-esteem; how did he steel himself to face the contempt? *How did he mobilize his initiative and self-assertion?* What forces within him resisted surrender, and enabled him to hold fast to his goal of achieving equality? What force of character prevented regression to that state of self-abasement, self-contempt, and hopelessness which was typical of Negroes marooned in the rocky, barren Berkshires, or stuck in lifelong menial work in Massachusetts towns?

The powerful blows of color prejudice were first struck during Du Bois's childhood. The earliest he reported at the very beginning of his greatest literary work, *The Souls of Black Folk*. At the age of thirty-five it was still his most painful memory. The white boys and girls in his school had brought visiting cards to exchange. Everyone had enjoyed the game until

one girl, a tall newcomer, refused my card—refused it peremptorily.
. . . Then it dawned upon me with a certain suddenness that I was different from the others . . . shut out from their world by a vast veil, to creep through; *I held all beyond it in common contempt,* and

lived in a region of blue sky and great wandering shadows. That sky was bluest when I could beat my mates at examination-time or beat them in a footrace, or even beat their stringy heads. . . . *Why did God make me an outcast and a stranger in mine own house?*

. . . . It is a peculiar sensation, this double consciousness, this sense of *always looking at one's self through the eyes of others.* [Emphasis added.]

The rigidly controlled detachment which he exhibited toward whites thereafter was clearly his defense against the hurt they had caused him. His specific rationalization of his rejection by them was that in decency, idealism, and intelligence it was *he* and not the white person who was superior, and he could gain nothing through contact with them. It was a favorite defense of middle-class Negroes.

A child in American society, in learning that he is a "Negro" or a "black," suffers a damaging blow to his self-esteem and self-respect. He can protect himself for a few years from the pain of rejection by denying the realities of the color barrier and of his inferior position in relation to whites—just as any young child, when confronted by external attacks upon his ego, defends himself by denying the reality of the danger. He denies its existence through fantasies, words, or acts. For instance, a child who feels his father is a threat may fantasize that he himself is a lion, or a giant, and wields more power than his dangerous father. The child may deny reality by words—by telling himself, when his mother is hospitalized, that "she's just gone to visit Grandma." Or he may learn as a baby to defend his ego against fear of separation from his mother by playing an age-old game: the mother hides her face with her fingers and pretends she's gone away. Then she suddenly removes her hands from her face, and laughingly reassures the baby that she is back. The baby laughs and begs "Do it again!" He enjoys this affirmation that his mother, even when she has to leave him, will always return quickly. This psychological process, achieved by fantasy, word, or act, is called "denial." In young children it apparently happens automatically.

Such fantasies, which protected Du Bois's ego by denying the realities of his fatherlessness and his dark skin, served him well as a child. Fantasies of a handsome cavalier father protected his ego from the reality—the pain—of having been deserted and left dependent upon charity. Such denial-by-fantasy is common and *normal* in the young child, whose sense of reality is poorly developed.

But Du Bois clung to his fantasies during adolescence and much later, constantly erecting a façade to protect his ego from shame. Such an effort to live behind a mask, consciously maintained even at the age of ninety, was *not* normal. Its defensive and irrational nature is indicated by the *excess* to which he carried it throughout his life.

In his *Autobiography,* the truth about his early life and his genealogical descent is liberally mixed with—if not obstructed by—such fantasies. Although Du Bois was an able historian and highly skilled in documentary research, he offered no evidence to support his quite romantic genealogical tales, except for reference to a notice in the *Berkshire Courier* of his parents' marriage. But the notice is *not* quoted, only claimed. Du Bois refers twice to other records, but produces none except one unidentified quotation saying that the first black "Burghardt," an African called "Tom," served in the American Revolution. He offers no evidence of the length and place of Tom's service. The truth is that his Burghardt "genealogy," at least in the eighteenth century, is supported by no hard evidence. Furthermore, it is written in a romantic, heroic, pseudopoetic style: "I was born by a golden river" (in actuality, the Housatonic was polluted and muddied by the paper mills); and "Burghardts lived on South Egremont Plain [!] for near 200 years"; and "from these were born a *mighty* family, splendidly named" (although none achieved anything of note). All the women, he writes, were beautiful; his Grandfather Du Bois, he claims, married three beautiful wives in succession, and "loved women in his masterful way." His own father, who deserted him and his mother, and whom he admits he never saw, becomes—in his fantasies—"small and beautiful of face and features, just tinted with the sun!" This saccharine prose is a conscious revival of childhood fantasies that were created originally to defend his ego against the stigmas of being the son of a ne'er-do-well deserter and of being black in white-dominated Great Barrington. Perhaps his fantasies also sought to suppress his worst fear—that of being illegitimate like his half-brother, Idelbert.

Against these deep-seated fears, then, Du Bois retreated into compensatory fantasies in which he became the descendant of two lines of strong men and beautiful women. It is important to notice here that among the beautiful women he did not include his mother (who in a sense was responsible for the loss of his father): ". . . she had a heavy kind face."

On the other hand, at seventy-two, he wrote in *Dusk of Dawn* an unemotional analysis of his environment—a cool appraisal of the town's weak social-class system—accurately identifying its tiny upper group of millowners and executives, its unpretentious Yankee middle class of farmers, merchants, and artisans, and its slum population of German and Irish immigrant millworkers. Beneath them, he said, were the twenty-five to fifty in the Negro population, whose men were waiters in the summer hotels (and tried not to starve the rest of the year, since the millowners hired no Negroes then or later), and whose women were domestic servants like his mother. The only claim he makes for the Burghardts in this second autobiography is that he knows of only *one* illegitimate birth in either his grandfather's or the two succeeding generations, which includes his own generation and his children's. In other words, he asserts that his mother's first son, Idelbert, was the only illegitimate child, and therefore that he himself was *not* illegitimate.

He also states explicitly in *Dusk of Dawn* that he had no genealogical records on either side.

> Absolutely legal proof of facts like those here set down is naturally unobtainable. Records of birth are often nonexistent, proof of paternity is exceedingly difficult and actual written record rare. In the case of my family I have relied on oral tradition in my mother's

family and direct word and written statement from my paternal grandfather; and upon certain doubt of the substantial accuracy of the story that I am to tell.

Of my own immediate ancestors I knew personally only four; my mother and her parents and my paternal grandfather. *One other I knew at second hand—my father. I had his picture.* I knew what my mother told me about him and what others who know him, said. So that in all, five of my immediate forebears were known to me. Three others, my paternal great-grandfather, and great-great-grandfather, I knew about through persons who knew them through records; and also I knew my collateral relatives and numbers of their descendants. My known ancestral family, therefore, consisted of eight or more persons. None of these had reached any particular distinction or were known very far beyond their own families and localities. They were divided into whites, blacks and mulattoes, most of them mulattoes.

The history of his white Du Bois ancestors, as claimed by their descendants, is the same as that given twenty-eight years later in the *Autobiography*. The colored Alexander Du Bois, his own father's father, born in 1803, left only a sketchy diary, which omitted many years of Alexander's life in Haiti, his marriages, and the early life of his son, Alfred, who became the father of W. E. B. Du Bois. But relying on his mother's account, Du Bois wrote that his father, Alfred, had never been able to get along with his own father, Alexander. Later, at fifteen, Du Bois, met this grandfather and found him a proud, aloof man.

As I knew my grandfather, he was a short, stern, upstanding man, sparing but precise in his speech and stiff in manner, evidently long used to repressing his feelings. I remember as a boy of twelve, watching his ceremonious bow, the way in which the red wine was served and the careful almost stilted conversation. I had seen no such social ceremony in my simple western Massachusetts home. The darkened parlor with its horse-hair furniture became a very special and important place. I was deeply impressed. My grandfather evidently looked upon me with a certain misgiving if not actual distaste. I was brown, the son of his oldest son, Alfred, and Alfred and his father had never gotten on together.

The boy Alfred was a throwback to his white grandfather. He was small, olive-skinned and handsome and just visibly colored, with curly hair; and he was naturally a play-boy. My only picture of him shows him clothed in the uniform of the Union Army; but he never actually went to the front. In fact, Alfred actually never did much of anything. He was gay and carefree, refusing to settle long at any one place or job. He had a good elementary school training but nothing higher. I think that my father ran away from home several times. Whether he got into any very serious scrapes or not, I do not know, nor do I know whether he was married early in life; I imagine not. I think he was probably a free lance gallant and lover, yielding only to marital bonds when he found himself in the rather strict clannishness of my mother's family. He was a barber, merchant and preacher, but always irresponsible and charming. He had wandered out from eastern New England where his father lived and come to the Berkshire valley in 1867 where he met and married my brown mother.

And so, at seventy-two, Du Bois still cherished a romantic fantasy of his father as a "gallant and lover," gay and irresponsible, but saw him more realistically than before—he admitted that he may have been "in trouble" with the law, yet insisted that he had married Du Bois's mother. Clearly, he felt ambivalent toward his father; at times critical, at times admiring. This oscillation between romantic fantasy and objective realism was typical of his writing (his objective scientific works in contrast to his oversentimental and childishly romantic novels) as well as of his relationships with people.

Despite the fact that there was no white-collar work for any Negro in Great Barrington and that none had completed high school, Du Bois and his family were determined that he should matriculate. The high-school principal wisely assigned him to the college preparatory curriculum, and he was graduated at the head of his class in 1884 at the age of sixteen. His mother lived to see him graduate, but died that fall.

Although Du Bois expresses no grief over the loss of his mother, and seems to have been as emotionally detached from her as he was from his wife later, he *was* grateful to his mother for having taught him to achieve. She had taught him that his only chance to escape the hopelessness of being a Negro in Great Barrington was to outdo whites in his studies and life's work. She had taught him—as every black middle-class parent strives to teach his child—that to escape the humiliation of poverty and racial discrimination, he must study hard and aspire to reap the rewards of education. As Du Bois reported in his *Autobiography,* his mother held that

> the secret of life and the loosing of the color bar lay in excellence, in accomplishment. If others of my family, of my colored kin, had stayed in school instead of quitting early for small jobs, they could have risen to equal whites. On this mother quietly insisted. There was no real discrimination on account of color [she taught] . . . it was all a matter of ability and hard work.

This was the typical middle-class Negro effort to deny the inescapable nature of the color barrier. (Inescapable for Du Bois because although he became the greatest sociologist in America, he was not recognized by white scholars or offered a post in a white university in his own country.)

Du Bois, like many millions of other educated Negroes later, was taught to internalize white middle-class values; that is, to learn, to achieve, to work hard, to deny oneself pleasure, and to renounce the magnificent sexual vitality and sensualism of the underclass Negroes. The black middle-class code actually was in some ways even more stringent than the value system of the white middle class. It taught Du Bois to work harder and renounce more than a white boy of his low economic status would; and it encouraged him to commit himself to academic achievement as the highest goal, whereas most working-class whites—among older Americans as among German, Swedish, and Irish immigrants—put education last, and money or politics first.

Du Bois realized quite clearly, as he wrote, that his mother had started and encouraged him along this upwardly mobile climb. He found the journey exhilarating but endlessly demanding, difficult, and burdensome. With no money to buy school texts and no parents to help teach him, he started out handicapped in comparison to middle-class white children. But his mother insisted that he outdo them. She pushed because she felt it a matter of his life or death: death, as an unskilled black or a ne'er-do-well like his own father; life, as the nearest one could come to the status of a middle-class white professional, without actually being one.

Du Bois wrote that he was relieved when his mother suddenly died. He felt "free." Du Bois may well have silently resented his mother's pushing him all those years. For she herself had failed, and, by disgracing them, was actually responsible for their downward mobility. Although rationally he saw that she had chosen the only course which could satisfy him, he had to bear the burden of gaining and holding the first place in his class, and of overcoming poverty, shame, and color. He felt sorry for his mother, he nursed her, and he expressed his concern and solicitude for her. But these are not love. In fact, they might have been defensive expressions of guilt from resenting her for having disgraced him.

In any case, Du Bois became restrained, *unexpressive*—perhaps even cold—toward women. He refers to his wife as "my woman" in the German fashion, as *Hausfrau;* until after her death he seldom mentions her, except to say that they were sexually incompatible. Given the manner in which his Grandfather Burghardt was dominated by his wife, it is still doubtful the Burghardts treated their women in this way. And his Grandfather Du Bois—having had more wives than Du Bois could trace—was a *gallant* who wrote poetic love letters to the last woman he married. Du Bois wrote lyrically of the beauty of Negro women at Fisk, but he was actually rude to many women. We know of only one love affair, that with his first wife, which is never described. My belief is that he was afraid of women—after all, he claimed he was "raped" by his landlady in rural Tennessee. No doubt he wished to keep them at arm's length, and therefore was rude to them in one way or another. In the mid-1930s, when he was sixty-seven, I heard him address the graduating classes at Howard University. He spoke on the "racial suicide" being practiced by Washington middle-class Negro women—that our most highly educated women were producing few or no children. This statement was indeed a fact, but a commencement platform and an audience of 2,000 mothers seemed scarcely the place or time to make the accusation. I also remember his reading a paper to a group of white upper-class women, Philadelphia Main Line Quakers, who had invited him to talk in celebration of Negro History Week. Du Bois treated these powerful, wealthy, high-status white women as if they didn't exist; he literally did not look at them, did not express any kind of relationship with them, made no appeal to them of any kind, not even for justice. He was completely withdrawn, apparently invulnerable to whatever they might think or feel about him; he was not a man, but a cold dissector of history.

Attending a Negro college, Fisk, did something to loosen his rigid sexual defense system; certainly it increased his ability to enjoy life. In addition to having adolescent crushes on girls, he made the acquaintance of many Negro men. As editor of a college paper he learned the skills of editing, writing, and running an organization. In his account of his life there, he reveals—as he seldom does—a feeling of being genuinely accepted, and of accepting others. He liked his white Yankee Fisk professors, whom he found both able and honorable.

The city of Nashville, however, was a "cracker" society in which lynchings were frequent. These occurred not only within Nashville, where Fisk is located, but also in neighboring districts. Du Bois was quickly taught that his status in the South was that of something subhuman.

On a Nashville street, 71 years ago, I quite accidentally jostled a white woman as I passed. She was not hurt in the slightest, nor even particularly inconvenienced. Immediately in accord with my New England training, I raised my hat and begged her pardon. I acted quite instinctively and with genuine regret for a little mistake.

The woman was furious; why I never knew; somehow, I cannot say how, I had transgressed the interracial mores of the South. Was it because I showed no submissiveness? Did I fail to debase myself utterly and eat spiritually dirt? Did I act as equal among equals? I do not know. I only sensed scorn and hate; the kind of despising which a dog might incur. Thereafter for at least half a century I avoided the necessity of showing them [whites] courtesy of any sort. If I did them any courtesy which sometimes I must in sheer deference to my own standards of decency, I contrived to act as if totally unaware that I saw them or had them in mind. . . .

Murder, killing, and maiming Negroes, raping Negro women in the '80's and in the southern South, this was not even news; it got no publicity; it caused no arrests; and punishment for such transgression was so unusual that the fact was telegraphed North.

Lynching was a continuing and recurrent horror during my college days; from 1885 through 1894, 1700 Negroes were lynched in America. Each death was a scar upon my soul.

Identification with such despised downtrodden people breeds contempt for oneself, Du Bois wrote. His mother had hoped that by developing his abilities and by hard work he would save himself from poverty and manual labor. *But what would save him from self-hatred and from self-contempt?* That disease requires another cure. Forty-eight years later Du Bois analyzed his own racial self-contempt, bred by caste and class. While he still was young, he could drop his conscious defense at times, as in his admiration for his white professors at Harvard: William James, Albert Bushnell Hart, Frank W. Taussig, and George Santayana. But as the years passed and he discovered the well-nigh universal grip of racism upon America and England—receiving, at no time, recognition for his research from white universities—he refused invitations to meet such prominent white men as George Bernard Shaw and two Presidents of the United States, and to spend weekends with H. G. Wells. He feared that they would try to condescend to him, and after many years of having been snubbed and segregated, he was not willing to accept even inadvertent condescension. If they wished to see him, let them come to him! Or perhaps he held against Shaw and Wells—

although they were Socialists, as he was—some expression of racism in their writings. Or, possibly, he was affirming his defiance of whites.

As to Presidents, he realized that even had he accepted the opportunity to meet them nothing would have come of it since he was *persona non grata* to all of them. For, as a political scientist and historian, he understood the crippling effects of their racial policies. He attributed Booker T. Washington's successes with Theodore Roosevelt, Andrew Carnegie, and the northern capitalists to Washington's willingness to preach subservience to Southern Negroes. In contrast, Du Bois constantly urged them to work to get their political and economic rights.

Of course the two men had been born and reared in entirely different environments. Du Bois, born in Massachusetts, had attended white grammar school and high school, and had led his class. Washington had lived in slavery until he was seven or eight, and then had been taken to West Virginia, where he worked at nine in a salt furnace and in a coal mine, and later, as a houseboy for a retired Northern general and his Yankee "school-marm" wife. Then, starving, he had walked his way to Hampton Institute, where he became the protégé and, later, adopted son of General Samuel C. Armstrong, who taught him that the only hope for Southern Negroes was to be servile workers for Northern industrialists. General Armstrong sought to implant in Washington the same doctrine he had previously passed on to native Polynesians in Hawaii—that they were inferior mentally, could master only manual skills, and must be subservient to whites. All this was meant to reconcile Negroes to giving up their political and social gains of 1867–1877, and to accepting disfranchisement, inferior and segregated education, and plantation peonage. The powerful white Northern capitalists on Armstrong's board at Hampton saw his doctrine as support for their plans to exploit the South economically.

Although Du Bois was defiant, he also realized early that his own emotions were ambivalent and that his identity was split with regard to "race." At times he was ashamed of his color and his "race"; at other times he was proud of his "Negro blood" and aggressive in defense of the rights and abilities of his "people." In his books, he is pulled apart before our very eyes, like a man twisted on a rack. What recourse is there for a Negro American who wants to be accepted as an American, but is constantly rejected by the "only true Americans"—whites?

The imperious nature which, many thought, characterized Du Bois was most obvious in his fantasies of becoming a second Bismarck. His commencement address at Fisk was not on Douglass or abolitionists, but on Bismarck. "Bismarck was my hero. He had made a nation out of a mass of bickering peoples. He had dominated the whole development with his strength. . . . This foreshadowed in my mind the kind of thing that American Negroes must do, marching forth with strength and determination under trained leadership." When, later, he studied in Berlin, he adopted the dress and mustache of a young Kaiser Wilhelm II. Du Bois followed this fashion for the rest of his life; he sported a gold-headed cane, held not like a dandy, but, rather, like a diplomat or head of state. It was part of his mask and of his policy to outdo whites at their own games.

Fortunately, however, living and teaching at backwoods schools near Fisk helped him to understand poor blacks and to enjoy living and working with them. He helped poor rural blacks organize a school, taught it for them, lived with them, and came to enjoy the incomparable vitality of their children and their songs. These summers in the backwoods broadened and deepened his knowledge of the Negro people—their terrible poverty and handicaps, their endurance and indomitable courage. He learned then not to fear getting his hands dirty; later, as professor of sociology in Atlanta University, he set up research projects in Georgia and Alabama, where he was able to keep in constant touch with poor Negroes on plantations and farms. The image of Du Bois as a fop and Fifth

Avenue editor was unjust. Until he was sixty, he knew more about Southern rural blacks in America than did anyone else.

At Harvard, Du Bois suffered social rejection, but he claimed there were compensations. "I was there to enlarge my grasp of the meaning of the universe," Du Bois wrote of his years in Cambridge. He enjoyed studying psychology under the great William James, history under Albert Bushnell Hart, and economics under Frank Taussig. He also met immutable barriers against Negroes, set up by the sons of New England Brahmins. In recalling his exclusion from the Harvard Glee Club, and his failure to meet any Brahmins socially, Du Bois claimed he did not feel rejected. (He took refuge behind his old defense of denial.) Seventy-five years later, he still maintained in his *Autobiography* that being a pariah among students at Harvard did not much disturb him, for William James often had invited him to his home, as had Hart—and the blow had thus been softened. Furthermore, he says, he enjoyed the educated and lovely colored girls of Boston much more than he would have the cold Brahmins.

"I was happy at Harvard, but for unusual reasons," he wrote fifty years later. "One of these unusual circumstances was my *acceptance of racial segregation . . .*" which he said he had learned to accept in the South at Fisk. But this "reason" was exactly that given by whites, North and South, for segregating Negroes: "they are happier together." Du Bois said the difference was that he planned to organize Negroes when he went out into the world, and "break down the boundaries of race." In the meantime he would "forget as far as possible that outer white world."

The fact that this pose was a conscious form of denying reality is made clear by his next paragraph from *Dusk of Dawn:*

> Naturally it could not be entirely forgotten, so that now and then I plunged into it, joined its currents and rose or fell with it. The joining was sometimes a matter of social contact. I escorted colored

girls, and as pretty ones as I could find, to the vesper exercises and the class day and commencement social functions. Naturally we attracted attention and sometimes the shadow of insult, as when in one case a lady seemed determined to mistake me for a waiter. A few times I attempted to enter student organizations, but was not greatly disappointed when the expected refusals came. My voice, for instance, was better than the average. The glee club listened to it but I was not chosen a member. It posed the later recurring problem of a "nigger" on the team.

In general, I asked nothing of Harvard but the tutelage of teachers and the freedom of the library. I was quite voluntarily and willingly outside its social life. I knew nothing of and cared nothing for fraternities and clubs. Most of these which dominated the Harvard life of my day were unknown to me even by name.

I was in Harvard but not of it and realized the irony of "Fair Harvard." I sang it because I liked the music.

Actually, he sang "Fair Harvard" because he was not clear how he felt. Half a century later, however, he saw Harvard as the reactionary defender of capitalism, and saw the men who owned and controlled it as the guardians of reaction. At the height of post-Reconstruction industrialization in 1896 they were making "Harvard rich but reactionary. This defender of wealth and capital, already half-ashamed of Sumner and Phillips, was willing finally to replace an Eliot with a Lowell. The social community that mobbed Garrison, easily hanged Sacco and Vanzetti." At the time he wrote this, Du Bois was not a Communist; on the contrary, he was advocating black economic nationalism, segregated business, and Negro cooperatives.

Du Bois received his A.B. from Harvard in 1890, his A.M. in 1891, his Ph.D. in 1895. Between his first graduate work and the time he completed his doctoral dissertation on the suppression of the slave trade to the United States, he had the tremendously liberating experience of spending two years studying at the University of Berlin and traveling in Germany, Italy, France, and England. In spite of his A.B. *cum laude* and A.M. from Harvard, and letters of praise from his professors, Du Bois had to fight for his tiny scholarship for study in Germany under more able social scientists than any at Harvard. He had read a speech by the head of the board of the Slater Fund (for Negro education), ex-President of the United States Rutherford B. Hayes, who offered European education to "any young colored man in the South whom we find to have talent for art or literature or any special aptitude for study." Du Bois wrote ex-President Hayes asking for a scholarship. He was told the program had been dropped. Indignantly Du Bois deluged Hayes with recommendations from the leading scholars at Harvard, only to receive the same reply. Du Bois then "impudently" accused him of bad faith. Hayes finally apologized, promising to take up the matter the following year with his board. Du Bois had to wait another year, during which he received his A.M. and prepared a paper which he read before the American Historical Society. He again applied to Hayes, whose board granted Du Bois a very small scholarship of $375, with the offer to lend him another $375, to be renewed possibly for a second year. Du Bois was overjoyed. In fact, he had imposed upon the Slater Fund to the extent that their original offer had specified "any young colored man in the South"— and Du Bois was from Great Barrington, Massachusetts.

His European diary offers one the opportunity to view Du Bois more objectively, entirely outside the American racist environment. At first, he felt joyfully emancipated from the bonds of the American racial system.

> They did not always pause to regard me as a curiosity, or something sub-human; I was just a man of the somewhat privileged student rank, with whom they were glad to meet and talk over the world; particularly, the part of the world whence I came.
>
> One annoyance I met here and all over Europe: the landlord would hasten to inform me beamingly that "Fellow Americans just had arrived." If there was one thing less desirable than white "fellow Americans" to me, it was black "fellow Americans" to them.
>
> Of greatest importance was the opportunity which my *Wanderjahre* in Europe gave of looking at the world as a man and not

simply from a narrow racial and provincial outlook. This was primarily the result not so much of my study, as of my human companionship, unveiled by the accident of color. From the days of my later youth in the South to my boarding a Rhine passenger steamer at Rotterdam in August 1892, I had not regarded white folk as human in quite the same way that I was. I had reached the habit of expecting color prejudice so universally, that I found it even when it was not there. So when I saw on this little steamer a Dutch lady with two grown daughters and one of 12, I proceeded to put as much space between us as the small vessel allowed. But it did not allow much, and the lady's innate breeding allowed less. Soon the little daughter came straight across the deck and placed herself squarely before me. She asked if I spoke German; before I could explain, the mother and other daughters approached and we were conversing.

Before we reached the end of our trip, we were happy companions, laughing, eating and singing together, talking English, French and German and viewing the lovely castled German towns. Once or twice when the vessel docked for change of cargo, the family strolled off to visit the town. Each time I found excuse to linger behind and visit alone later; until once at Dusseldorf, all got away before I sensed it and left me and the prettiest daughter conversing. Then seeing we had docked she suggested we follow and see the town. We did; and thereafter we continued acting like normal, well-bred human beings. I waved them all good-bye, in the solemn arched aisles of the Cologne Cathedral, with tears in my eyes.

The high point of his sojourn with Germans occurred during his first two months there. In Eisenach, beneath Luther's Wartburg, he lived in the home of the Rector of the Wartburg, as a paying guest in the company of students from all major European nations. He was fully accepted by the family and students, and he and Dora, the blue-eyed daughter with "lovely skin coloring," fell in love.

Dora always paired with me, first to correct my German and then by preference. Once we all went to the annual ball of the upper middle-class folk in the town. It was formal and a little stiff. The carefully gowned matrons sat around the walls of the room, knitting and gossiping and keeping watch over the demure white-gowned girls in their charge. The fathers sat at tables and drank beer, I danced with all the girls of our home; then bowing from the waist ventured to ask other young ladies to whom I had been introduced. Then came the *Damen Wahl* [Ladies Choice], I drew back, but it was unnecessary, for my card was filled for every dance.

I was very fond of Dora Marbach and as I well knew, so was she of me. Our fellows joked about us and when I sang the folk song of *Die Lora am Thore* [Lora at the Gate], little Bertha invariably changed the name to "Dora." We confessed our love for each other and Dora said she would marry me "gleich!" [at once]. But I knew that would be unfair to her and fatal for my work at home, where I had neither property nor social standing for this blue-eyed stranger. She could not quite understand. Naturally I received much advice as to marriage plans. One lady told me very seriously *"Sie sollen heiraten eine hellblonde.* [You ought to marry a blonde.]" But I knew better.

Since we know Du Bois usually "denies," this story is probably exaggerated. He "protests too much" that he was loved; more likely he was accepted without prejudice, which in the light of his constant fears of being rejected by whites appeared to him to be passionate love. As we know, he was not a man with whom women were at ease, and he was certainly not one at whom they threw themselves. At any rate, during his last two years in Europe, he never again mentions a woman. He made no male friends of his own age, except another outsider, an Englishman. On numerous occasions he claims that he chose to be alone—and he did travel alone on most of his European tours.

Why was he alone so often, especially when he was in a university with 5,000 registered students? It is clear that Du Bois not only was shy with women, but did not trust men. His father's desertion left him unsure of a man's loyalty or affection, and as a result he could not get along with men who were in authority. But his two best friends, John Hope and Joel Spingarn, were quite shy and mild, and Du Bois remained their friend for more than thirty years. Beneath a mask of cold detachment were shyness and what he called "sickly sentimentality." On his twenty-fifth birthday in Berlin he says he invited in no one, although he was "a little lonesome and far away from home and boyhood friends." He thought of his dead parents, went to hear Schubert's *Unfinished Symphony,* and had a curious ceremony in his room "with candles, Greek wine, oil and song, and prayer." This was a ritual dedicating his library to the memory of his mother. He also wrote at that time an oath to guide his life:

Night-grand and wonderful. I am glad I am living. I rejoice as a strong man to win a race, and I am strong—is it egotism—is it assurance—or is it the silent call of the world spirit that makes me feel that *I am royal and that beneath my sceptre a world of kings shall bow.* The hot dark blood of a black forefather is beating at my heart, and I know that I am either a genius or a fool. O I wonder what I am—I wonder what the world is—I wonder if life is worth the *Sturm.* I do not know—perhaps I never shall know: But this I do know: be the Truth what it may I will seek it on the pure assumption that it is worth seeking—and Heaven nor Hell, God nor Devil shall turn me from my purpose till I die. I will in this second quarter century of my life, enter the dark forest of the unknown world for which I have so many years served my apprenticeship—in the chart and compass which the world furnishes me I have little faith—yet I have nothing better—I will seek till I find—and die. There is a grandeur in the very hopelessness of such a life—Life? And is life all? If I strive, shall I live to strive again? I do not know and in spite of the wild Sehnsucht [yearning] for Eternity that makes my heart stick now and then—I shut my teeth, and say I do not care. *Carpe Diem* [Seize the day!—that is, enjoy the present]. What is life but life, after all? Its end is its greatest and fullest self—and this end is the Good: the Beautiful is its attribute—its soul, and Truth is its being. Not three commensurable things are these, they are three dimensions of the cube. Mayhap God is the fourth, but for that very reason he will be incomprehensible. The greatest and fullest life is by definition beautiful, beautiful—beautiful as a dark passionate woman, beautiful as a golden-hearted school girl, beautiful as a grey haired hero. That is the dimension of *breadth.* Then comes Truth—what is, cold and indisputable.

Apparently he had adopted the *Weltanschauung* of the "Sturm und Drang" writers, probably influenced by Goethe's *Die Leiden des Jungen Werthers*. At any rate, his inner reality was as distant as possible from his façade of cold withdrawal. And what Tamburlainian ambitions!

At Wilberforce College, a Negro African Methodist Episcopalian church school in Xenia, Ohio, where he first taught, Du Bois's imperiousness and rudeness were frankly expressed and he was constantly in hot water with the President and the Trustees. During his second year there (1895), however, he completed a masterly dissertation, received his Ph.D. from Harvard, and had his dissertation published as the first volume in the Harvard Historical Series (*The Suppression of the African Slave-Trade to the United States of America, 1638–1870*). As a result he was offered a one-year appointment by the University of Pennsylvania. His rank, *assistant instructor*, was unknown at any reputable university. But he was attracted by his duties, which were to conduct and write a study on the social and economic condition of the Negro population of Philadelphia. The salary was $900 a year, including his research expenses. He had no office on campus and was neither accepted by the white faculty, nor invited to faculty meetings. Despite the fact that his book *The Philadelphia Negro* (1899) proved to be an unparalleled work of empirical research for many years afterward, he was not retained by the University of Pennsylvania, nor offered a post later. The University simply had wanted him to conduct one study of the Negro population because the Negro population of Philadelphia was beginning to encroach upon its grounds.

Before leaving Wilberforce, Du Bois married a student, Nina Gomer, whose father was the Negro chef at a Cedar Rapids, Iowa, hotel. Her mother, Du Bois said, was a "German hausfrau," so that he clearly had not forgotten the blue-eyed Dora with whose family he had lived in Germany. After giving a few facts about their trip to Chicago and a reception at Wilberforce, Du Bois scarcely mentions her again until the review of his life written when he was over ninety. Clearly Nina Gomer was only a *Hausfrau* to him—the mother of his son and daughter. He says she had no interest in sex, that the life went out of her after the early death of their son, and that thereafter she had no interest in social life. He always referred to her as "wife," that is, "wife says" or "wife thinks" or sometimes as "woman"—no doubt a habit he picked up in Germany, and one which inflated his defenses against the fear of women.

In 1897, Du Bois read a paper at the forty-second meeting of the American Academy of Political and Social Sciences in Philadelphia. In it he announced his intention to carry on a continuous scientific study of American Negro life, and his determination that this research should be objective and free of racial bias—a goal to which he devoted the next thirteen years of his life at Atlanta University.

> The American Negro deserves study for the great end of advancing the cause of science in general. No such opportunity to watch and measure the history and development of a great race of men ever presented itself to the scholars of a modern nation. If they miss this opportunity—if they do the work in a slipshod, unsystematic manner—if they dally with the truth to humor the whims of the day, they do far more than hurt the good name of the American people; they hurt the cause of scientific truth the world over, they voluntarily decrease human knowledge of a universe of which we are ignorant enough, and they degrade the high end of truth-seeking in a day when they need more and more to dwell upon its sanctity.

In that same year, 1897, he presented to the head of the United States Bureau of Labor Statistics a detailed plan for the study of Negro laborers, skilled workers, and professionals in selected Southern areas, which resulted in his doing a series of such studies. But the Bureau destroyed his reports without publication, except his study of Farmville, Virginia.

In the autumn of 1897, when he was twenty-nine, Du Bois was invited to Atlanta University as professor of sociology, and asked

to take charge of an annual institute on Negroes in cities, parallel-
ing Hampton's and Tuskegee's Farmers Institute. Du Bois greatly
expanded this plan, and during his thirteen years there he published
fifteen sociological reports dealing with a great variety of black institutions: Negro occupational groups, health, morality, crime, et
cetera. His faith in changing the attitudes of whites through appeals to reason and objective research continued to be his strongest
motivation, and he planned studies of Negro life not simply for
another ten years but for the next 100 years: "I laid down an ambitious program for a hundred years of study." With his first two
books published by two Ivy League colleges, Harvard and Pennsylvania, and fifteen reports by him and his black students published by Atlanta University, he had become one of the most
proficient social scientists in the United States. The concise, clear,
and well-organized *The Negro Family*, written by Du Bois and his
students, for instance, remains, in its clarity, organization, and objectivity, equal to anything published thereafter on the black family.
With his training at Harvard in history and political science, and in
Germany in sociology, government, economics, and quantitative
techniques, Du Bois became an exemplary social scientist. One has
only to compare the clarity, thoroughness, and empiricism of *The
Philadelphia Negro* (1899) with W. I. Thomas and F. Znaniecki's
The Polish Peasant in Europe and America, published two decades
later, to see how much of a forerunner Du Bois was among American empirical sociologists. His work has little or none of the be-
fuddled social psychological sentimentality of *The Polish Peasant*.

Du Bois also influenced the most productive black social scientists and creative writers for the next forty years. Indeed, it was Du
Bois, not Alain Locke, whom writers of the "Negro Renaissance"
of the 1920s, most admired as a writer. At Atlanta, Du Bois also
taught the *upward mobility dream*, with its powerful incentive and
hope, to black students, demanding that they work to equal and
surpass whites. Following his inspiration, thousands of efficient and
determined black teachers—ranging from Ivy League honor grad-

uates who taught in Dunbar High School, Washington, D.C., to those in poor Southern "training schools," which whites would not dignify with the name "high schools"—insisted on hard work and achievement from their black students. Black principals demanded excellence, as did the man in charge of the Mobile County Training School in Alabama who insisted that hundreds of black youngsters (including Albert Murray, today a gifted writer) come to school at 6:00 A.M. to master their grammar. There was Hazel Harrison at Tuskegee, who, as Ralph Ellison recalls, had been one of Busoni's pupils, had known Prokofiev personally, and had even played from his original scores for her own Tuskegee students. From such highly trained and gifted black teachers, Ralph Ellison and many other black students often had opportunities to learn what was not yet taught at the vast majority of white American colleges.

For the best years of his life, Du Bois steadfastly strove to ascertain the nature and meaning of behavior in the black society, with the honest hope of alleviating—through the therapy of reason and truth—the vast race hatred in America. He set the highest criteria of objectivity for himself, and during those years—with his gift for writing—he showed himself to be a social scientist of great ability and the highest professional ideals.

But he came to realize that the black middle-class belief that education would overcome white prejudice and white oppression had led him into a blind alley. As had most educated blacks, he found that whenever he sought to compete with whites professionally, he met the impasse of color. No white college or university ever offered Du Bois a teaching position, and none in the United States ever offered him an honorary degree. Yet he had published the classic history *The Suppression of the African Slave-Trade,* had gathered the data for and had written the most outstanding American empirical sociological work (*The Philadelphia Negro*), had carried out the most thorough and objective studies of any racial or ethnic group in America (the series of fifteen Atlanta University

Studies of the Negro Problem), and had published one of the most enduring and critically acclaimed essay collections of our time, *The Souls of Black Folk*.

In the meantime, however, he had learned, firsthand, of the oppression and lynching of blacks in Georgia and lived through that horrible day when the amputated knuckles of Sam Hose, a black farmer lynched by whites, were put on display in the window of a white store in Atlanta. Du Bois had to live with the brutal fact that 200 to 300 blacks in the South were lynched each year—over 2,700 had been lynched during his years teaching there. His defense had been to withdraw from all contact with Southern whites. He would not ride the segregated streetcars, but walked wherever he went. He would not attend segregated theaters, lectures, or meetings. He lived and moved entirely within the black community. His was the typical stance of the middle-class Negro: "Stay away from whites; live in your segregated world." In his daily life in the South he tried to deny reality; he told himself, "It is not I who am inferior; whites are the oppressors and murderers—they are my inferiors." But by 1910, after twenty-three years of research, and after witnessing the Atlanta race-riot murders, he realized that his intellectual work and his morality were powerless to stop lynching, peonage, or terrorization. Furthermore, he saw that, unlike Booker T. Washington, he had no actual *power*, either political, social, or economic; and finally he realized that he had withdrawn from social and economic reality. By limiting himself to research, he had—in his own works—"tried to isolate myself in the ivory tower of race."

In view of his devoted mother's exacting middle-class training, which taught him to abhor violence, one would not expect Du Bois to respond like Douglass, with counterviolence. One feels certain he never refused to move back in the bus and never tried to ride in the whites' cars in a Jim Crow train. He led no boycotts or demonstrations involving violence. He never took the physical risks which Professor John A. Davis, whose work he praised, took in

1935 by leading black boycotts and by picketing white stores that refused to employ blacks.* Du Bois did not champion the boycott—the Negro's most powerful weapon—as Professor Charles G. Gomillion did at Tuskegee, as King, Reverend Fred L. Shuttleworth, and SCLC did in Montgomery and Birmingham, and as the black college students did in Greensboro, N.C., Nashville, and Atlanta. In short, Du Bois in the South, like all other middle-class blacks in those days, had practiced, not physical confrontation, but *withdrawal* into a separate black subordinated society.

Despite avoiding the activist's role, however, he found himself after twenty-three years of research, not only without the necessary funds ($2,500 to $5,000 a year) to continue his unrivaled sociological studies, but also convinced that his work had had no influence in gaining a modicum of justice for blacks, and that this failure was due to the fact that he had no organization behind him, and, therefore, no power.

Earlier, in 1905, he had decided to attack openly Booker T. Washington's leadership and work, which Du Bois felt only maintained Negro servility. Du Bois felt, too, that Washington discouraged collegiate education for Southern Negroes—although Washington wanted it for his own children and even persuaded Andrew Carnegie to finance his daughter's musical education in Europe.

Accordingly, Du Bois invited Negro leaders from seventeen states to meet at Fort Erie in Canada, and on July 9, 1905, twenty-nine men from fourteen states met to plan an attack upon segregation, discrimination, and disfranchisement in the United States. From this meeting arose the "Niagara Movement," incorporated on January 31, 1906 in the District of Columbia. Booker T. Washington, as a result of this opposition, persuaded white foundations to cut off financial support for Du Bois and for Atlanta University. The

---

* Dr. Davis and Attorneys Belford Lawson and Thurman Dodson took the cases to the U.S. Supreme Court and won the right for all consumers to picket. See *New Negro Alliance* v. *Sanitary Grocery Co.,* 303 U.S. 555 and 303 U.S. 542.

battle lines were drawn—and Washington had been the chief aggressor.

In the same year that Du Bois founded the Niagara Movement, a violent race riot broke out in Atlanta. Du Bois rushed home from one of his rural projects to try to protect his family. A race war on his very doorstep—an attempted massacre started by whites—must have convinced Du Bois that he could do nothing to change the situation in Atlanta; he would need a Northern base from which he could influence Congress and the North.

Du Bois found this platform in 1910, when he was invited to join a few white liberals and Socialists led by William English Walling, a Socialist from the Midwest, Mary White Ovington, a social worker, and Oswald Garrison Villard, a publisher and a philanthropist, in forming the National Association for the Advancement of Colored People (NAACP). As editor of the *Crisis*, which he had founded in spite of opposition from the chairman of the NAACP's board, Du Bois soon became the best-known leader of the Negro civil-rights movement. He attacked lynching, disfranchisement, segregated schools, and a hundred forms of racial discrimination. Over the following two decades, his independence of judgment, his fearlessness, and his powerful intellectual grasp of the Negro's problems served to educate both the Negro middle class and the liberal white world.

Nevertheless, Booker T. Washington had succeeded in driving out the most able man in Negro education by seeing that his funds and those of Atlanta University were cut off. During that time, foundations, white philanthropists, and most Negroes thought Washington wise in emphasizing trade schools and industrial education for Negroes, and Du Bois unrealistic in emphasizing college training for the "talented tenth." Once driven away, Du Bois did not return to Negro education until twenty-two years later.

In the period between 1902 and 1910, at the height of their confrontation, Washington appeared much more realistic and farsighted. *The opposite has proved to be the case.* Only a few years after his death, Tuskegee had to become principally an academic teachers college, owing to the pressure of students whose parents wanted them to attain white-collar or professional positions. Du Bois foresaw this movement toward white-collar status. By 1980, basic technological and economic changes in American society had more than doubled the proportion of blacks holding white-collar jobs. It has been precisely this increase in the black middle class—from less than 10% of the total black population in Southern cities in 1940, and from little more than 15% in Northern cities, to a rate twice as high now—which both economically and educationally has constituted the most significant force in the move toward that racial equality Du Bois so ardently desired.

But whose educational philosophy prevailed? The answer lies in an analysis of employment statistics. According to the U.S. Department of Commerce and the U.S. Bureau of Labor Statistics, only 12.8% of all black workers had white-collar jobs in 1957. For 1980, the same federal sources reported 40%. Today *four out of every ten black workers have white-collar jobs. During the last twenty years, the percentage of blacks holding white-collar jobs has increased five times as rapidly as that of whites*.

Contrast this increase in black white-collar workers with that of black "craftsmen and foremen," whose numbers constitute only 7% of the black working population. Since the Second World War, the previously rigid barricade against black white-collar workers in federal bureaus and in business and industry has gradually weakened. Not so, however, in the *craft and building unions*.

The large increase in the proportion of blacks holding middle-class occupations has resulted from the change in the basic technology of American and Western societies. This change has led to rapid increase in semiprofessional and computer-created jobs *among whites*. As the *new* types of white-collar, small-executive, and skilled work available to *whites* increased after 1950, there was an exodus of whites from federal bureaus, from clerical jobs in business, and so on. Many employers, including the Post Office and federal offices, had to use black white-collar workers to replace whites who had taken better-paying jobs in the many new types of electronic industries, including the expanding field of symbolic manipulation and data analysis. In Chicago, for instance, nearly half of all bank tellers—responsible but poorly paid workers—are blacks.

The great increase in employment of blacks in white-collar positions has taken place chiefly in the following fields: (1) professional, technical, and kindred work, in which the proportion increased by 150% and (2) clerical work, in which the increase was more than 200%. The increase began slowly in the 1940s as a result of the Fair Employment Practice Committee, established by President Franklin D. Roosevelt's executive order 8802, which, in turn, was based upon the original guidelines and plans of the New York State Fair Employment Practice Committee (the first in the nation), which had been made effective by Professor John A. Davis of the City College of the University of New York.*

Nearly twenty years later, the black civil-rights movement of the late 1950s and early 1960s culminated in federal laws which afforded minimum case-by-case sanctions against job discrimination on federally financed work. Moreover, the black civil-rights movement—notably the work of Martin Luther King, Jr., the Southern Christian Leadership Conference, and the Southern Nonviolent Coordinating Committee—changed the middle-class white image of the educated black. The effectiveness, intelligence, and middle-class self-control which King displayed on nightly television changed the whites' image of educated blacks from that of an alien, primitive, and lazy group to that of a group of genuinely middle-class people: purposeful, committed to the Protestant ethic, and highly responsible. This new image of the educated black emerged at exactly the same time (the mid-1960s) that the image of white educated youth had shifted to one representing rebellion, radicalism, and destruc-

---

*After the Second World War, the most effective work in job integration also was that of Professor John A. Davis, acting as a member of the New York State Commission Against Discrimination.

tion of the middle-class work ethic. White educated youth now seemed ready to scorn the middle-class ideals of hard work and self-renunciation. The new positive white view of educated blacks made them more acceptable to whites in middle-class jobs, and accelerated the rise in the proportion of blacks who obtained white-collar jobs. But that increase had begun ten years before, in the early 1950s, with the turn of technology toward electronics and computerization.

The sharp rise of income among black middle-class families since 1960 results from the holding of multiple jobs. The wife may work as teacher, nurse, social worker, or secretary, and earn between $8,000 and $23,000 a year in Chicago; while the husband may work as a teacher, salesman, or assistant personnel officer, at times working two jobs, and earn from $12,000 to $30,000 a year. The joint incomes in such middle-class black families vary from $25,000 to $45,000 per year and enable them to buy a home, a car, and to educate their children.

Most of this increase in white-collar jobs held by blacks results from the employment of women. Their income constitutes the added factor which makes it possible to meet middle-class goals, including educating one's children in private schools (rather than in ghetto schools controlled by gangs) and aiding one's children in college and professional school. The types of well-paying jobs held by large numbers of black women are quite numerous and the total number is increasing. Most educated black women today work as teachers, librarians, social workers, nurses, secretaries, computer operators and programmers, newscasters (especially on television), bank tellers, typists, clerks in federal bureaus, and clerks and carriers in the United States Postal Service.

The relative acceptance of the educated white-collar black has not been matched, however, by similar recruiting of the *skilled black working class*. Owing to discrimination by white unions, blacks have not been able to enter apprentice programs in any significant numbers; as a result, the proportion of blacks in the North becoming licensed plumbers, machinists, steelworkers, or journeymen in other trades, including nearly all the skilled building trades, has *not* increased significantly. For instance, in 1957, only .5% of blacks were carpenters. Today it is still less than 1%. In 1957, mechanics and repairmen constituted 1.8% of black workers; they are still only about 2%.

So time and the rise of the monopolistic, politically protected trade unions has led to an ironic outcome of the famous Du Bois–Washington debates on the relative need for "industrial" (trades) education on the one hand, and for college education on the other. Neither Du Bois nor Washington decided the ultimate outcome of the struggle between the two policies. The pivotal force was the racial barrier set up by white craft unions and most of the member unions of the American Federation of Labor, who have proved more thoroughly racist in excluding blacks than has any other group in America, including the Mississippi white planters.

Actually, fifty years ago, it was already evident that Negro "industrial" education was passé. By that time, the so-called industrial schools, which had never had the money and equipment to teach artisans, and especially machinists, had all begun to concentrate upon training elementary and high-school teachers. By 1925, both Tuskegee Institute and Hampton Institute, its mother, had become primarily academic teachers colleges. Some "industrial" schools upgraded their course in agriculture into a much more popular college course in veterinary medicine; others added college courses in nursing, building construction, and, finally, in 1953, engineering.

Thus, historically, Du Bois's educational philosophy was the one to prevail. One has only to look at the U.S. Census of Occupations for blacks, as we have already done, to learn that the black white-collar, semiprofessional, and professional groups have increased far more rapidly than skilled blacks. Every day, new gains are made in the employment of the college-trained black. The largest white universities have increasing numbers of black professors. Chemical firms, for example, have had black chemists since the Manhattan Project in 1944–1945; many black chemists have headed their own laboratories in white firms, and their numbers in white universities and plants are still on the increase.

But not so with black skilled workers. As late as 1966, it took a federal injunction, obtained by William R. Ming in the United States District Court of Northern Illinois, to stop the erection of a new federal building in Chicago because not one black steel-construction worker was employed. In the years following, only a handful of blacks was admitted by the United Steelworkers. While blacks in growing numbers secured white-collar and small professional positions, *blue-collar* blacks could not penetrate the construction job market, except to push wheelbarrows. Booker T. Washington greatly underestimated the stubborn and prevalent racism in white craft unions; but Du Bois attacked them often, both in his earlier research and in the *Crisis*—as Douglass had, long before. Du Bois had the common sense to recognize that power and money in this society usually go to those with knowledge and education—not to plumbers, carpenters, and machinists, or to workers that black "industrial" schools were training: shoemakers, tinsmiths, bricklayers, and auto mechanics. He emphasized education for the ambitious, the academically oriented—and this is precisely the class that is maintaining the black community today, and that has become necessary to the white economy. White-collar and professional work has proved an easier route to good income, good housing, and the education of one's children than have trades—an easier route by far. In his educational prophecy and policy making, Washington was merely an excellent politician; this fact was evident to Tuskegee, Hampton, and the black land-grant colleges fifty years ago.

Of course, Du Bois never seriously addressed the very bottom group in the urban black community. His only contact with the most deprived urban blacks took place in his gathering data in a Philadelphia ghetto. He had been taught by his mother to admire the ambitious, the studious, the achievers, and, like the rest of his society—black and white—he expected no great desire for self-improvement or achievement from lower-class blacks. In fact, Du Bois did not like the rabble—the *lumpen proletariat*. He was ill at ease with their way of life, their sexual freedom, their violence. This feeling he made clear in his reaction to the followers of Marcus Garvey in Harlem. But he was a magnificent leader of the Negro middle class—aspiring, aggressive, hard-working, articulate.

His greatest influence upon middle-class and upper-working-class Negroes was exerted during his years as editor of the *Crisis*; especially the years between 1915 and 1925. Through incisive and often moving appeals to join in the battle against segregation and lynching, he became the spiritual leader of middle-class Negroes. In his accounts of lynchings, he wrote with anger and gall, and at times, it seemed, with the very blood and agony of the dying Negro. For middle-class Negroes of my father's and of my own generation, his descriptions may well have been the most powerful and terrifying experience of their lives. The majority of those Negro children and adolescents who would become scholars, teachers, lawyers, and professional men between 1920 and 1950 read the *Crisis* each month, as a family magazine. One can be certain that *none* of them has forgotten Du Bois's descriptions of lynchings. They were as vividly portrayed as if the sweat rolled down his own face and the fire consumed his own body. He wrote of burnings at the stake, of the castration of black men, and of the disembowelment of pregnant black mothers. He wrote as if his own flesh cracked and popped in the searing fire; as if his own eyes bulged from their sockets; as if his own heart had finally burst—his mouth crying out in the insupportable, final agony. The *Crisis* molded a generation with the sensitivity, anger, and moral indignation of their spiritual leader, Du Bois. Forty years later, rejected by American blacks, he would write that the words, the maxims, the goals enunciated by black leaders of the 1960s were his own words, taken from his own mouth.

Despite the opposition he met at the very start from Oswald Garrison Villard, son of William Lloyd Garrison's favorite daughter and chairman of the NAACP's board, Du Bois threw himself vigorously into the work of building what would become the most effective journalistic force against racial oppression. In four years, the membership of the NAACP rose to only 6,000, but the *Crisis* had 34,000 subscribers and at least five times that many readers. In eight years, it had over 100,000 subscribers annually.

Villard had opposed the appointment of Du Bois as editor for fear he would attack Booker T. Washington and the Northern capitalists. Specifically, Villard hoped Andrew Carnegie would donate funds to the NAACP, but Carnegie and Theodore Roosevelt had long been Washington's most powerful friends. Although Du Bois did not use the *Crisis* to attack Washington, Carnegie gave the NAACP nothing. And Theodore Roosevelt, running for President as a Progressive, labeled Du Bois "a dangerous person" when Jane Addams and Joel Spingarn presented him with Du Bois's statement on race which had been suggested for the Progressive Party's platform. The Progressive candidate proved far from progressive on the color question.

Three of the white founders of the NAACP were Socialists: Mary White Ovington, William English Walling, and Charles Edward Russell. A year after the founding, they persuaded Du Bois to join the Socialist Party. Of these, Mary Ovington became Du Bois's loyal supporter and adviser in his repeated confrontations with Villard. Both men had quick tempers, both tended to be uncompromising, and Villard certainly had some of the white abolitionist's condescension toward Negroes. Du Bois never had tolerated a white man's condescension; and the fact that Villard had a Southern wife and that no Negro—not even Du Bois—was ever invited to their home increased Du Bois's distrust.

Mary Ovington, however, learned what Villard and most of the "white-people-know-best" breed never learn: that Negroes must and can gain their own freedom, make their own decisions, stand on their own feet. Ovington reminded Villard during the first year of the NAACP that "I find myself still occasionally forgetting that the Negroes aren't poor people for whom I must kindly do something, and then comes a gathering such as that last evening and I learn they are men with most forceful opinions of their own."

With Ovington's help as a buffer against Villard, and the later advice of the more tactful James Weldon Johnson (*God's Trombones*; *The Autobiography of an Ex-Colored Man*), who later ran the Association as executive secretary, field organizer, and money raiser, Du Bois had ten highly productive years. His editorials were often magnificent in logic and force, and his writing became tight—free of false eloquence and sharply honed. His only rival was H. L. Mencken; and as Du Bois addressed crimes more offensive to a universal civilized morality than did Mencken, his writing wielded more power. He soon became known all over the world as the most able spokesman for the Negro Americans; with the organization of the first three Pan-African Congresses, Du Bois became the acknowledged spokesman for all Negroes.

In fact, the Pan-African Congresses that he organized were never effective against the colonial offices of England, France, and Belgium. Only twelve Africans attended the 1919 Congress in Paris. The United States and England had tried to prevent the first Congress, but Du Bois succeeded in organizing it through dogged determination and with the help of the Senegalese member of the French Parliament, Blaise Daigne, who was granted permission by Clemenceau to hold it in Paris. "The results of this meeting were small." The later meetings in London, Brussels, Paris in 1921 (with thirty-nine Africans, thirty-five American Negroes, and thirty-nine blacks from Europe), London in 1923, and New York in 1927 received publicity and stimulated a few Negroes and liberals to be interested in African independence, but accomplished nothing else. A subsequent Pan-African Congress was proposed for Tunis, North Africa, in 1929, but the French Government refused permission. Yet, as Du Bois wrote in 1939, "the idea is not entirely dead," for some of the African "radical" students in London in the 1920s became leaders of the independence parties in their colonial homelands thirty years later. These colonies did indeed become politically, if not economically, independent. In his effort to bring together the Negro people of the world, Du Bois had been far more foresighted, not only than most American Negroes, who wanted nothing to do with Africa, but than the Africans themselves.

In Du Bois's political experience, well-known white American liberals did not act in the interest of American Negroes. Theodore Roosevelt refused to include a platform statement promising Negroes equal treatment, as suggested by the NAACP and Du Bois; and at the 1947 Paris meeting of the Human Rights Commission of the United Nations, Eleanor Roosevelt, along with Jonathan Daniels, *prevented* consideration of a petition from the NAACP, written by Du Bois, in behalf of Negro Americans. (Americans had no African colonies, but they had supported European colonial powers; in return, no European nation would vote to consider the "colony" of blacks within the United States.) This experience and many others taught Du Bois the tremendous power of the forces maintaining the oppression of Negroes in the United States. By the time he was retired from the NAACP in 1934, he considered that organization only a small, ineffective effort against insuperable power. He wrote then:

> If . . . the NAACP has conducted a quarter-century campaign against segregation, the net result has been a little less than nothing. We have by legal action steadied the foundation so that in the future, segregation must be by wish and will and not law, but beyond that we have not made the slightest impression on the determination of the overwhelming mass of white Americans not to treat Negroes as men.
>
> If you have passed your resolution, "No segregation, Never and Nowhere," what are you going to do about it? Let me tell you what you are going to do. You are going back to continue to make your living in a Jim-Crow school; you are going to dwell in a segregated section of the city; you are going to pastor a Jim-Crow church; you are going to occupy political office because of Jim-Crow political organizations that stand back of you and force you into office. All

these things and a thousand others you are going to do because you have got to.

Discouraged and depressing words, but it was the bottom of the Great Depression and Negroes were suffering more than ever. Du Bois was correct in saying that such catastrophic times required new defense strategies, but certainly not the kind he proposed, and for which the NAACP retired him. Briefly, he advocated a tightening circle among Negroes, producing and selling their own goods, and "buying Negro." This incredible plan was essentially that of Booker T. Washington's National Negro Business League, founded more than thirty years before. To this, Du Bois added a call for Negro cooperatives on the model of those he had observed in Denmark.

For as long as the *Crisis* remained self-supporting, and James Weldon Johnson was executive secretary, Du Bois was protected. But when Walter White, a man as vain, but not as gifted, as Du Bois, succeeded Johnson as executive secretary, Du Bois's old hostility toward male authority figures was unleashed. Each distrusted, feared, and envied the other, but White held the money and the power. By the middle of the Great Depression, the *Crisis* no longer was self-supporting, and Du Bois, incredibly enough, had embraced the cause of a separatist "black economy." This program would have been directly antithetical to the Association's policy of no segregation and no racial discrimination of any kind. Garvey and his followers earlier had ridiculed Du Bois's efforts to be accepted by whites; now, fourteen years later, Du Bois, it seemed, was joining the separatists and black nationalists.

Although he never said so, it is likely that as he found his differences with Walter White irreconcilable and found White determined to force him out, Du Bois thought seriously of returning to Atlanta University, where his best friend, John Hope, was now president. Frightened of destitution as he neared seventy, and knowing that eventually he would be going to an all-Negro University, he set out to rationalize his position, namely, that Negro professionals must work for segregated Negro institutions, churches, colleges, public schools, and insurance companies, or for Negro clients and patients. The NAACP had been trying to break up an invulnerable system which would last another hundred years. Its efforts had met with very little success. Facing the greatest economic disaster in years, the Negro had to forget the hopeless effort to win civil rights through the courts; and had to concentrate upon making a living and keeping off the public dole. If, as President Roosevelt had estimated, one-third of the Nation was ill-fed, ill-clothed, and ill-housed, twice that proportion of Negroes were. Du Bois's rationalization was appealing: you can't eat civil rights.

The reality was that he would be penniless if he were retired by the Association. He would have no choice but to depend upon John Hope for an appointment at Atlanta University. This was no time, then, to start a new "radical" program and risk alienating the foundations that supported Atlanta University; foundations that had their own representative—"overseer," as the Negro faculty called her—on the grounds to keep the faculty in check. After all, Du Bois had been forced to leave Atlanta once before when foundations had cut off his funds because he had attacked Booker T. Washington. The system was no different a quarter of a century later.

His financial position must be taken into account in order to understand both his "black economy" separatism, and his last, brief, Communist period. He was paid only $1,200 a year for thirteen years at Atlanta (1897–1910), and $2,500 a year for his first five years with the NAACP. The following eighteen years, he was paid $5,000; there was no raise. At age sixty, he had lost all his savings due to the slum deterioration of a five-flat building he had bought in Harlem. He had no savings or insurance—the Negro company had gone bankrupt.

Forced out in 1934 by White, Du Bois returned at sixty-six to the new graduate school at Atlanta University as the chairman of the sociology department. There, after a six-year struggle with the white treasurer, he succeeded in getting $1,000 per year to publish *Phylon*, still the best scholarly journal on the sociology and culture of the American Negro. He wrote and published three volumes during the next ten years, including a revealing history of the Negro during Reconstruction; and he began a fourth, his mammoth *Encyclopedia Africana*. Nevertheless, he was retired without notice in 1944, at the instigation of the same powerful white treasurer. Back at the NAACP by joint invitation of the President, the Chairman, and the Executive Secretary, he again took up his work in the African field. In 1945, he sent statements and appeals on behalf of American and African Negroes to the planning sessions for the United Nations, and in 1946, drew up the appeal to the Human Rights Commission of the United Nations, which was tabled on a motion by his own United States delegation. Between the ages of seventy-six and eighty, he attended the Pan-African Congress in England, wrote a book on colonies and one on Africa, edited two others, and wrote many articles, pamphlets, and newspaper articles.

Finally, having again been forced out of the NAACP by White, he returned, at eighty, to lecturing and writing and became more strongly socialist. On April 3, 1951, he and the other officers of the small, unimportant Peace Information Center, which lasted only six months, were indicted by a grand jury in the nation's capital for not having registered as agents of a foreign power. He was handcuffed and prosecuted by the United States Justice Department, but was freed by a disgusted federal judge who threw the case out of court for lack of evidence.

Nevertheless, he was ostracized by all Negro institutions except the black press, blackballed as a speaker, and hounded for the rest of his life by the State Department and the FBI. His passport was withdrawn, not because there was any evidence of his working for Communist Russia, but as a lesson to 20 million other Negroes who might be influenced by his example.

In Europe, Africa, and Asia, however, he was welcomed and

celebrated, given honorary degrees, and invited to speak on national television. Even England welcomed him, although his political views were disliked there. In his *Autobiography* he wrote:

> . . . I received every courtesy. I had tea on the terrace of the House of Commons, I had tea where I had last been entertained by Kier Hardie, I met several members of Parliament, and spent many Sunday afternoons with Donald Ogden Stewart and Ella Winter. There I met James Aldrich and Katharine Hepburn. I saw Paul Robeson and his splendid production of *Othello*. Lawrence Bradshaw, sculptor of the great head of Karl Marx, did my head.

But hounded in America and driven to the point of destitution, he joined the Communist Party at ninety-three, and in the last year of his life went to Africa as a voluntary exile, to die on the very day Martin Luther King, Jr., led his triumphant Freedom March on Washington—August 28, 1963. King's own assassination soon followed, and, thus, the two greatest Negro leaders of the twentieth century died within five years of one another; one at ninety-five, the other at thirty-nine.

It remains only to summarize and interpret the evidence on Du Bois's personality. He was an enigma to friends as well as to enemies. Faced with his inscrutability, his biographers have dealt only with symptoms. These external traits are often antithetical: he was vain but shy, pompous but uncertain of himself, defiant but anxious to be accepted. Ambitious to lead, he was essentially retiring and withdrawn. Longing to be admired and worshipped, he often was rude and scornful.

On the exterior, he affected an imperious manner; sported a Kaiser Wilhelm II mustache, his Van Dyke and cane; was rude to women and openly hostile with men. Fundamentally, however, he was insecure and feared rejection. The mass of evidence we have from Du Bois, from his second wife, Shirley Graham, and from his contemporaries suggests that his childhood insecurities persisted throughout his life. He still feared rejection and still wanted—more than anything in life—acceptance from men and love from women.

His fantasies about his undistinguished ancestors and his ne'er-do-well father were defenses against the shame he felt for his and his mother's pauperism and for the stigma of his father's desertion. His fantasies provided an escape from Great Barrington, where he was regarded as a poor "darky," and probably an illegitimate one. In the deepest sense, his brilliant career was a reaction to and compensation for the disgrace of his mother. His mother's own family, he wrote, was ashamed that she had borne an illegitimate son, Idelbert.

Most of all he was lonely, for, according to his writings, he grew to sixteen without a single black or white friend. Typically, he tries to deny his isolation by saying he joined the white boys' games and was accepted by them. But his constant denials make it clear that he *felt* alone, exposed, isolated; furthermore, he often writes of building a wall around himself to keep from being hurt.

After his mother's death he was completely alone. He made no close friends at Fisk, Harvard, or the University of Berlin. At Fisk, he says, he dated colored girls, but names none. Nearly eighty years later, he names a few Fisk friends (men) who had become prominent. At Harvard, he was either in his room in a Negro family's home or in the library. He claims he dated Negro girls from Boston, but again he names none; these affairs, like those at Fisk, may have been only fantasies. Basically, he was an ascetic—one whose constricted personality contrasts dramatically with Douglass's heartiness and vitality.

To Berlin he was a foreigner without background or roots. The most significant incident in his European diary is his birthday celebration in his room—alone. It was a symbol of his emotional life: hypersensitive, devoted to a dream of leadership, and dedicated to his disgraced mother, who had set his feet on the lonely path of accomplishment, an unconscious projection of her own ambitions and dreams.

After her death and his departure for Fisk, he apparently never saw any of his relatives again. In the deepest sense—in family bonds—he was a man without ties. He married twelve years later and remained married for fifty-three years, but in describing himself in his *Autobiography* he admits he was never close to his wife, nor she to him.

In estimating his own "character," Du Bois claimed he had four or five friends who were women—all of them co-workers in the NAACP or in research. Except for them, women always regarded him as rude and pompous. This rudeness was a defense against two fears: that they would discover his sexual shyness, and that, like his mother, they would try to control and direct him.

Like most children rigorously trained for achievement, Du Bois must have unconsciously resented his mother. The first hint we have of this resentment is his account of his mother's death. He writes that she died unexpectedly in the autumn after he was graduated from high school. Then follows a passage which openly expresses his *relief*, and virtually confesses "I was glad!"

> *I felt a certain gladness to see her at peace at last,* for she had worried all her life! Of my own loss I had then little realization. That came only in after years. *Now it was the choking gladness and solemn feel of wings!* At last, I was going beyond the hills and into the world that beckoned steadily. [Emphasis added.]

Perhaps Du Bois was so accustomed to thinking of himself first that he was not subject to the depression and guilt which usually follow the death of one's mother or father. Grief is universal and the death of a loved one leaves one feeling guilty because one has survived. But years later, when he wrote the account, he remembers only a powerful surge of new energy. One concludes, then, that Du Bois told the truth when he wrote he was relieved by her death. *Relieved of what?* Of her pressure upon him to achieve, to save them both from destitution, to restore their good names and reputation, and to outdo all whites. As he later wrote, it was too much to want to outdo all whites, many of whom were as able as he.

His relief was only temporary, of course, for his mother's conscience was *within him*. Just as he says he could not moderate the rigid Yankee puritan controls upon his sexual drive and capacity to enjoy life, so he never could relax the inner pressure of his mother's voice to achieve, to produce, to attain. Since he still felt driven, he wanted no more domineering women in his life. Hence his marriage to a docile *Hausfrau*, whom he kept docile; hence his efforts to keep all women at a distance. Mary White Ovington and two or three other women, recognizing his great ability, put up with this behavior. Others refused, so he got along as poorly with women as he did with men, perhaps even more so, for if a man was mild and modest like his two best friends, John Hope and Joel Spingarn, Du Bois could prove a loyal friend.

Far more helpful than his own conscious analysis of his personality in his *Autobiography* are his *unconscious associations* through which he unwittingly reveals his emotions. At the beginning of *Darkwater*, written when he was fifty, he wrote a credo, a formal statement of his fundamental beliefs:

> I believe in Pride of race and lineage and self; in pride of self so deep as to scorn injustice to other selves; in pride of lineage so great as to *despise no man's father*; in pride of race so chivalrous as neither to offer *bastardy to the weak nor beg wedlock of the strong*, knowing that men may be brothers in Christ, even though they be not brothers-in-law. [Emphasis added.]

In this one sentence he denies the three basic sources of his insecurity: his feelings of inferiority from his color or race; his feeling of rejection from his father's desertion; and the fear that he was illegitimate. No doubt the most damaging of these was the rejection by his father.

In the Negro, as well as in the white, middle class, the illegitimate child is in the most "exposed" of all social positions. The child and his mother become "loners." Whether Du Bois's mother and father actually were married or not, he knew at the age of three or four that his father was gone, but not dead. Du Bois never saw his father. In a sense, his brilliant ambitions and career were reaction-formations to the feeling of exposure and shame as a child.

In his *credo* Du Bois also denies his shame in being a Negro. This was largely conscious. He had been aware since early life that Negroes were universally regarded as inferior, stupid, and immoral compared to whites. His plans to train, improve, and lead them, expressed in his oath in Berlin on his birthday, were a reaction to the stigma of being black. Twenty-seven years after that oath he claimed in his credo, "I believe in Pride of race." He had been teaching it for twenty-seven years. But at sixty-five he wrote in the *Crisis*, "First of all comes the fact that we are still ashamed of ourselves."

Negroes are not ashamed of middle-class and professional blacks, he pointed out; they are ashamed of lower-class blacks. Du Bois was one of the first to use the concept of social class in studying Negro life and was quite honest about himself and other professional Negroes. ". . . this upper class of colored Americans are ashamed—both directly and indirectly of this mass of impoverished workers," and "desperately afraid of being represented before American whites by the lower group, or being mistaken for them, or being treated as though they were part of it." Since Du Bois made no field studies of Negroes' feelings on this subject, his view must have been based on an analysis of his own feelings.

> They are embarrassed and indignant because an educated man should be treated as a Negro. They are ashamed and embarrassed because of the compulsion of being classed with a mass of people over whom they have no real control and whose action they can influence only with difficulty and compromise and with every risk of defeat.

Since childhood—when the white girl in his Great Barrington school rejected his card in a classroom game—to his exclusion later by the Harvard Glee Club, by the University of Pennsylvania faculty, and throughout his life, Du Bois responded to racial rejection as he had responded to rejection by his father. He denied it by building fantasies of outdoing whites and overcoming their rejection. But what he most wanted was *acceptance as a human being*—as a person of the same species, and with the same rights, as whites. This is what every Negro American wants.

Du Bois never got such acceptance. Instead, like all middle-class Negroes, he felt himself a member of a pariah caste. He was the first scientist to describe its psychological effects accurately. Using an image later developed by Richard Wright and Ralph Ellison, and possibly suggested by Plato's image of the cave, he wrote the most insightful and powerful account we have of the effects of this caste system upon both blacks and whites.

> It is difficult to let others see the full psychological meaning of caste segregation. It is as though one, looking out from a dark cave in a side of an impending mountain, sees the world passing and speaks to it; speaks courteously and persuasively, showing them how these entombed souls are hindered in their natural movement, expression, and development; and how their loosening from prison would be a matter not simply of courtesy, sympathy, and help to them, but aid to all the world. One talks on evenly and logically in this way, but notices that the passing throng does not even turn its head, or if it does, glances curiously and walks on. It gradually penetrates the minds of the prisoners that the people passing do not hear; that some thick sheet of invisible but horribly tangible plate glass is between them and the world. They get excited; they talk louder; they gesticulate. Some of the passing world stop in curiosity; these gesticulations seem so pointless; they laugh and pass on. They still either do not hear at all, or hear but dimly, and even what they hear, they do not understand. Then the people within may become hysterical. They may scream and hurl themselves against the barriers, hardly realizing in their bewilderment that they are screaming in a vacuum unheard and that their antics may actually seem funny to those outside looking in. They may even, here and there, break through in blood and disfigurement, and find themselves faced by a horrified, implacable, and quite overwhelming mob of people frightened for their own very existence.

Under such conditions, he points out, it is impossible for the entombed "to make the outer world understand their essential common humanity." This is the most profound comment ever written on Negro life in America.

It was precisely his desire to make whites understand his "essential common humanity," this hunger to be accepted, which motivated his herculean efforts for nearly nine decades. The wish for acceptance by whites and for justice fitted in with and was reinforced by his longing to be accepted by his father. But as he was deserted by his father, so was he distrusted and rejected by whites. For the dominant white society demanded submission. Booker T. Washington accepted submission and was elevated; he dined with the President and was regarded as a friend by both President Theodore Roosevelt and Andrew Carnegie. Du Bois refused submission, demanded justice, finally challenged capitalism, and was destroyed.

But for ninety-three years of life in the United States, he had endured the unremitting drain of a terrible loneliness. Under that lifelong burden, he wrote twenty-two books—seven of them major works—and fifteen Atlanta University reports; he trained a generation of sociologists and leaders, and published his stirring editorials in the *Crisis*, which for twenty-four years rallied Negroes to defend themselves.

He had become the spiritual father of the most effective black leaders of his day, including Martin Luther King, Jr. The excellence of his work and his incorruptibility as a civil-rights fighter made him—as he had dubbed his Jewish friend Spingarn—"a knight *sans pareil*." Martin Luther King, Jr., the greatest of all American Negro leaders, and possibly the greatest American of his time, saluted Du Bois: "He has not died. . . . The spirit of freedom is not buried in the grave of the valiant."

4

Mightier Than the Sword: Richard Wright, Creator of *Native Son*

Richard Wright's works stand as the most effective literary attacks against the system by which American whites have subordinated blacks. Although Du Bois in *The Souls of Black Folk* and Fanon in *The Wretched of the Earth* wrote with greater eloquence, as essayists they could not evoke the terror and pity aroused by Wright in his best fiction. For sheer power, there is no tour de force in modern English fiction which can equal *Native Son*, and there are few short stories in Western literature that have the tragic effect of "Bright and Morning Star" and "Fire and Cloud."

A few critics claimed, following the publication of *Native Son* (1940), that Wright exhibited nothing more than raw emotional power, and that his work lacked discipline, style, and narrative skill. But one cannot regard as artistically unsophisticated a man who studied the novels and letters of Dostoevski, the prefaces of Henry James, the works of Conrad, Joyce, Gertrude Stein, Kafka, Malraux, and Hemingway; a man whose first serious writing, poetry, was influenced by Whitman, T. S. Eliot, and the surrealists; who read literary criticism by Waldo Frank, Joseph Wood Krutch, Van Wyck Brooks; whose own teaching and work greatly influenced one of the most able novelists of our time, Ralph Ellison, as well as the unsurpassed essayist James Baldwin (*vide* the comments of Edmund Wilson); a man who later was regarded in France as one of the greatest creators of existentialist fiction. Rather, he must be viewed as an artist of miraculous talent, who by genius and hard work transcended the enormous obstacles raised by deep Southern racism against the cultural and educational development of any Negro. As a black sharecropper's son, Richard never had a "full year" (five months) in school until he was twelve years old, and that "education" took place in a segregated black school whose teachers had no college training. Indeed, when one looks at an old photograph of the four-year-old boy standing in front of a miserable shack on the plantation where his father worked—when one remembers that his father was illiterate and unskilled, and that the son would remain virtually illiterate until he was twelve—it is difficult to comprehend that this same individual published a successful volume of stories by the age of thirty, and a Book-of-the-Month Club selection by the time he was thirty-two. The only possible explanation lies within the man himself—the miracle of his unbreakable will, his fierce pride, and powerful aggression and initiative which drove him to do the impossible.

Richard Wright was the angriest, and yet the most influential, of all black writers. To find the sources of his anger we begin with his early years in the Mississippi county where he was reared, go on to analyze his basic personality structure, and, finally, trace the dominant influence of his anger upon his creative work.*

Wright's reactions to his early environment developed his fierce determination and stubborn will. The dominant force in that environment, stronger even than the racial system of oppression, was his sadistic maternal family. Wright may have allowed his public to believe that his character and behavior were formed by the impact of racial oppression by Mississippi whites; indeed, at times he encouraged the reader to accept this view of his emotional development.† One needs only to read his *Black Boy*, however, to understand that Wright considered his family the primary source of his anger

---

*This essay deals entirely with the influence of Wright's personality upon his fiction. His achievement in the existentialist movement with Jean-Paul Sartre and Simone de Beauvoir, his part in the founding of La Société Africaine de Culture, and his work for Présence Africaine are not discussed.

†Michel Fabre, a man of good intentions but of incredible naïveté both about black life in Mississippi and about the psychology of personality, has published the most detailed biography of Wright: *The Unfinished Quest of Richard Wright*. Unfortunately, Mr. Fabre lacks scientific objectivity about the Mississippi social and economic system in which Wright was reared, and is not equipped to deal with Wright's emotional development. He has no knowledge whatever of Wright's basic emotional conflicts, and apparently no interest in learning their continual working in his behavior, his fantasies, and his writing.

and his hatred. Nevertheless, Wright probably did not recognize that his reactions to his family's attacks gave rise to his greatest strength: his fierce determination to assert himself and to stand up against apparently insuperable opposition.

Although as time went on he developed powerful defenses against admitting his need for love from either his mother or his father, he was less ambivalent about his father, and saw him more clearly. At the time of Richard's birth in 1908, Nathaniel Wright was an illiterate sharecropper, working rented land on "half-shares" about ten miles south of Natchez, Mississippi, near a ragged line of ravines and bayous called "The Devil's Backbone." Nathaniel Wright was a man of great vitality, a lower-class man who had suffered none of the sexual constrictions that were routine in his wife's family. According to both his son and his wife, Nathaniel Wright was a man with winning ways; a hardy man who laughed easily and robustly. When his wife brought him to the police court in Memphis in an effort to gain support, Nathaniel smiled and laughed his way into the good graces of the white judge, with the result that his helpless and abandoned wife and children were awarded nothing.

Whether his "upward" marriage had been the result of his own ambition, which seems unlikely, or of his wife's desire to be saved from the austerity of her own family, we do not know. We do know that Nathaniel Wright was a rural, lower-class man and a great favorite with women—always a good sign of vitality. The woman he finally married, however, was from a long, grim line of puritan matriarchs; a woman who felt that all natural enjoyment, whether it be sex or Sunday baseball or card playing, was a cardinal sin; a schoolteacher who wished to convert him, to save him from perdition, and to run his life.

When the bottom fell out of the cotton market in 1914, Nathaniel Wright took his family to Memphis, and worked as a porter and janitor. A short time later, he deserted his wife and two children to live with another woman. His son attributed this desertion, as he did almost all negative traits of blacks, to the destabilizing effect that racial oppression and urbanization wreaked on rural blacks. It is clear that Nathaniel Wright left his wife because he did not wish to be saved for the church, because he did not like to have his life directed for him, and because he did not wish to be controlled by a dominating woman. In fact, he exhibited the same kind of behavior which his son developed soon after, namely, a revolt against matriarchy; both males rebelled against those viragoes in their lives who insisted on keeping a man in his place. Richard Wright's father rebelled against his wife's domineering nature, as he had previously rebelled against her religious doctrine of hell and damnation for those who worked on Saturdays, who danced or played Sunday baseball, or who simply sought to enjoy life. Nathaniel took life easily and had the capacity to enjoy it. Nevertheless, he was a workingman; he always had a job, and was still working when Wright saw him twenty-five years later.

Wright's mother's family consisted of a clan of obsessively religious and sadistic women. They were the members of a revivalistic religious sect, whose credos they used chiefly as excuses for projecting their own hatred, anger, and sadism upon others. I have never read of so violent a clan of women. Wright's mother nearly whipped him to death when he was four, and his grandmother rained blows upon his head; his grandfather, too, threatened to "get my gun" in order to enforce their sadomasochistic "morality." The boy's early experiences with his grandfather, grandmother, mother, and aunts, gave him reason to hate them. His Aunt Jodi disliked him, his Aunt Addie tried to crush him. His grandmother, when he was eleven or twelve years old, tried to hit him, missed, fell down the steps, and sprained her back. His Aunt Addie kicked all doors open before her, then shut them behind her so that she might kick them open again. A woman of uncontrollable, raging temper, she would beat Richard in school, where she was his teacher, and then again at home. Fearing her attacks, he kept a butcher knife in his bed to protect himself at night. His mother forced him to stand up against a gang of boys that twice had beaten him; she sent him back the third time with orders to fight or stay out of the house unless he wished *her* to whip him. She thrashed him for writing obscenities which he did not understand and for a variety of other real or imagined misdemeanors. These women tried to beat him into submitting to them, and to the white world. In this unrelieved environment of sadistic puritanism, criticism, rejection, and beating, Wright developed into quite a sadistic child, who must have felt that while Mississippi whites were dangerous enough, the women in his own family were even more so. If a "cracker" talked to him, he simply had to bow his head and grin; but when his grandmother or aunts yelled at him, he was forced to cringe and be prepared to fight off blows. A four-year-old whose mother beats him to near death is bound to fear and hate her. That Wright was filled with hate at that age is made clear enough by his attempt to burn his sick grandmother.

It was a family of infinite sadistic inventiveness. The trait was apparent in Richard himself—for instance, in hanging a kitten until it was dead; it was evident in his mother's wrath when she forced him to pray over the kitten after he had buried it, and to ask God not to kill him (her own son) in his sleep; it was clear in the rage of his uncle, who was determined to beat Richard at the age of fourteen because he did not like the way the boy had answered his demand at five o'clock in the morning to be told the exact time; and in the maniacal rage of his Aunt Addie, the prim schoolteacher, who whipped him and threatened to kill him for no reason except that she simply hated the very sight of the boy. To Richard, *home*—whether in Natchez, Jackson, the orphanage in Helena, or Memphis—meant isolation, suffering, rejection, curses, and blows.

Nathaniel Wright was born and reared within a plantation system in which the land was owned by whites but the work was done by blacks. White landlords governed black workers by intimidation and terror; as late as 1933 to 1935, when I interviewed landlords and tenants in Mississippi's Adams and Wilkinson counties, this practice was still widespread. During this period, black tenants were intimidated by the occasional whipping and shooting of their fellow blacks. Interviews with planters as well as with tenants in these counties revealed that most whippings resulted from either (1) the landlord's charge that a tenant had stolen or deserted his crop, hurt or killed the livestock, or refused to perform his work at the time appointed by the landlord, or (2) the tenant's accusation that the landlord had cheated him in the settlement of their accounts. In some instances, terrorization was used to enforce deference to whites, for although the system usually insured a hierarchical deference to the landlord, there were some black tenants who occasionally refused to act as deferentially as some whites expected. When such a black tenant was "impudent" or "too smart," slowing the wheels of the efficient plantation, "a good whipping" helped oil the system.

One white landlord in Adams County, where Nathaniel Wright was a tenant on half-shares, even admitted that he had instructed his sons to shoot or hang disrespectful black tenants. "There was one black tenant out our way not long ago—he was on a place near ours—who was getting too smart. I told my sons that if he didn't behave, they ought to take him out for a ride and tend to him, and tell him that if he didn't stop talking and acting so big, the next time it would be a bullet or a rope. That's the way to manage them when they get too big." Another white planter, in Wilkinson County, said that he had recently beaten one of his tenants who "didn't do anything but he had that insolent kind of manner about him." A powerful federal official in Wilkinson said, "When a nigger gets ideas, the best thing to do is to get him under ground as quick as possible."

The wife of a prominent white planter in Wilkinson County who frequently whipped his black tenants claimed that whipping was the best control: "Whipping is the way they usually do. It is the best way. We can't afford to send them to jail because we need them on the farms; so they just take them out and give them a good beating, and that teaches them. It is a good way. It frightens them and they are all right after that. If they whip one, it frightens the others enough to stop them. The men who do the whipping were out again last night, but I don't think they got any. A lot of the men from here went down to help them. That's the way they do to help each other out that way."

Another white landlord stated he had beaten one of the black tenants for mistreating a mule. "He started to run, but before he could get away, I hit him so hard with the bull whip that the shock just stopped him in his tracks. I then gave him half a dozen good ones." The same white landlord told how he had whipped another black tenant and also a third tenant for something which had actually been done by the landlord's own cousin. "One day my cousin had gone to town in the wagon with a Negro, and when they got back I noticed that the mule had a long whip cut on his back. I called the Negro up and told him I was going to whip him for cutting the mule. He knew I wouldn't stand anything like that. I took a piece of grass plow line and thrashed him a bit with it. Afterward he told me that my cousin had cut the mule. But he should have told me that before, and I wouldn't have hit him." Another white landlord reported that when a black tenant had refused to endorse his government subsidy check to the landlord in payment for supplies, he, the landlord, had called the black tenant up before the other tenants and pulled out his clasp knife. In the presence of the others, he had told the black man that he was "going to cut his throat from ear to ear." The tenant endorsed the check. This same landlord also carried an automatic revolver when he went among his tenants.

The system of racial oppression on the plantation reached extremes of inhumanity in the whipping and beating of black women. A pregnant black woman was beaten by a white landlord when she refused to work because of her condition. A white landlord in Wilkinson County recounted his having beaten a black woman for stealing until "her head was all covered with blood." In another case, he had whipped an old black woman because she had insisted upon coming between the landlord and her son, whom the landlord was trying to whip. "I didn't want to whip the old woman but I finally had to. I just let her have it with the bull whip and gave her a good beating, then I whipped her son." These incidents are all too reminiscent of Wright's descriptions—especially in "Bright and Morning Star." But these are incidents in Adams and Wilkinson counties in the 1930s. In 1908, when Richard Wright was born, his father must have had to confront an even more terrifying system.

Wright's father was at the bottom of the black society and well beneath all whites. For in Natchez, and in Adams County—both in 1908 and in the period between 1933 and 1935—there was a social class system, just as there was in every American and European town. It was a dual social class system, one in the white community and another in the black community. My co-authors for *Deep South*, the Gardners, and I made a study of both. I also gathered data on the Negro class system that had existed thirty years earlier, that is, around the turn of the century.

The findings make it clear that neither Wright's father nor his grandmother nor mother would have known the Natchez black middle class. His mother's status as a country schoolteacher would not have won her acceptance in Natchez, for there a normal-school diploma was a prerequisite to teach. She had married a farm tenant, and no wife of a sharecropper would have been accepted in the middle-class Negro groups in Natchez, either then or at any later time.

Near the turn of the century, according to my informants who had lived at that time, "colored" people of Natchez acquired prestige chiefly by virtue of their white or light skin and the status of their occupations. My informants agreed that thirty-two Negro families, totaling 150 individuals of the highest status group among "colored people," shared some distinct traits. This general group was composed of a rural high-status Negro group and an urban high-status group. The rural group consisted of a rather large number of colored planters, all of whom were white-skinned except for one family, who were reddish brown but had white types of hair. Of the Natchez high-status Negro families, four were light brown or yellowish brown, with white types of hair; one was reddish brown with straight or wavy hair; and two were medium brown in color with white types of hair. All others in the Natchez prestige Negro group in 1900—amounting to more than three-fourths of the total—were olive, light yellow, or white in skin color and had white types of hair. In occupation, they had been proprietors of rather large stores catering to white trade, or contractors, artisans, or teachers. One had been a lawyer, and three had held or were holding jobs in the federal government. Among this "blue-veined," light-skinned group, there were a few of lower occupational status. For instance, two had been waiters, and one had been a coachman for a well-to-do white family, and one the leader of a dance band. The great majority, however, had been proprietors or artisans.

Most of this group in 1900 were the children of white fathers. Some were children of upper-class planters; one was the son of a former mayor of Natchez. Some of them had been sent away by their white fathers to be educated in the leading Negro schools and colleges, and a smaller number had inherited considerable real estate from their white fathers. Three of these high-status Negro families had been free for at least a generation before the Civil War, and members of two of these families had fought with the Confederate Army.

Within both the rural and the urban Negro prestige class, there were several friendship groups, all of whose members were white or light yellow. These cliques made up the so-called blue-vein society, similar to those found in Savannah, Charleston, Washington, D.C., Philadelphia, and New Orleans. This group possessed the highest status among Negroes, because the other Negroes looked up to them, resented them, and envied them. In the Adams County rural area, the blue-vein group consisted of six families, four of which were related by blood. A member of the leading family in this group told me in 1934 that "thirty years ago if a child turned out black or dark, it was too bad for him." The dark children born into these families, like dark children in the New Orleans Creole families, were sent off to live with dark relatives in other places. In Adams County, this blue-vein group of rural families still distinguished themselves from the Negro middle class as late as 1933 to 1935; even the younger members insisted that they were not Negroes. They pointed out that until recently their families had not been treated as Negroes by whites, but had constituted a group of intermediate status, resembling that of the colored Creoles in Louisiana at the turn of the century.

In Natchez itself, the blue-vein clique was larger and more exclusive. Even brown-skinned members of the middle class, who attended the larger balls, were excluded from the smaller affairs. Like the rural groups, the members of this urban blue-vein clique around 1900 not only regarded themselves as a different "race" from the Negro group, but were so regarded by upper-class whites, *to whom many were blood kin*.

These standards of Negro class status have now, of course, changed, and the emphasis is chiefly upon occupation and education, as in all other urban black groups. But during Richard Wright's childhood, his parents, his grandmother, and he would have been *quite aware* that there was such a blue-vein, high-status group, which had, on the whole, more money and higher occupations. Both his grandmother and his mother, it is true, were "respectable" people and good church members with middle-class ambitions. But since his mother was not qualified to teach in Natchez or in Memphis, and since neither his grandmother nor his grandfather had skilled or white-collar occupations, they had little chance of retaining their rural middle-class status in the city. In fact, Wright's family was on the skids; Mrs. Wright had married an illiterate sharecropper who, with the collapse of cotton prices, lost even that work. In Jackson, Mississippi, where Richard Wright spent most of his childhood and all of his adolescence, he lived in a class system similar to that of

Natchez. There would have been slightly less emphasis upon light skin, but more emphasis upon occupational level and education.

Wright's hostility toward middle-class Negroes is expressed throughout his writing. It is true that Wright learned to hate white people in Mississippi, but it is accurate to say that he did not hate them any more than he hated the Negro high-status group, or, in fact, any more than he hated blacks in general. His hostility to the Negro bourgeoisie was deep and bitter. Later, in Chicago, he found a tremendously complex Negro class system, whose top rungs were occupied by physicians, officials of black insurance companies, lawyers, and a few businessmen. Many from the blue-vein groups of Natchez, New Orleans, Atlanta, Athens, and other places in the South had migrated to Chicago, with the result that in 1935 Richard Wright found in Chicago a Negro upper-middle class that had a higher concentration of white skin than any other similar Negro group in the United States. Richard, at that time, was "on relief," although it is important to notice that he was on a white-collar WPA project and very early had made contacts with Professor Louis Wirth and Horace Cayton at the University of Chicago.

Wright rejected both the Negro bourgeoisie and the Negro working class. Time and again he made it clear that he had little use for either class—that he never enjoyed life among Negroes. The year *Native Son* was published, I attended a house party given for Wright on Fifty-first Street in Chicago. During the host's years working in the Post Office, he had been Wright's friend; now he (the host) had risen into the lower bracket of one of the Negro insurance companies. The guests were white-collar workers and professional people. Except for one or two white book reviewers from the Chicago papers, everyone was Negro. Wright seemed completely out of place in this Negro middle-class group; I have never seen a man more unhappy at the celebration of his own triumph. Actually, of course, he had little in common with the group, since few of them read serious books or bought them. They were not interested in the world of literature where Wright's future lay, but in the world of insurance companies, business, and school-teaching; Wright himself wanted the acclaim of the powerful, the well-to-do, and the literary world. *That world was white*, and I believe Wright deliberately and coldly fashioned *Native Son* with the purpose of seizing the attention of white readers and holding it, regardless of the cost to the self-esteem of the Negro middle class.

Native Son indeed won Wright the attention and acclaim of the white world. He had engineered *Native Son* so that it could not be ignored by whites, and it made him the center of white attention both here and in Europe. He was a man who went after what he wanted, and what he wanted was what the white man had. He knew that to attain it he had to get their attention; this he did in the man-beast, Bigger. The fact, simply put, is that Wright hated blacks as deeply as whites did.

His hatred of blacks in general is essentially a projection of his hatred and contempt for himself for being in the lowly position of a black. His own words say it best:

> After I had outlived the shock of childhood, after the habit of reflection had been born in me, I used to mull over the strange absence of real kindness in Negroes, how unstable was our tenderness, how lacking in genuine passion we were in those intangible sentiments that bind man to man, and how shallow was even our despair. After I had learned other ways of life, I used to brood upon the unconscious irony of those who felt that Negroes led so passionate an existence! I saw that what had been taken for our emotional strength was our negative confusions, our flights, our fears, our frenzy under pressure.

In more direct language, he wrote: ". . . riding trains, autos, or buggies, moving from morning till night we went from shack to shack, plantation to plantation. Exhausted, I filled out applications. I saw a bare, bleak pool of black life and I hated it."

In Wright's work, there are also a few blacks with courage, or strength, or love. Among these are the woman in "Bright and Morning Star," and the man in "Fire and Cloud." His gallery of thieving, murdering, and hypocritical whites is no larger than his cast of equally murderous, hypocritical, and thieving blacks, except that the blacks at times suffer from guilt. Wright's black antiheroes also suffer from self-hatred and self-loathing. *The self-hatred and self-loathing, of course, are Wright's own, which he projected onto his fictional characters.*

Why did he hate himself? Richard Wright's response to his family in childhood led to three basic conflicts. The first was a conflict between his wish to be dependent or submissive—that is, all the things which his puritanical and dominating mother and grandmother wanted him to be—and the opposite desire: the wish to be his own man, to hold his head up and direct his own life. In spite of the constant attacks upon his ego by both his family and the dominant white racist society, he solved this conflict well, and excelled. His second conflict was between a need to trust and a deep-seated distrust of women as well as men. Most damaging of all was the unresolved conflict between his hatred of his parents and his guilt over that hatred. It was this guilt that led him to hate himself.

He solved the first conflict by learning to be aggressively *independent*. As a child he had learned that his very survival as a self-respecting and self-directing individual depended upon fighting back. Although he never started fights, he did not accept whippings, he did not back down, he did not demean or debase himself in order to gain acceptance. He never forgot that he could not get what he wanted out of life unless he stood up for himself. And he always fought racial injustice. More than that, he aggressively went after what was due him. When Wright wrote his first story in the eighth grade and had it accepted by the editor of the Negro newspaper in Jackson, Mississippi, the boy typically demanded to be paid. His grounds were just—he should have been paid for his work—but how many boys of fourteen would demand payment from an editor? (At any rate, one would have thought he would be discouraged when both his grandmother and his Aunt Addie told him only a fool would ask for payment.)

Much of Wright's anger was transformed into initiative, ambition, and the drive to achieve; that is, his rage was channeled *away* from its naturally *destructive* aims toward more socially acceptable goals such as literary work. Wright learned that his anger in actual life served as a motive force to make him stand up and fight for himself. He was expressing this anger openly when he was only four. Throughout his life, he would offer fiery and indomitable resistance against all efforts to humiliate and subjugate him. I can think of no other major writer whose spirit was so irreconcilable and whose indignation toward black and white exploiters alike remained so fierce. Compared to Wright, even Frederick Douglass seems to have been a compromiser and a politician, especially in Douglass's later years.

In this respect, the contrast with James Baldwin, his protégé, is most enlightening. Baldwin wrote at least five essays on Wright, some of them obviously hostile, most of them painfully ambivalent. But one, "Many Thousands Gone," is an extremely insightful piece, written in a style that marks Baldwin as one of this country's leading masters of prose. Near the end of this essay Baldwin takes an incredible stance—at least it would have been incredible to Richard Wright. Baldwin identifies with white liberals! Oh, he attacks them as usual, just to get their attention, but he then implies that white and black liberals are a *solid* group, insofar as ideals are concerned. Their mutual good will, if examined, Baldwin writes, will "lead us back to our forebears, whose assumption it was that the black man, to become truly human and acceptable, must first become like us." What "us"! What "forebears"! It would have been impossible for Wright to have written such a passage. It is true that he put similar words into the mouth of the white Max in the concluding passages of *Native Son*. But to have thought of his forebears as the same as those of white liberals, and of his roots as the same as theirs, would have seemed a joke to Wright. Apparently not to Baldwin, however, who has often written of American white society in such a way as to indicate that he was able to identify with that society in many ways and quite deeply. Wright could not so identify, although he often analyzes this process of identification intellectually.

Wright experienced Baldwin's hostility in 1950. In 1948, when Baldwin arrived in Paris, Wright befriended him and gave him money. Two years later, Baldwin asked Wright to find a publisher for his essay "Everybody's Protest Novel." Wright got it published; he did so, apparently, without having read it. The essay was a searing attack upon Wright's own work. The day after its publication, Wright discovered Baldwin's treachery and at once told him he wanted nothing more to do with him. But in 1953 Baldwin again tried to borrow money from Wright. They met in a café, where Baldwin tried to justify his previous behavior. After a dispute over Baldwin's specious claim that Wright was the "father" who had to be killed so that the "son" (Baldwin) could develop, Wright wrote to a friend, "This man disgusts, there is a kind of shameful weeping in what he writes." Wright considered Baldwin subservient and groveling; at that time, and with people upon whom he was dependent for money and patronage, he indeed may have seemed so. Certainly he had neither the force nor the independence of Wright.

Wright's initiative, ambition, and career-drive were all forms of healthy aggression. Thus, he was able to handle most of his anger successfully by transforming it into a powerful competitive drive. This realistic and indignant anger was effective, inflexible, and incorruptible. It was his flaming moral indignation and his powerful will, after all, that carried him to the pinnacle of literary fame from the depths of being a half-starved "boy" who worked at menial jobs and could boast only an eighth-grade education in the miserable black schools of Jackson, Mississippi. Through indomitable ambition and daemonic work, he made writing his weapon against the white racist system; he tempered it like hot molten steel, sharpened it to a point, and drove it straight into his target—the heart of that system. At times in his Chicago WPA days, he may have seemed to temporize or compromise, but this behavior, like that of the mother in "Bright and Morning Star," was merely a stratagem to enable him to attack the system again.

Wright chose the man's part; he was the antithesis of those hesitant, indecisive, and small guilty spirits that oppression often creates. Dostoevski has described the typical psychology of this self-pitying, whining type of oppressed person in his *Notes from the Underground*:

> Apart from the one fundamental nastiness, the luckless mouse succeeds in creating around it so many other nastinesses in the form of doubts and questions, adds to the one question so many unsettled questions that there inevitably works up around it a sort of fatal brew, a stinking mess, made up of its doubts, emotions, and of the contempt spat upon it by the direct men of action, who stand solemnly about it as judges and arbitrators, laughing at it till their healthy sides ache. Of course the only thing left for it is to dismiss all that it does not even itself believe, creep ignominiously into its mouse-hole. There in its nasty, stinking underground home our insulted, crushed and ridiculed mouse promptly becomes absorbed in cold, malignant and, above all, everlasting spite. For forty years it will remember its injury down to the smallest, most ignominious detail, and every time will add, of itself, details still more ignominious, spitefully teasing and tormenting itself with its own imagination. It will itself be ashamed of its imaginings, but yet it will recall it all, it will go over and over every detail, it will invent unheard of things against itself, pretending that those things might happen, and will forgive nothing. Maybe it will begin to revenge itself, too, but, as it were, piecemeal, in trivial ways, from behind the stove, *incognito*, without believing either in its own right to vengeance, or in the success of its revenge knowing that from all its efforts at revenge it will suffer a hundred times more than he on whom it revenges itself, while he, I daresay, will not even scratch himself. On its deathbed it will recall it all over again, with interest accumulated over all the years. . .

Having said that Wright was a strong man, an independent and self-directing man, one must add that he was also a man in conflict, a suffering man. He never was able to resolve the conflict in his feelings for his father. To review, when Richard was six, his father took the family to Memphis because the price of cotton had collapsed. Away from his wife's matriarchal clan, and in the freer life of the big city, Nathaniel Wright found himself unwilling to put up with his wife's compulsive puritanism and her authoritarianism, and so deserted her and the two boys. Richard then went hungry, as he did chronically for the next ten or twelve years. He wrote in *Black Boy*, "the image of my father became associated with my pangs of hunger, and whenever I felt hunger I thought of him with a deep biological bitterness."

He resented his father not only because his father had deserted him and let him go hungry, but also simply because his father wielded authority. Wright felt that "he was cruel," although he makes no record of having been whipped by his father. The truth is that he was at war with his father; shortly after their arrival in Memphis, he writes, "I had my first triumph over my father." His father had been working at night and sleeping during the day. One day a stray kitten came into the yard; Richard and his brother played with the kitten and the noise kept his father from sleeping. His father got up, came to the back door, and tried to quiet them. Finally—his efforts unsuccessful—he yelled, "Kill the damn thing. Do anything, but get it away from here." Richard pretended to believe that his father had seriously ordered him to kill the kitten, although his brother argued that his father had not literally meant what he said. Nevertheless, the young Richard put a noose around the kitten's neck and hanged it until it was dead.

This act of defiance he called his first triumph over his father. "I had made him believe that I'd taken his words literally. I was happy because I had at last found a way to throw my criticism of him into his face. I had made him know that I felt he was cruel." He resented his father's authority; later he described similarly resenting the preacher who ate his mother's food, because "like my father he was used to having his own way."

More tangibly, his father's desertion meant that Richard and his brother and mother had little or nothing to eat. His mother finally brought his father to court in an effort to make him support her and the children. His father, it seems, clowned and won over the judge, so that the judge denied support to the children. Starvation did not intimidate Richard, however. When his mother asked him to beg his father for food or money, he refused. "I did not want to see him."

His resentment toward his father, which develops irrationally in all little boys at the age of three or four, had in Richard's case, therefore, a basis in objective reality. His father had mistreated him and his mother, deserted them, and laughed in their faces. Richard wrote, "If someone had suggested that my father be killed, I would, perhaps, have become interested." He was able to express the death wish against the father directly, and even could threaten attack. When his mother took him to his father's place to ask for train fare back to Mississippi, his father laughed and said he had no money. Richard threatened his father, saying: "I'll take that poker and hit you!" His mother then suggested that he stay with his father, and his father told him, "You'll get plenty to eat," but Richard lashed out, "I'm hungry now, but I won't stay with you!" Little Richard made the best of this desperate situation by defending his self-respect and his pride; he chose the only healthy way to react to a rejecting and unjust father, which is to accept nothing so as not to depend upon him. This the six-year-old Richard did, but at a life-long cost, for every little boy wants his father to protect and love him. Wright must have yearned for such a father, a father who would have loved and protected him.

No other man appeared to help little Richard; none of his uncles treated him as a son, with the exception of one uncle in Greenwood, Mississippi, who tried to be a father to him after his mother had suffered a paralytic stroke. Unable by then to accept a filial relationship with a man, Richard left this uncle within a few weeks. We know, however, that Richard Wright longed for a loving father, because years later he went back to Mississippi to see his father for the first time since their break in Memphis, and for the last time. He found his father old, toothless, and broken, but still smiling. They stood in a field trying to talk, the father now at his lowest rung—a laboring "hired hand"—the son now an internationally known author. The father obviously felt no resentment, but Richard was trying to see if there was any love, any bond at all. He had gone back to try to "find" his father, in this sense. Richard commented: "The psychological gap between us that had been wrought by time made us regard one another with tension and forced smiles, and I knew that it was not the myth of blood but continued associations, shared ideals, and kindred intentions that make people one."

What of his love relationships with women? In the whole of *Black Boy*, there is not one tender scene with the mother; not one memory of love from her or his grandmother or *any* woman. There is one pseudo loving scene: When he is leaving home his mother begins to weep and say, "Take me." But that is not love, and Wright never would have mistaken it for love. He would have taken it to be what it was—a claim of dependence.

It is quite possible that Wright never felt close to women (he married two, both were white, both quite able). He did not feel at ease with black middle-class women, he claims, because he felt their parents always judged him in terms of how much money he could make. As to the underclass or folk black, no loving ever resembled that of Bessie or Bigger. Neither rings true, the "love" scenes are stilted, forced. The scene in *Black Boy* with Bess, a girl of seventeen who was the daughter of Wright's landlady on Beale Street in Memphis, is ludicrous, incredibly naïve. And Wright still couldn't do any better with love scenes in his novels or stories ten or twelve years later.

In other words, he, too, was a sexual puritan at heart, like his mother, his grandmother, and his aunts. He was skittish about love because he felt disappointed, hurt, and rejected by them. He, in fact, had once been abandoned by his mother, who had put him into an orphanage after her husband had deserted.

In his basic fear of and resentment toward women, Wright resembled Du Bois. But their development differed. Whereas Du Bois's resentment was *unconscious*, Wright's was quite *conscious* and developed into an open pitched battle with his grandmother, mother, and aunts. He always *knew* he feared and hated them; Du Bois on the other hand, having repressed his resentment, consciously thought he respected, even revered, his mother. Wright, whose fear and hatred were conscious, attempted to work them out through his novels. But Wright's sense of guilt still pursued him. He attempted to expiate it by supporting his mother financially for the rest of her life.

Like Du Bois, Wright was poor at courtship and at giving himself over to a love relationship. Very late, certainly for a man whose father was a folk black and a "charmer" with women, Wright did begin a more active sexual life with women, when he was twenty-eight or twenty-nine. But he always found reasons to reject or break off with most of them. The Negro women, he thought too middle class, or too interested in money, in social status, in social life, or too unsophisticated and nonintellectual, or, simply, boring. Even white women always had to take the initiative and court him. He feared all women would reject him. Yet socially he presented a fierce front.

Michel Fabre, his official biographer, concludes that Wright wanted white women because possessing a white woman "was his revenge for the years of sexual and emotional frustration during adolescence—a way of eradicating painful memories." This statement, like most of Monsieur Fabre's efforts at psychology, is completely meaningless. *What did white women have to do with Wright's adolescent sexual frustration and painful memories?* He had nothing to do with white women in Mississippi except that once, by chance, he saw one naked. However, he quickly repressed that memory and it was not dredged up until he studied with Dr. Frederic Wertham, a psychoanalyst, thirty years later.

To the Negro man of that day, a white woman became attractive and desirable simply because she was forbidden to him by law. He also attributed ideal characteristics to her, such as intelligence, culture, beauty, affection. Fabre says that Wright's two white wives had all these traits, and that Wright's choosing them was as simple as that. But Fabre's deep ethnocentrism often appears in his attempts to deal with the American race system, of which he knows little and understands less. Wright was never a chaser of either black or white women. He was too *ambivalent about women* and too afraid of being rejected to pursue them actively. Thus, while he won his struggle to become independent, he lost his second major conflict, that between trust and distrust. His distrust of life and of people began in his earliest years. The hostility toward his mother, which he showed at the age of four, five, and six arose from a feeling of distrust, which was expressed most fully and most memorably in the hallucinations *he suffered after his mother had whipped him to the point of death*.

Erik Erikson has pointed out that trust of life and people develops in the first year or two of life, that it has to do with the nursing relationship between mother and child. If the child feels safe and warmed and loved by the mother, and if his earliest experience at the breast is pleasant and rewarding, he will expect always to have enough, to be treated well by people and the world, and to be generally fed with the milk of human kindness. But if his experiences are of the opposite type, if he receives a sour breast, a bad tit, if the mother is so anxious or so unable to express her love that the child feels unwarmed and unwanted, then the child's reactions are generalized from these early bad experiences *to life in general*. He expects nothing good of other people.

As a young child, Wright experienced a breast fantasy, particularly after his mother had beaten him very severely.

> Whenever I tried to sleep I could see huge wobbly white bags, like the full udders of cows, suspended from the ceiling above me. Later as I grew worse, I could see the bags in the daytime with my eyes open, and I was gripped by the fear that they were going to fall and

drench me with some horrible liquid. Day and night I begged my mother and father to take the bags away, pointing to them, shaking with terror because no one saw them but me.

This is a fantasy of the "bad tit," of the mother offering poisonous milk; it expresses distrust. Throughout his life, Wright suffered this basic distrust, which made it difficult for him to have intimate, close feelings toward anyone. It accounts for the lack of feeling he shows toward the characters in his novels.

His emotional distrust of people was turned into a chronic suspiciousness. His almost paranoidal fear that he was being watched resulted from the fact that his grandmother, mother, and aunts actually had watched and spied upon him continually. Their hostile, critical, and lacerating eyes had followed his every act. Since Wright had internalized this "watching conscience" of his mother and grandmother, it follows that the "spy," the watcher, the judger, is *himself*. That is to say, the "watcher" is a part of him, learned in childhood, and surfacing involuntarily in adulthood. Later Wright actually *was* watched and spied upon by government agencies, both French and American, but his oversuspicious nature at times apparently reached a neurotic stage in which the "inner voice" of his watchful and censuring mother and grandmother continually tortured him.

Wright's hostile "death wishes" toward his mother and grandmother were very powerful and lasted throughout his life. Most of the time, of course, these death wishes were unconscious; that is, they were repressed. And, fortunately, Wright was capable of partially sublimating them by writing out his fantasies in novels. One finds, throughout his works, men assaulting and murdering women (in *Native Son*, in *The Man Who Killed a Shadow*, and so on). One does not have to look too far beneath the surface to read their meaning. In fact, one could infer Wright's hostile death wishes quite validly simply by reading his fiction, without knowing anything about his life. Consider, for example, that the first story ever to impress Richard, the story that led him to begin his reading, was

"Bluebeard and His Seven Wives"! The account in *Black Boy* of hearing the story read by his aunt unmistakably reveals his identification with the subject:

> She whispered to me *Bluebeard and His Seven Wives* and I ceased to see the porch, the sunshine, her face, everything. As her words fell upon my new ears, I endowed them with the reality that welled up from somewhere within me. She told how Bluebeard had duped and married his seven wives, how he had loved and swained them, how he had hanged them up by their hair in a dark closet—I stopped her constantly to ask for details. My imagination blazed. The sensations which the story aroused in me were never to leave me.

When his mother interrupted the story and scolded him because he wanted to hear the end of it, she told him, "You are going to burn in hell." (In later life, Wright was tortured by hallucinations and nightmares in which he saw himself as a devil with a long tail.)

> Not to know the end of the tale filled me with a sense of emptiness, loss. . . . I vowed that as soon as I was old enough I would buy all the novels there were and read them to feed that thirst for violence that was in me, for intrigue, for plotting, for secrecy, for bloody murders. . . . Ella's whispered story of deception and murder had been the first experience in my life that had elicited from me a total emotional response.

The unconscious and unacted tragedy of Wright's inner life was indeed that of Orestes, who was caught between his love of and filial piety toward his mother and his hatred of her. Wright suffered throughout his life for his unconscious hatred of his mother and grandmother, and the resulting guilt. He punished himself severely with a variety of masochistic burdens which he inflicted upon himself. In the penultimate year of his life, for instance, he was still sending his mother and aunt money that he did not have to spare. The medical care he provided and his concern about their health were expressions of his guilt and frustrated love (reaction to the opposite).

His deepest conflict, then, was that between his conscience and his resentment against his mother. Wright was tortured by guilt for his own hatred because he, like his mother and grandmother, had a puritanical conscience. This deep-seated and unconscious guilt led him to the self-loathing and self-contempt that are manifest in *the male characters of his novels*. The angry conscience of his mother and grandmother, which he internalized in early childhood, punished him as he felt those women would have, had they known of the feelings he harbored against them.

A writer of fiction continually projects his own emotional and moral conflicts upon the fictional characters he creates. When Wright, day after day and year after year, sat down before an empty sheet of paper to write a story and create "characters," what actually came out of his mind, imagination, and emotions was a reflection of *himself*: his own conflicts, his own history, his own basic hostility, distrust, and fierce desire for independence, his own love-hate-guilt conflict over his mother. A writer can write only what is within him; upon each character he tries to create, then, he projects aspects of his own conflicts, loves, and hates.

As one grows older, moreover, one's unsolved emotional conflicts and defenses become—through years of repetition—more strongly reinforced (learned), more crystallized, and rigid. In Wright, this repetition and the increasing compulsiveness of his hate, guilt, and suspiciousness account for the deterioration of his creative work after his early thirties. For nearly thirty years more, he unsuccessfully tried to solve his basic personal conflicts by writing his own story over and over.

But a writer has to learn first to face *himself* objectively. He must be able to see his own bias or neurosis if he is to be able to look at his "fictional" characters objectively. After his first three published books, however, Wright fell victim to perseveration and kept trying to solve his personal problems by "expressing" them in his fictional characters. His protagonists in his later works no longer are courageous farm tenants, or a struggling poverty-stricken black boy, or an existential monster from the lower depths; they become versions of himself in his Chicago and New York days, *a very sensitive, proud, conflicted, alienated, middle-class man*. It was this unsolved and crystallized conflict—not his residence in Paris—which accounted for the marked decline in the quality of his later fiction.

But if he failed in his later years as a novelist, he had already—in *Uncle Tom's Children*, *Black Boy*, and *Native Son*—shown himself to be a writer of power and ability. No American novelist of his time, except Faulkner, equals Wright in narrative power; the stature of his protégés, Ellison and Baldwin, is further testimony to his greatness.

Wright had an important but unacknowledged role as a liberator of his people, a role such as perhaps no other twentieth-century American writer, white or black, has had. *He freed educated Negroes from the fear of expressing anger at their persecution, segregation, and exploitation.* His hoarse, rage-filled, confrontational, and completely incorruptible voice was that of a "new Negro," throwing off the age-old repressions formed under slavery and peonage, and demanding—down to the lynch-holes and gullies of Mississippi—to be free.

Wright freed middle-class Negroes, their writers, and spokesmen from the "Uncle Tom" role. He freed them from the back-bending, grinning, and yielding; from tipping their forelocks in obeisance to all the invincible white "massas," and from that involuntary fear of the bull whip, and the shot in the dark, which kept cotton tenants like Wright's own father in line on Mississippi plantations. *Wright called upon his Negro reader to break the lock step of the imprisoned and defeated, and to stand up, as he had had to do, and act the man.*

To have power such as Wright's is to be the most influential kind of leader; one who is capable of changing the spirit of a people. In helping them to *free themselves* from their inner repressions, to express their anger, he enables them to release the energy that has been tied up in the act of repression—in the "damming up" of anger. He frees them from the inner bonds upon their initiative.

Middle-class people, white or black (including lower-middle-class people like Wright's grandmother), are generally frightened of their own anger. They teach their children not to express it, but to swallow it. And since to show anger toward whites is physically very dangerous, black parents teach their children to hide such anger, to disguise it. Wright took the all-important first step in dealing with repressed conflict: *he articulated the anger*. He spoke with such force as to startle the nation into attention. "Bigger" was unreal, larger than life, but a dread symbol of what our society was producing. (As a symbol he took his place beside other names representative of American culture: Huck Finn, Moby Dick, Hester Prynne.) Negro writers had protested before, but none with such effect. Wright gave other Negro writers the courage to express their anger. Wright "broke open the dams" and the white world learned that they would have to contend with the Negro's anger.

On the personal level, Wright was a tragic man—defeated by the same unconscious forces that defeated Oedipus, Hamlet, and those who never resolve and master their earliest conflicts or untoward circumstances. This is the human dilemma, and it is not surprising that Wright failed to conquer it. But he did enough. He handled his rage by transmuting it into such powerful symbols as made the nation attend and listen; and, in his finest stories, he gave catharsis to the enraged American Negro. Most important of all, he paved the way to greater freedom for all writers who followed him, black or white, to tell the truth about the existentialist rage of the oppressed.

5

Amazing Love: Martin Luther King, Jr.

. . . in the last resort we must begin to love in order
that we may not fall ill, and *must fall ill if*,
in consequence of frustration, *we cannot love*.

SIGMUND FREUD
On Narcissism: An Introduction

A foreign reporter who accompanied Martin Luther King, Jr., on all his marches in the Deep South wrote, "I have seen many mass movements, but nothing like this. It is one of laughter and song."

King felt himself a warrior for God. He communicated this to his beleaguered and often bloodied campaigners. These "soldiers"—often only high-school children—faced jail with good spirits and good consciences. Buoyed by high spirits, these youngsters were able to confront white state troopers and policemen. It was indeed, as the foreign correspondent wrote, an incredible revolution. In the face of savage dogs, electrified cattle prods, and powerful fire hoses their adolescent laughter and song moved the world, and finally shook America out of its racial complacence.

But the singing and laughing were, in reality, only a defense against a constant fear. Fear rode every Negro who demonstrated in King's campaigns—fear of being beaten, or shot, or lynched. It was the same fear that had broken Richard Wright's father on a Mississippi plantation, and had driven King's own grandfather off a Georgia plantation.

But King realized that this oppression of Negroes by whites in the South was only one example of the mutual hatred between ethnic, "racial," and national groups all over the earth. In time, King posed the central problem of our age. Our dilemma rests in whether mankind can learn to *control and convert* a chronic anger and desire for revenge, or whether our pattern of group violence and economic exploitation must *continue compulsively*, with no relief.

How may one learn to convert contempt for or hatred of members of another "race," or class, or nation into conciliation and understanding? How may whites and blacks in America, or the world proletariat and the world bourgeoisie, or the Irish and the English, the Iranians and the Americans, the English and the Argentinians, or any hating groups, for that matter, learn to deal with and resolve their mutual distrust?

We have yet to discover the solutions to hatred between contiguous national groups, or within the same nation. Hostility at a greater distance we may feel permissible—*chacun peut tuer son mandarin*. That is, everyone can in fantasy "kill his own Mandarin," who is so far away as to be unreal (for scarcely any one of us knows a real Mandarin personally). But we are amazed when *neighbors* hate each other, since, for example, in Belfast every Protestant at work or somewhere rubs elbows with a Catholic—or the other way around—and in the South, except in a metropolis, almost every white knows some Negro.

Yet it is precisely this violence—between nations in close proximity, between groups living within a relatively small region, or within families where social ties are shared—that erupts most often. Murder in the family is and always has been more common than any other type of murder. Simply put, violence springs from the emotions, and the most *violent* emotions are love and hate. Hatred is strongest, of course, between (1) those who have the closest and most frequent contacts, (2) those at different levels in a status system, and (3) those taught by their cultures to contemn or hate one another.

Social anthropologists are aware that each group teaches its members that its own habits, customs, and values, its own religion and ethics, are superior to those of any other group, society, or nation. Each society indoctrinates its members with a firm belief that they are superior to the members of any other group. Depreciation of and contempt for the "outsider" are natural consequences. To be centered on one's own way of life (*ethnos*) is to profess ethnocentrism. All peoples and nations are *ethnocentric*; all believe themselves right and the "other" wrong. Each wants to preserve its group, and maintain its "superiority." Such an encysted sense of innate superiority felt by whites was the real disease with which King had to contend.

It has often been said that King adopted Gandhi's technique of militant but nonviolent demonstrations. Actually, this technique was practiced by labor unions years before Gandhi, and dates from Thoreau's essay "Civil Disobedience," which was Gandhi's inspiration. King's religious background, dogma, and ritual were, in fact, entirely different from those of Gandhi, whose religion was that of a small, archaic, esoteric, and severely masochistic sect. Whereas Gandhi was ascetic, masochistic, and sexually puritanical to the point of celibacy (he demanded this, too, of his followers, the *satyagrahis*), King was an athlete in college, fond of good clothes, loved women sexually, and enjoyed eating. Whereas Gandhi hated the fact and practice of procreation—in other words, advocated race suicide—was a poor father, and was basically suicidal, King wanted and enjoyed his children, and was a loving and good father. More-over, King dealt with a more difficult problem than that which Gandhi faced. Gandhi tried to heal hatred between the English conquerors and the oppressed Indians; both groups were of the same basic physical stock, Aryan, and the Indians had a far older culture than the English. But King represented a completely de-spised "racial" group, Negroes, who never had been integrated into Anglo-Saxon society. King and his followers were recent descendants of chattel slaves, owned by the white ancestors of those very whites from whom King was trying to win concessions and respect. If one is to accept Erikson's profound analysis of Gandhi, he was far less loving and honest, and far more masochistic and hypocritical than King.

Someone has written that the great author Franz Kafka, who died in 1924, portrayed a world that—at the time of his works—appeared monstrously unreal, *but one that has been coming true ever since*. Martin Luther King, Jr. seems to have had the same kind of prophetic insight, but his vision was of a better future, a future in which reason and conciliation would save us. Now, suddenly and spontaneously, mankind has arisen to condemn the insane preparations for nuclear war. Generation after generation, we have felt doomed to bear the horror of war, and we have borne that horror through two World Wars, Korea, and Vietnam, and into the present promise of a *compulsive plunge into nuclear war*. But, with this new movement, it now seems possible that healing and ultimate sanity—the drive for self-preservation—will save our children and grandchildren from annihilation.

In this Age of Fear, one sees few men of hope and courage. There was, of course, Governor Adlai Stevenson, who, at the time of the Cuban missile confrontation, spoke for life. Just after Russia had placed its atomic missiles in Cuba, when the two crazed world giants were threatening life itself, Stevenson joined two eminent scientists in a public discussion of our chances for survival in a nuclear war. One soon learned that the gentlemen of science knew infinitely more than Stevenson about the physiological effects of the bomb. For an hour and twenty minutes they piled up images of death, starting with the overwhelming argument that there is no defense against nuclear missiles. They then proceeded to describe the range of monstrous deaths and the even more terrible deformities we can expect. They painted horrible images of the Inferno in the final blast, the treacherous fallout sliding in upon us all, the burns and blindness and bone cancers of the survivors. Finally, they portrayed the future offspring—the progeny of gene mutations—bred under atomic radiation, and grown into a generation of monsters. At this point, the world seemed a hopelessly insane place, where life itself was subject to the mad whimsey of the nuclear powers. Why plan? Why bear children? Why work? Such goals are empty rituals in a world where every hope has vanished. When fewer than ten minutes of the symposium were left, the scientists turned to Stevenson to ask how we might escape the labyrinth in which they and the politicians had entrapped us. "This reminds me of a story, gentlemen," Stevenson replied, "which I believe you have left me just time enough to tell. Last month my niece, who is becoming a young lady, was enjoying her sixteenth birthday party, and her uncle, as one is apt to do on such occasions, expressed his surprise at her growth. 'My dear,' he said, 'in just a few years you will be twenty-one. And what do you want to be then?' And my niece, dancing away, her cheeks flushed, her eyes sparkling, cried, 'Oh, I want to be *alive! Alive!*' "

Stevenson concluded, "And so do the Russians, so do the Chinese, and so do *we*. I am certain we will all feel just as strongly about *living* tomorrow, and a year from now, and a generation from now." Stevenson had expressed our thirst for life—not death; the determination to seize and explore life's possibilities for creativity and strength, and to go for love—not hate and despair.

Of course, King, like Kafka, was not understood in his day. King pictured the future world united by the love of mankind. To make such a world, and to save ourselves from mutual annihilation, he said, we must learn how to change our hatred for "outside" groups into what he chose to call "love" for the outsider. This love for the once hated white or Negro, or German, or Russian, or Japanese, or Irishman, or Englishman, King said, "*affirms the other unconditionally. It seeks personal fulfillment of the other.*" That is, the "love" which binds men together includes forbearance and the willingness to be patient because one is *no better* than his enemy, and he is *no worse* and *no different*. This is not the philosophy that advocates the turning of the other cheek; rather, it exhorts one to set an example of one's best self, to inspire—and shame—the "other" to rise to *his* best.

This search for a new way of life, which turns compulsive and repetitive fear and hatred into reconciliation, King called the "*weapon of love*"; "*weapon,*" the metaphor is proof that there is both *aggression* and *love* in King. The love is a drive for affiliation, a love of mankind; the aggression is the determination to *change* others, to reform.

Several years ago, on the anniversary of King's birth, I heard the extemporaneous remarks of two white television commentators on a coast-to-coast telecast. They had covered King's marches in Birmingham and Selma. One man, now very prominent, said, "I'm Southern-born, and lived in the South for my first thirty-one years. But King changed me. He taught me to examine myself and to understand what blacks felt and had to bear at the hands of whites." The other man, from Atlanta, added, "He did the same for me and many other whites. He called it love, I call it the ability to understand. I guess it comes to the same thing. It was as if the *blinders* were lifted from my eyes. King made it possible for many whites like me to become free men." Free from what? From the sickness of hate.

These chance remarks astounded me, because, being a Negro, I'd thought only of the effects *upon me* of segregation and discrimination. I had not thought, except very abstractly, of the tremendous emotional and psychological burden placed upon whites by a system that treats fellow human beings as pariahs, outcasts. But here were two hard-boiled white newsmen testifying to the pain of that burden.

Owing to the past seven decades of war, our ethics and our morality with regard to violence have become schizophrenic. Since 1914, Europe and America have been bled in a succession of wars that have piled more than 61 million deaths—and far more injuries—on a dropping birth rate. This birth rate, in itself, is insufficient in most Western nations to maintain their populations. After the First World War, many of England's young men were dead, crippled, or suffering "war psychoses" and the effects of poison gases. Women were left celibate. In one London rooming house after another, young women lived in lesbian marriages—their accommodation to a world without men. Twenty-one years later, the Second

World War finished off the already grievously reduced English and French. So the seeds for the collapse of the Maginot Line and the shambles at Dunkirk had been sown a generation earlier, in the First World War.

Western society has since been locked in its dance of death, grimly holding out for revenge on the Continent, in Vietnam, Ireland, the Middle East, and even in the Falklands (for an injury done 150 years ago). Since 1945, we have been primed for nuclear annihilation. In the rush to death, the two giants, insanely bent upon destruction and suicide, have armed themselves with a myriad of nuclear bombs, set to fly in ten seconds and capable of killing a population of 200 million souls a hundred times over.

The certainty of death has taken the meaning out of life. Death has become the one reality, the constantly-at-hand final sanction of Western society. For the past sixty-three years, we have seen our sons face weapons that are capable of shattering steel itself but are used to splatter the genitals, brains, and the tender, utterly miraculous human body.

The West is dying of the effects of its compulsive hatred, and its obsessive wish for revenge. Why does nothing seem likely to stop our suicidal and murderous descent into extinction? Because the basic morality of the Western world fell apart in the First World War. (Even prior to that slaughter, the middle classes had lost their faith in the Judaic-Christian religion and in the earlier traditions of humanistic moderation, which had begun to die during the Industrial Revolution.) The First World War finally undermined *the West's entire basic moral code of behavior*. Disillusioned, the middle classes were ready for the knockout blow—a complete loss of faith in any morality and a complete loss of hope.

It was Hitler who dealt that final blow to the moral code of the Western middle class, which until that point had been based on truth in dealing, even-handed justice, observance of law, mercy, and the belief in the ultimate possibility of moral and social improvement. Hitler established, instead, the code of force, guile, fraud, and genocide. The old value systems had been the source of the middle class's identity, its sense of purpose and self-approval. Now the middle class has no reason to work and seize life. It is left in a void, with no purpose, no self-justification, no hope.

Nevertheless, the vestiges of that old morality die slowly. A few years ago American prisoners of war returned from North Vietnam. Nearly all these men were aviators who had let loose an inferno of napalm and fiendishly contrived antipersonnel fragmentation bombs—during the heaviest "saturation bombing" of all time—upon a rural population with no aircraft to defend itself. Yet, as one listened to and looked at the faces of these returning bombers of helpless women and children, one saw the expressions and heard the words of the typical "nice" middle-class young man, the "good" son. Returning to America, they still expressed, with nonaggressive words, the "decent" attitudes of the "good" middle-class boy. But the fact remained that they had killed hundreds of thousands of children, mothers, and noncombatants.

There is no way to understand this paradox—*which is the world of our time*—except to realize that we live in moral chaos, *in a schizophrenic society whose own values and sense of reality are split right down the center, just as were the personalities of those aviators.* Our right hand neither knows nor wants to know what our left hand does. Remembering Hiroshima and Nagasaki, we sit and wait for the final incineration that will execute our friends, our family, our children, our grandchildren—and end all life.

This is the world and the America in which King came of age. He learned Atlanta's and the South's two-faced system of "democracy." In that brutal caste system, every Negro was treated as childish, primitive, stupid, and each was stamped by law as inferior to whites. It was a society which believed neither in Christianity (its own "white" churches excluded Negroes) nor in democracy (it had disfranchised 99% of Southern Negroes), and had rigged its courts of justice against the Negro (including the Supreme Court of the United States until 1954).

Knowledge of this society was ground into King by his daily experiences in Atlanta. But between his nineteenth and twenty-fifth birthdays, he was educated in a different climate, in university classes on religion and philosophy at Crozer, at Harvard University, and at Boston University. Under the leading white scholars in those fields, King learned how and why America and the West were being destroyed by hatred, by war, and by the death of the white man's God. King was always perfectly aware, therefore, of the nature of hatred and its life-or-death implications. He chose to confront the cycle of hate first in Montgomery in 1955, and finally in 1966 at the White House, where Lyndon Johnson and his war party claimed they were "winning" the war in Southeast Asia.

The basic cause of chronic hostility between whites and blacks—the behavior which King wanted to change—was the fact that the larger economic, political, educational, and legal systems all operated and cooperated to subordinate blacks to whites. In spite of democratic political dogma, and a Constitution which was conceived by the general public as guaranteeing equality of citizens before the law, the machinery of Negro subordination still worked smoothly.

The problem King faced first of all was how to reduce and, if possible, have declared illegal the local legal systems for the intimidation and segregation of Negroes, and to do so in a nonviolent and nonhating manner. His method was to start with peaceful confrontations in "white-only" situations in order to underscore the harsh realities of segregation, and to bring the feudalistic treatment of all Negroes out into the open through television, radio, and newspapers. By peaceful demonstration, without any show of hatred or violence, he hoped to change the feelings and the thinking of American whites. His method seemed weak indeed in comparison with the tenacity of age-old hatreds, the long history of more than 32,000 lynchings of blacks, and the brutality with which segregation and subordination were enforced by white police and state troopers.

King had also to face the problem of Negro attitudes. It is a fact *that all systems of subordination arouse mutual hostility between the subordinating and the subordinated groups,* owing to the unequal distribution of power and privileges. For a person of the subordinated group (a black), his hostility *hides his fear* of the aggressive, dominant group. His *anger is defensive,* and is often an unconscious effort to preserve his self-respect under constant public attack and derogation.

The black's fear of whites becomes chronic, an anxiety felt in all his relationships with whites, whether at work, in stores, theaters, or buses. Before King's work, a system of legal taboos against Negroes existed everywhere in the South, the Border States, the Plateau States, and in most large Northern cities. All American blacks, therefore, could readily identify with King's campaign. Even Northern whites—due to King's protests—came to realize why they never saw blacks in "their" white public restaurants, hotels, or schools.

In the long-standing, state-controlled Southern system of segregation, the hostility of the lower group was constantly exacerbated by repeated discrimination and insults, but their anger was hidden from whites. In fact, the anger often was *repressed* and hidden from the Negro himself, since it is *painful* to be continually angry over mistreatment which one cannot oppose or prevent. Generally, however, the black's hostility toward whites takes one of these four courses: (1) He may express it as *overt* aggression toward whites. But this course is suicidal—or at the very least doomed to fail—for whites are far more powerful and can destroy his career, or have him jailed. (2) As John Dollard has pointed out in explaining the high incidence of intragroup violence among lower-class blacks, he may transfer his anger from its real cause—a white—and direct it toward another black. In thus displacing his anger, and expressing it against another target—a black—he avoids any necessity for swallowing his feelings, and thus gains a modicum of self-respect. (3) He may transform or sublimate his hostility toward whites into *aggression to achieve within the black world*. This process has been the source of most upward economic mobility. The majority of black physicians and lawyers in the North, for instance, is comprised of those who hated the South and fled. That is, their antagonism against Southern whites is palliated by succeeding and flourishing within the black's own status system. Finally, (4) he may turn his hatred of whites *inward,* upon himself. This process leads to "Uncle Toming," playing the fool, pretending stupidity, and other self-derogating behavior. The extreme of this self-punishing adjustment is suicide, which is still rising at a far higher rate among young Negro Americans than among young whites.

Martin Luther King, Jr. was born in Atlanta, Georgia, at noon on January 15, 1929. He became the first great Negro-American leader born of securely married parents of good economic position. Ironically enough, as the only black leader who took to the streets with his supporters, King was also the only leader born to a highly religious and stable middle-class family. He was likewise the only leader whose father did not early desert or deny him. Martin was his father's pride and joy.

Writing fifty-two years after Martin's birth, his father remembered Martin as having been "smart as could be, always a gentleman—destined to be some one special." His grandmother, who was closest to him, called him "Child of God, Child of God."

Always a gentleman! The typical middle-class boy is well trained, seldom rebellious, and basically intimidated in his enjoyment of the human drives of sex and aggression. But in Martin's case he was *not* crippled sexually: his magnificent widow remembers, "Martin was all man." Nor was he crippled in his courage to stand up aggressively for himself and for his people.

"*Always a gentleman.*" A great achiever. A brave leader. "*Child of God.*" White fathers and mothers who often saw King on their television screens, could easily have thought him the son whom they themselves had borne or desired or imagined, the child they themselves had nurtured, sacrificed for, sent to college and professional school, to afford him every opportunity. Here he was—a hero!—before their very eyes. They identified with King as *their* leader; he changed the image of the educated black in the minds of American whites.

But today's child psychologists would say it was not his parental training but *parental love* which made him a strong and responsible man. For he had the incredible good fortune to be loved by both his mother and father. So he was indeed a child of God in the sense that he was one of those happy individuals who seem "blessed by the gods" from birth.

His personality seems to have combined his mother's intelligence and tenderness with his father's stubbornness, endurance, and fortitude. In his autobiography, his father makes no bones about being less intelligent verbally than Martin's mother. But he is and always has been a remarkable man in his own right.

Martin's father, called "Michael" or "Mike" by his mother (a name which he kept until she died, after which he took the name his father gave him at birth, "Martin Luther"), was born in 1899 about forty miles southwest of Atlanta. Mike King's own father (James Albert, young Martin's grandfather) was a violent alcoholic—a poverty-ridden sharecropper working on a white man's plantation. Fierce-tempered, James Albert used his fists or grabbed a shotgun when provoked, and was known to attack whites as well as his own family members. A typical lower-class man with respect to intrafamily violence—he beat his wife—he was, nevertheless, a hard worker. He tried to provide for his family, and undoubtedly he loved his wife, Delia, as she did him. (In the Negro lower classes, as I found in the 1930s in Mississippi, spouses fight with their fists instead of harrying each other with mutual resentment and verbal torture, as a great many middle-class spouses do.)

Having lost part of his right hand in an explosion in a rock quarry, this James Albert, father of Mike King, sank to the status of sharecropper on the plantation of a white man who systematically cheated both his black and his white tenants. The James Albert King family, therefore, despite the fact that both parents and their nine children worked hard raising cotton, were destitute; even the mule they used for plowing belonged to the white landlord, who stole their share at "settling time."

All Negroes were oppressed, but here—as in Richard Wright's Adams County, Mississippi, home—Negro farm tenants and their children were openly terrorized. As a boy, Mike saw a Negro man lynched by white sawmill workers. "He was dead, just a few feet in front of me." Mike had seen the drunken whites rob this man, beat him to death, and hang him from a tree. The body was swinging just a yard in front of him. Martin's father never forgot this lynching, he says, and always hated whites until his son, Martin, Jr., taught him to forgive.

Southwest Georgia has always been a primitive, Negro-hating area with a large "poor-white" population. Mike King's parents shared the violent culture pattern of the whites. One day Delia, his mother, gave Mike a bucket of milk and a pod of butter to carry to a neighbor whose cow was sick. On the road, the boy was stopped by the white sawmill owner and told to fetch a bucket of water from a spring. Mike explained that his mother had already given him an errand to do. The white owner beat him, kicked him in the head, and white workers smashed his nose. Mike went back to his mother covered with blood. His mother asked, "Who beat you?" Her voice was steely, deadly. "Who was it, son?"

She took Michael back to the mill. The millowner was still laughing with his workers about the lesson he'd just taught the "little nigger."

"Did you do this to my child?" Delia asked.

"Yeah, woman. What'n hell you goin' do 'bout it?"

Delia tackled him. She had done heavy work all her life and was stronger than he. She beat him in the face. Other whites tried to pull her off, but she knocked them back while sitting on the millowner. Then she crushed his nose and left.

Beaten by a black woman, the white man tried to keep the matter quiet. So did Delia, for fear James, her husband, would become involved. But James learned, got his shotgun, and went after the millowner. Fortunately, the owner had left the mill. But a white posse later came to the Kings' cabin, and therefore James had to leave Stockbridge for three months. When he returned, he was drunk and demoralized, and he remained so thereafter.

James did risk his life, however, to protect Mike. At the close of the crop year, when the landlord was "settling" accounts with his tenants, little Mike, who was "good at figures," reminded his father to get payment for his cottonseed as well as for the cotton itself. Since the landlord had always cheated James Albert of his seed money, he threatened to beat the boy. His father, although knowing he would be kicked off the land for intervening, told the landlord not to touch his son. James and his family of ten were then given until sundown to leave the farm. They slept out of doors for days, because no other landlord would accept James King as a tenant. James proceeded to drink up the seed money.

Mike thus saw only the angry and violent side of his father, who was incapable of expressing the love he actually felt. As a young adolescent Mike was in the predicament of anyone who tries to live with an alcoholic. Alcohol releases the inhibitions upon fear, jealousy, hatred, and other strongly inhibited emotions; and alcoholics soon become hostile, vengeful, and belligerent. The child who has to deal with such a powerful and unjust parent may (1) try to outwit him, or (2) avoid him, or (3) divert him by playing the clown, or (4) swallow his anger and allow himself to be demeaned and intimidated, or (5) openly show his hostility.

As a small boy, Mike had to hide his anger and avoid his father as much as possible. But by the age of fourteen, it seems, he came to identify with this same powerful father, for he attacked and stopped him when he found him beating his mother. The boy's behavior was as angry and as violent as the father's, but James Albert promised never to strike Mike's mother again, and he never did. He threatened, however, to kill Mike if Mike ever attacked him again.

We know Mike identified at least in part with this domineering father, for he himself became, first, an authoritarian father who thought he should try to control his children's lives (for their own good) and, second, an ultimate authority, indeed a God-figure for thousands of his church members in religious, political, civic, and financial affairs. But Martin Luther King, Sr. (Mike) also identified in larger part with his strongly nurturing and self-sacrificing mother. Delia could *show* her love, and from her Mike learned what she could teach: loyalty to and responsibility for one's children. In Atlanta, from the age of eighteen, Mike paid his own and his sister's expenses in a private grammar school, and sent money to his mother on the farm. This was the loyalty and devotion to family which he had learned from his mother. Since James Albert provided only a "bad-father" example, Mike's most remarkable achievement has been that he became an absolutely devoted father to his own children. This unselfish protecting behavior can be attributed to his mother. She fought a powerful white man with her fists to warn him and other whites not to touch her son; and she sacrificed money Mike was giving her at fourteen, when he worked as a fireman on the railroad—money she sorely needed. Because the job was very dangerous, and too heavy for a boy, however, she went to the yard office of the Southern Railroad in Atlanta to demand that he be fired. (She always put his best interests above her own.) Later, when he no longer could stand his father's abuse, she told him to go to Atlanta to live and work—that is, she advised him to forget her plight, and save *himself*. He owed his mother his life, not only physically but also spiritually; he internalized *her* courage, *her* tenacity, and, above all, *her* devotion to her children.

Although severely deprived culturally during his first eighteen years, Martin Luther King, Sr. had a natural gift which burst, at last, through its cultural fetters. Such ability is not uncommon to persons born into poverty and under oppression. The first part of

his autobiography represents by far the best-told and most powerful story of a Negro farm tenant, except for those by another man
who was virtually illiterate until he was twelve, Richard Wright.
The story of the lynching that Mike witnessed at the age of ten is
the most convincing descriptive account of a lynching in literature.
Whereas most such accounts have been written by persons who
have never been present at a lynching, Mike's description reads like
what it actually is—an account by an observer standing only a few
feet away. It is stark horror.

Leaving the plantation for Atlanta at eighteen, he worked days
and attended school at night. The Atlanta school put him "back,"
into fifth grade, and as a result he was ridiculed by the children and
discouraged by most of his teachers. But he memorized, went without sleep, drove himself relentlessly, and entered high school at
twenty-one. There, the ridicule by his freshman classmates, who
were thirteen and fourteen, was much worse. But he persevered in
what others thought a hopeless quest, even while financially supporting his family. His father exhorted him to quit and return to
the plantation. One day James Albert came into the high school
and had the Negro principal send for Mike. Reeking of liquor and
now thoroughly broken, Mike's father ordered his son to return to
help on the farm. With the principal's help, Mike held him off.

Preaching in a number of villages in order to support himself,
Mike graduated from high school at the age of twenty-five. Already
married to the daughter of one of the two leading Negro ministers
in Atlanta, he was determined to go to college, and he applied to
the registrar of the leading Negro men's college in the South,
Morehouse. The registrar gave him "some little tests." He failed
them all, and was denied admission. He then asked to be allowed
to take remedial courses to qualify him for entrance. The registrar
again refused and told Mike, in effect, that he was too stupid and
too "countrified" to do college work. Finally Mike walked unan-
nounced into the office of John Hope, the president. Dr. Hope was
Du Bois's best friend, and like Du Bois he believed strongly in

education for "the talented tenth." Mike made his plea for admission, confessing how many times he had been refused and how utterly he had failed the entrance tests. Hope said absolutely nothing. He handed Mike a note to the registrar. To Mike's amazement, Dr. Hope had instructed that he be admitted to the college. Enraged, the registrar sent him off to class.

A hundred times that year and the next Mike wanted to give up. But "Bunch," his wife, herself a teacher, encouraged and pushed him. "A grown man can't quit." Mike failed freshman English twice, but received a D the third time. He had to repeat many courses during the next four years, but with summer sessions and evening classes he finished Morehouse at the age of thirty-one! By that time he had three children: Christine, born in September of 1927, Martin Luther, Jr., born on January 15, 1929, and Alfred Daniel, born in July of 1930.

From the start, Martin, Sr. tried to give his son everything in life he himself had missed, including the love and support of a father and the complete education essential to a successful career and a full life. But in the effort to shape and guide the life of one's son, it is all too easy to dominate, and so destroy his initiative, his self-assertion, and his capacity to achieve adult independence. Who wants a son at twenty-five or forty who still feels and acts *dependently,* as if he were still a child? The image which Martin, Jr.'s biographers seem to give of his father is that of a parent who hovered over his son; who sought to protect him, guide his career, keep him close all his life. He is the faithful-unto-death father, who, after his son became the target of white dynamiters in Montgomery, followed him into every dangerous confrontation with Southern "law" officers in an ongoing mission to protect him from being murdered by Southern police. He was irrational in this, because, in reality, he could not possibly keep hostile police or other hidden assassins from shooting his son if they had chosen to. Nor could he prevent the cops from using their favorite means of murdering Negro prisoners—that is, shooting them "when trying to escape," with only other cops as witnesses. He was probably irrational, but only as are millions of other loyal and devoted parents in America, who would freely give up their own lives to save those of their children.

This precious son, born when his sister, Christine, was about fifteen months old appears to have been as much loved by his mother, Bunch, as by his father. Certainly Martin, Sr. felt at times that she loved him too much; so much that she, like her own mother, who called him "Child of God," might be placing him in danger of becoming spoiled. But when Martin, Sr. wrote his autobiography at eighty-one, he saw his wife as having been a loving compromiser between his own constant efforts to dictate to or "guide" his sons and those sons' efforts to direct their own lives. It is known that Martin took his problems first to his mother and broached his educational and career plans first with her, so that she might prepare his father for any disappointment in store for him. Often, Daddy King says, his wife would explain to him her understanding of the sensitive and imaginative Martin or the rebellious Alfred ("A. D."), and he would change his demands upon his sons accordingly. Bunch, as he called her, was a careful middle-class organizer of husband, children, and home. She determined the children's chores, allowances, and savings; and the use of time for work, study, quiet, play, meals, and prayers.

But Lawrence Dunbar Reddick, who is our only observer of the whole King family, wrote that Martin's mother's mother, Mrs. A. D. Williams (the grandmother who called him "Child of God"), was closest to him. He and everyone in the family called her "Mama." "A woman of health and spirits," Reddick wrote, "she radiated cheerfulness. She and Martin were each other's favorites." They each did special little services for the other. When she died suddenly of a stroke, Martin apparently jumped from his second-story window. He sank into melancholia. His father, the preacher, tried to restore Martin by telling him it was not his fault that "Mama" had died, but God had decided it was time to take her to him. Martin, Sr. was, remarkably enough, making God the guilty one, and denying the basic human truth discovered by Freud—that survivors of a loved one feel guilty for having lived longer.

Martin, Jr.'s childhood, then, was filled by essentially the same kind of childhood-identification objectives—hero, heroine, and villain—which we found in his father's childhood. The father was dominant and somewhat frightening, and the mother figure was a split one: a female, his grandmother, who was loving, nourishing, and indulgently gratifying; and a second female, his mother, who was an organizer and completely trustworthy. These were strong, spirited, admirable people.

With secure bonds of kinship, then, Martin Luther King, Jr. started out like Everyman on his journey through life to his inevitable meeting—only a few years away—with Death. His ego was strengthened in his very first years by learning to deal with a father who was tenacious, stubborn, enduring, and responsible. The child dealt with the unconquerable adult by adopting the father's traits, that is, by incorporating his spirit. This identification with his father made Martin, after the age of three, increasingly stubborn but patient, determined but enduring and responsible—the image of his father.

On the journey, King had to solve conflicts within himself as well as with the world. Often discouraged, apparently defeated, he proved to be resilient and determined; he never collapsed or turned back. *He had no guide to protect him from the dangers inherent in encouraging haters to love one another.* He had only his own maturing insight into mankind, his sense of reality, his own stubborn will. These—insight, sense of reality, and will—constitute the basic faculties of the ego (the "I," the Self).

One of the most outstanding psychologists of individual development has been Erik H. Erikson. Elaborating the findings of an even greater and more creative psychologist, Freud, he identified the basic psychological crises met in childhood and adolescence. The first crisis is met in nursing and weaning; the struggle is to learn to trust one's mother, or mother substitute. *The outcome may be either trust or distrust of people.* The second crisis, also met in the first two or three years, arises from the mother's demand that the child learn to keep himself clean—that he control the evacuation of his bladder and bowel. In this crisis, the child develops either "will or its opposite, willfullness" ("I'll do what I want!"). But the society requires that the child develop *self-control* and a sense of *responsibility* at this time (ages two to four) and maintain it henceforward.

These two earliest periods must have gone well, although we have no witnesses to document the child's responses. The critical phases in the development of King's ego were: *first,* his struggle for self-assertion against the controlling hand and protective guard of his dominant father; and, *second,* his effort to find an identity of his own—quite apart from his father's. The difficulty of these two problems caused him to "linger" for seven years in graduate study. But internally he lingered even longer.

The other faculties that his ego had to develop were the ability to work (industry), the capacity to open up emotionally to the opposite sex (intimacy), and the capacity and desire to generate and create (generativity). These last three stages, as we shall see, he learned early and well. His difficult problems were (1) dealing with "authority," and (2) like Du Bois, fusing his identity as a black man in a society where one is *taught* to admire the "white" culture (there is, of course, no such thing) and to despise that of Negroes. Certainly, learning to stand up to his childhood father *peaceably* must have had something to do with his peaceful revolt against the suppressive laws and customs imposed on Negroes. In both cases, only patience and nonviolence would have won.

Since the only female survivor in his immediate family, his sister, Christine, was too young—at the time of his nursing, weaning, and toilet training—to remember his responses to these most formative experiences, we shall simply infer that they seem to have been benign. As to nursing and trust, he loved to eat and he enjoyed people. Both James Baldwin and Bayard Rustin—two perceptive observers—were impressed by his genuine warmth toward and acceptance of people. One must emphasize, too, the great influence of his maternal grandmother, who, Reddick says, was hearty, congenial, loved people, and especially loved Martin. As to his "doing his duty," everyone, including his wife, Coretta, found him highly conscientious and determined to fulfill all his obligations, not only to both his parental and his nuclear families, but also to the civil-rights organizations he led. We assume that he "did his duty" in toilet training to please his loved mother or grandmother, and did not develop the compulsivity, irrational fears, stinginess, and suspiciousness found in those too severely trained. And since women found him quite attractive—his wife wrote of him in her biography that she felt proud in that "he always made me feel like a real woman because he was a real man in every respect"—we may assume his early sex drive was not impaired by puritannical sex training in childhood. So, his early organically based drives were not damaged in childhood, but were handled leniently.

Reddick, who actually lived with King's parents and siblings, has, unfortunately, provided us with only three or four incidents from Martin's childhood. All deal with insults: from white salesmen, white policemen, the white woman shopper who called him "nigger" for absolutely no reason, and the white playmates whose mothers had told them they were too old to continue playing with "niggers." But this tells us only of the hatred that whites, trapped in the caste system, directed toward him. It tells us nothing about Martin.

His father had often told young Martin of much more terrifying experiences from his own childhood, including that of the lynching he had seen. Describing his life on the plantation near Gainesville, he had said:

> I lived when the black man had no rights that the white man was bound to respect. He wadn't nothin' but a nigger, a workhorse.
> I was a sharecropper. My father was a sharecropper . . . and whatever grew on the farm, they'd rob you out of it. Then you

wasn't supposed to question them. You just worked and let 'em take from you, and I lived in that.

But I think it did something to me from a child, as I came up in it, and *created a hate in my heart against whites*. See, I had seen 'em beat black people up, saw 'em lynch them and hang 'em up by a tree. And I promised to hate every white face I ever saw when I got to be a man.

His anger made a permanent impression on Martin, Jr.

Except for President B. E. Mays, Martin, Jr.'s former professors at Morehouse seem to delight in saying he was only a B student, who showed no real comprehension in his orientation courses in the great Western philosophers. He was, however, graduated from Morehouse College when he was only nineteen. Intensive research by Dr. Robert Daniel Hess and myself on white and black high-school students—first studied as seniors, and restudied nine years later after college—has shown that *adolescent performance is a very poor base for predicting any kind of behavior, including academic*. Martin, who was "an ordinary" student in philosophy at fifteen and sixteen, was an A student three years later in graduate study at Crozer, in Pennsylvania. There, among white students, he led his class, was valedictorian, and won a $1,200 fellowship for further study.

By the time he was twenty-two, in 1951, Martin had earned the bachelor of divinity degree as well as the bachelor of arts degree, but wanted to go on for the degree of doctor of philosophy. Why? He certainly did not need a Ph.D. to preach and minister to poor black congregations in small Southern churches, where he planned to work. He already had had seven years of higher education and had been accepted several years before as co-minister of his father's important Atlanta church. His father had hoped Martin would eventually return to help him carry the load of his large congregation. But Martin felt he was not "ready." What was this unreadiness to accept full adulthood? What was standing in his way? Perhaps his father understood, for he did not fight to make Martin stay with him; he furnished the money that Martin needed in addition to his $1,200 fellowship to attend Boston University full time and to take several courses in philosophy at Harvard.

One would have thought Martin planned to become a professor of philosophy at a university, and not the minister of a working-class Negro church. It is clear he was *psychologically lingering,* his ego trying to gather strength to assume his rights as an adult. To do this, he would first have to face his father in choosing a place to work, in choosing a wife, and in rearing his own family. As long as he remained a student, he could postpone all these decisions. There is no doubt that at twenty-two, Martin still was emotionally dependent upon his parents—his father even recalls that he telephoned them three or four times every *week* from Boston.

Soon after going to Boston University, he met Coretta Scott, a uniquely able, responsible, and handsome young woman from Marion, Alabama. She had spent six years in Lincoln School, an American Missionary Associations school in Marion. Its Northern white teachers lived and ate with their Negro students; for this they were ostracized by all local whites. From Lincoln School, Coretta Scott went to Antioch College in Ohio on a scholarship, where she stood up well to the "on-again, off-again" racism of the white faculty. Graduating, she received a fellowship for postgraduate study at the New England Conservatory of Music in Boston. It was here that Martin met her and fell in love with her. By Christmas of their first year there, they were "going steady."

His mother alerted his father to the fact that Martin no longer was telephoning them. Since the young woman to whom he was "almost engaged" in Atlanta also reported she no longer heard from Martin, his father suspected there was a new girl. Martin, Sr. decided to go to Boston, and to take Bunch as an intermediary.

In Boston he at once raised the question, but Martin avoided the matter until his father could meet Coretta. When Martin, Sr. saw them together, he was convinced that his son was deeply in love. He feared their love would lead to indiscretions—perhaps an illegitimate child—that would ruin their careers. Their infatuation, as he thought it, not only endangered their reputations in the puritanical society of the church, but also threatened their academic careers. But Martin was twenty-two; his father chose to wait.

Finally, on the afternoon he was about to leave for home, Martin, Sr. decided to confront the young lovers. Bunch took Martin into the kitchen of his little apartment to enable his father to talk to Coretta. The Reverend King discourteously challenged "what she had to offer" in comparison with the daughters of the "best Atlanta Negro families." This brought Coretta to her feet, her eyes blazing. "I have something to offer, Reverend King." Daddy King would, in later years, chuckle at this proud rebuff from his future daughter-in-law; but at that moment they were in conflict. In the kitchen, Martin already had told his mother that he was going to marry Coretta. His mind had been made up before his parents had arrived. (The very first evening he'd spent with Coretta, he had told her she had the four qualities he most wanted in his wife: character, intelligence, personality, and beauty. He was prepared for marriage, and quite deliberately searching for a wife. He had been delayed only by the fear that his father would not approve of a woman who was preparing to be a concert singer—one who was unknown to Atlanta Negro "society.") That same day he told his father that, although he realized Martin, Sr. did not think Coretta would be a suitable wife for a Baptist minister, he was going to marry her anyway. *He had developed self-assertion vis-à-vis his parents, where it must be developed if the son is ever to become an independent man.*

Martin's method of dealing with his father was much like his later strategy of resistance and conciliation with much more powerful authority figures in the Southern racial system and in the federal government. First and always he would listen, trying fully to understand the other's position. Then he would state his own position and the goals he wanted to attain. He listened patiently while the two positions were restated, attacked, defended. He might at times bargain, but he never surrendered. He usually got what he wanted from white society through his nonhating, nonangry, non-violent claims and his enduring faith in others. He even converted his father, who hated all whites, to reconciliation, and—his father says—to love of mankind.

But even as late as 1955, when he was twenty-six, Martin had to fight off his feelings of being less than "grown up," less than his own man. His ego was still embattled against feelings of dependency within, and by the external pressures his father brought upon him to remain a child. If his ego was to learn to direct its own course, it had to overcome not only the blows of society ("race hatred"), but also the attack from within—the feelings of dependency upon his father. Such a battle rages within each of us constantly. If the ego frees itself from inner attacks upon its strength, it will seek life, power, and adult independence.

For King this fight would be unremitting—it would require courage and fortitude of the highest order. It was no journey for an individual with a child's ego. King would have to deal with a white government that thrived upon robbing the poor and sacrificing the helpless—in war as well as in the slums. He would have to come to terms with governments based upon injustice, fraud, cunning, and force—against whose power every man had to fight to keep from being driven to slaughter. To overcome what lay ahead of him and radically change a system of Negro segregation which had survived essentially unchanged for 300 years, he needed a strong independent ego, and the courage of the explorers of the Hanseatic League: *Navigare necesse est; vivere non necesse* (It is necessary to explore; it is not enough merely to exist).

In June 1953, Martin and Coretta were married by his father at her parents' home, nine miles from Marion, Alabama, with a reception a few days later in Atlanta. Martin had completed the course work for his Ph.D., but his dissertation—the acid test—still had to be written. Candidates for the doctorate degree who claim they have completed course work sometimes neglect to add that the most difficult work is still to come. Many never complete the dissertation because they do not possess the requisite aptitudes of application and industry. The dissertation is the most demanding test of assiduity in the academic world, although seldom proof of either insight, creativity, or understanding. Since early elementary school, Martin had never lacked industriousness. He worked two years longer on his dissertation, "A Comparison of the Conceptions of God in the Thinking of Paul Tillich and Henry Nelson Wieman," finished it in the spring of 1955, and received his Ph.D. from Boston University.

Martin was sure of his identity by this time; he was a man certain of his sexual identity—a full man—whose wife felt fulfilled and satisfied, and whose father had begun to look up to him. If the identity which the ego integrates for itself in young adulthood is, as Erikson said, a fusion of all earlier identities—identification with one's father and mother, identity as a male or female, and identity as a member of an ethnic group, religion, and nation—then that fusion of identities is culminated in one's identity as "father" or "mother." For King this was achieved early. Many husbands cannot face the prospect of having children. They fear their child will "cut them out" of the wife's love and attention (what they married to get); it is usually the wife, not the husband, who first wants children. But King was precocious in this development—he often said he loved children. After Coretta's first pregnancy, he wanted seven more! He had a genuine drive for generativity, as Erikson called it. Such a drive means hope and faith, zest for life, and a bursting creativity, which was beginning to be apparent in his civil-rights leadership.

By the time his first child was born, he had embraced his full occupational identity as the minister of an urban middle-class Negro Baptist church. He had talked for years about ministering to the poor Negro masses, and that would come later, in his civil-rights work. But his first choice was an old, strongly middle-class church whose members were dentists, business proprietors, physicians, and even Ph.D.s who taught at the Negro Alabama State College. Coretta later wrote that this was a highly congenial setting for a man and wife who had spent a total of twenty-one years in higher education (twelve for Martin and nine for Coretta). The illusion of harmony, or, rather, the delusion, behind which middle-class blacks barricaded themselves in those days—even in a center of racist oppression like Montgomery, Alabama (which I knew well)—was torn to pieces, however, by a frail Negro woman, Mrs. Rosa L. Parks, whose name has become known around the world. Not for any great gift of achievement has the world saluted her, but simply because she refused to be humiliated and persecuted any longer for the color of her skin. After 300 years of lock-step obedience to the laws made by tyrants, she had decided simply, "Life isn't worth it." This was the same feeling which had led Douglass to stand up and fight the monster slave driver Covey. "To hell with it and you! You can beat me, you can shoot me, but you can't frighten me any longer!" King and Coretta called Mrs. Parks's protest a "stroke of heaven" or "God"—in fact, it was the magnificent human ego and spirit, always embattled and always resilient.

"Destiny," self-preservation, or courage—whatever one chooses to call it, the outcome was clear. Mrs. Parks's resistance engendered a force that blasted King's rather complacent church members out of their pews, and sent them forth to try to redeem their souls, that is, to *regenerate their self-respect after a lifetime of bending and bowing in Montgomery and of hiding their souls' faces in shame.*

From the hour tiny Mrs. Rosa Parks asserted her rights as a human being and shamed others into following her example, and from the time King accepted his congregation's call to lead them against the crushing power of the police, the courts, National Guard, landlords, commission merchants and banks, a regenerative force began to work in the leader and his followers. It enabled King to face—"confront" was his word—the following crises: (1) the Montgomery bus boycott, December 5, 1955 to December 26, 1956; (2)

the Birmingham demonstrations and "children's crusades," April 3, 1963 to May 10, 1963; (3) the Selma, Alabama, march and Bloody Sunday, March 21 to 25, 1965; (4) King's battle with the Black Power leaders; and (5) King's stand against the Vietnam war party and President Johnson.

Martin accepted the presidency of the Montgomery Improvement Association (MIA), December 5, 1955. Very quickly he instilled its members with his flaming indignation, his determination to rebel against injustice, and his belief in the inevitability of freedom and justice for God's warriors. The bus boycott consumed their days and nights—it lifted and inspired them. From a local issue, it rapidly grew into a nationwide cause, then into the Movement, then into an internationally acclaimed nonviolent revolution of the oppressed and powerless. The boycotters displayed only laughter and song to the white police and the cameras, but internally their fears increased with each confrontation. Every marcher was dogged by the fear of white violence, of the lynching with which King often was threatened, of death itself, as it was meted out to their companions: to Medgar Evers and other NAACP leaders and young ministers in the Movement; to white Mrs. Viola Liuzzo; to James Chaney, the white Andrew Goodman, Michael Schwerner, and the Reverend James Reeb, all of whom were beaten to death; and to John Lewis, who, like scores of other leaders of the Movement, suffered crippling skull fractures. But such was the elevation of spirit that King imparted, and such was the sweep and force of their own group spirit, that what in ordinary days had seemed insane and suicidal became inspired, uplifted, and heroic. Even today, there are many who wish they had been with them. For even if Freud is correct—if to turn the other cheek is insane— this was an entirely different kind of cheek-turning. It had an aggressive component. It was designed to make whites who watched it on television feel guilty and ashamed because they had supported and profited by a system of racial injustice and oppression. If a white felt no guilt or disgust with his own racial system, then it could no longer be said that he believed in Christianity or democracy.

The hand of Death lay constantly on King's shoulder. A month after he became the Movement's leader, he was arrested on a trumped-up charge of driving thirty-miles-per-hour in a twenty-five-mile-per-hour zone, even though—knowing the white officer had been following him—he had carefully driven below the speed limit. He was jailed without bail; his best friend, Ralph Abernathy, pastor of the First Baptist Church of Montgomery, was told he could neither see him nor provide bond. King feared, as did his followers, that he might be spirited away and lynched. But so many of his supporters gathered outside the jail that the police decided to release him on his own recognizance. The Kings' telephone rang constantly with threats of death, and curses at "you nigger." Finally, Coretta was obliged to take the phone off the hook after half past two every morning.

Less than two months after King became president of the Montgomery Improvement Association, his home was bombed, at 9:30 in the evening. He was preaching at Abernathy's church, but his wife and baby were at home. The tremendous explosion split the front porch, shattered all the windows, and plunged the house into darkness. Coretta, who was in the sitting room, was unhurt. She rushed into the second bedroom and found her baby girl, Yolanda, unhurt. Within moments their neighbors came, and, very quickly, many more Negroes, armed with shotguns and pistols, gathered outside the home. Even the children had sticks and stones. One Negro said to a white cop who was restraining him, "You got your thirty-eight 'n' I got mine. Let's shoot it out!"

This was the first critical test of King's ability to control his followers and himself—to maintain the discipline of nonviolence. His home was in an all-Negro ghetto. A large, angry crowd of blacks surrounded the house. Most were armed and ready to shoot if King were arrested or manhandled. They shouted abuse at the police. The policemen, the Mayor, and the Police Commissioner were the only whites present.

King came out of the shattered front of his house and held up his hand. Quietly, he said his wife and baby were all right and that he wanted the crowd to go home and put down their guns. "We cannot solve this problem through retaliatory violence. . . . Remember, if I am stopped, this Movement will not stop, because God is with this Movement."

God is our leader! This was the secret of Martin Luther King's ability to stir his followers, of his power to lift and inspire them. Clearly, King's view of the world, his religion, was nothing like Gandhi's. King believed in a Spirit with which he could communicate—both as an individual and within group sessions—through prayer and introspection. When the threats began in Montgomery, he prayed to God for strength and courage. "I can't face it alone," he told his father. Then, in the midst of his pleas for guidance and help, he felt the actual Presence of the Divine. King's relationship with his God was always that of an obedient son to a beneficent, understanding, and loving father. There seems to have been little or none of the defiance, resentment, and self-torturing doubt which the German Martin Luther, author of the Reformation, expressed so often toward his God. Yet Martin King had great cause to doubt and resent his God's "treatment" of Negroes.

That day in Montgomery his prayers seemed to perform a miracle. He told Coretta, "At the moment I *experienced the presence of the Divine* as I had never experienced Him before. [Emphasis added.]" It was this belief that he was a divine warrior destined to free the poor and the oppressed—those in chains and those broken by subjugation—that enabled him to face the constant threat of death during his next twelve years.

To be true to his divine revelation he had to fight off his father and all sensible men. His hovering father drove from Atlanta *that very night* and tapped at the window of a friend's home where Martin and Coretta were sleeping. Thinking it might be a white assailant, King would not open the door. In the morning, Martin, Sr. and Coretta's father both came to insist that they return "home"!

King refused—he would not desert his followers. Coretta insisted on staying with him. But Martin, Sr. was determined that they should heed the warning from whites and leave for good. He felt certain there would be other attempts upon their lives. The home of F. D. Nixon, founder of the boycott and the MIA, was bombed next, and, later, a smoking pile of dynamite sticks was found on King's porch. In the middle of February, shortly after the first bombing of King's home, a grand jury made a frontal attack on the MIA, and indicted ninety of its leading members—including King and Abernathy—for organizing an "illegal" boycott. The police immediately began to make arrests. King broke off a lecture tour in Nashville and hurried to Atlanta, where Coretta had been vacationing.

King's father already had decided it would be far too dangerous for King to go to jail in Montgomery, and had set up what would prove to be his final confrontation with his son. He had invited the most influential Negroes in Atlanta to discuss the Montgomery grand-jury indictments with King. The advisers he brought to his home included bankers, publishers of the largest Negro newspapers, heads of insurance companies, the presidents of Morehouse College and Atlanta University, bishops, and the most prominent Negro businessmen. Except for President Mays of Morehouse, who knew Martin always made his own decisions, they advised Martin not to return to Montgomery, where they believed he would certainly be killed in jail. Martin responded, "I would rather be in jail ten years than desert my people now. . . . I can't turn back. I have reached the point of no return." (There was the silence that follows a death sentence.) Daddy King burst into tears; tears from the rugged man who once had beaten his own father! Tears for a lost son he knew was signing his own death warrant; one that might be consummated next week, or next year, or in ten years, whatever the day of the inevitable assassination.

Martin, Sr. did all he could. He promised that if the fine were large, he would pay it. A minister himself, he admitted that his son must do *what he felt he had to.* King had used those very words many times; not in the sense of any "destiny," but of an inner moral necessity, and more, of *a promise made to that Presence in whose fire he himself would be consumed.* Later, as he moved through one test after another, he justified his acts solely on this ground: that they were what he felt he had to do. But each choice became more difficult because his position—the nexus in which he had to operate—grew more complex, until at last King stood face to face with the President of the United States and his war party, and confronted their monomaniacal involvement in the Vietnam War.

As for Martin, Sr., his effort to "save" his son by persuading him to back down failed when it ran head on into a will even more stubborn than his own. The "old man" henceforward had to be content to guard King and not to try to persuade or dissuade him. The father followed the son in all his arrests and tried to protect him; even from the cops in jail.

Is this love? Or is it acute anxiety? Is the willingness to throw one's own body in the way of danger to save one's son not love? The question is crucial because, given that King based his whole philosophy and campaign upon loving his enemies, *his* own life must have provided a convincing evidence of the power of love. But from whom? The only person with whom he had shared a consuming love relationship, according to his biographers, was his maternal grandmother. At her death, when he was twelve, he apparently tried to commit suicide. He had made an attempt even earlier, when he thought his brother had killed her by sliding down a banister and knocking her over. Professor Reddick says he and his grandmother had a world of their own, and constantly were doing "little things" for one another. Such early love from a woman could have powerful influence upon the affiliative drive of a boy. I am willing to settle for this relationship as the most formative of his positive social feelings, his "love of mankind."

Yet there is his father. Although King did not realize, perhaps, that his father loved him, he *knew* his father was prepared to lay down his life for him. I have presented the evidence of this willingness, and of Martin, Sr.'s early pride in his son. To King, his father appeared anxious, hovering—a manipulator. Behind these reaction-formations of his father, however, there is more than a basic father-son rivalry. There is much pride, and, eventually, much love.

The real source of the abundant love visited upon King was his God. Using philosophical concepts to explain King's concept of God can only lead to mysticism. But consider his "God" in psychological terms. King had been told since early childhood by his father—who was also his minister—and by his mother, grandmother, and Sunday-school teachers that God lives in Heaven, is good and loving, but also can be angry and punishing. None of this was real to him until he began to pray and to talk with God. It was *in this talking relationship,* mentioned earlier, that he felt the Presence, and—at least once in Montgomery, in January 1956, and again in Memphis, in 1968—heard the Voice. This God whom he visualized in his prayers and whom he always described as full of love and mercy became the very apotheosis of love and forgiveness to him. For "he is part of God, and God is part of him." *Had he projected his own loving nature—displaced it—onto his God?* This idea is best expressed in William Blake's poem "The Divine Image":

> For Mercy, Pity, Peace, and Love
> Is God, our father dear,
> And Mercy, Pity, Peace, and Love
> Is Man, his child and care.
>
> For Mercy has a human heart,
> Pity a human face,
> And Love, the human form divine,
> And Peace, the human dress.

King's message to blacks and whites was that as they grew in the love of mankind and became willing to suffer for its sake ("redemptive suffering"), they would gain increasing faith in the beneficence of life and creation, and they would thereby increase in love. He believed it was a cyclical process. Willing to take on the suffering, then, he returned to Montgomery to certain conviction and jail.

On November 13, 1956—a few days less than one year after the start of the bus boycott—the United States Supreme Court affirmed a decision of a special three-judge U.S. District Court declaring segregation on buses unconstitutional. It took thirty-seven days for the Supreme Court's order to reach Montgomery. In the meantime, the Ku Klux Klan had marched through the Negro area and had been laughed off the road; members of the White Citizens Council had warned that blood would flow in the streets; fifty Negro homes, including King's, were threatened with burning. On the first day of integrated buses, King, Abernathy, and others rode unharmed, sitting where they chose. Later, however, buses were fired upon, stoned. Negroes were dragged off and beaten; a pregnant Negro woman was shot. One January night, there was a planned guerrilla attack: Reverend Abernathy's church and home were dynamited. Two other Negro churches were completely destroyed, and a third was burned. King preached on his twenty-eighth birthday, January 15, 1957, begging his followers not to seek vengeance, but to meet hate with love.

Was he "chicken," "Cowardly!" as the SNCC and the Black Power spokesmen said? How? In the face of violence and death, King and his followers had stuck to their previously arranged strategy of battle. It was a new kind of battle, to be sure, but it had won their goal. King, his fellow ministers, and their followers had won the "impossible" without firing a shot. They had won a desegregated bus line; in a few years they would win desegregated stores, restaurants, and theaters. These were changes no one before King had expected in less than 100 years.

What did the whites get in Montgomery? They got physical

revenge. Beating "niggers"! Vengeance for losses they had incurred in "Yankee courts," including the highest constitutional court in the nation. Vengeance, and the determination to fight again to put the "niggers" back in their cages. But to answer vengeance with vengeance seems pointless. We know that some vengeful people are generals in our Army and Air Force, or admirals of our nuclear fleets. What happens, for instance, if such a President, or Secretary of State, or of Defense cannot control his or her rage against Soviet provocations? Certainly the white society will have to come to grips with the same life-or-death choice King faced, and will have to solve it as he solved it. Either that, or be annihilated by a war of extinction. This is exactly the choice blacks had in Montgomery, as King saw it.

King's philosophy has been made clear in our description of his tribulations during "Montgomery"; we do not intend to repeat this course with King's other major confrontations against segregation. Let us resume our way with his ego as it moves ahead n life's journey. Quite contrary to his biographers and critics, I believe it was after Montgomery that King's ego gained its greatest strength.

Everyone knows the barbarities of Bull Connor in Birmingham, the chief of police who set fierce dogs upon thousands of children, tortured them with electrified cattle prods, and stripped them with powerful jets from fire hoses. The horror of this Brown Shirt torture shown on television in every American living room brought so many protests to President Kennedy that he sent the able Burke Marshall to negotiate a settlement between King and Birmingham's business leaders. They agreed to most of King's original terms. This agreement, like that in Montgomery, was followed by days of rioting by both whites and blacks. But King's victory this time was much greater; it produced the 1964 Civil Rights Act, originally proposed by Kennedy after "Birmingham."

During King's last period, from 1966 to 1968, most of his critics proved thoroughly biased. These were the years of his struggle against the "Black Power" groups (Stokely Carmichael and Charles Hamilton), against the Black Panthers, against the various Black Nationalist groups, and against the Vietnam war party of Lyndon Johnson. His critics were far too quick to accept the media's propaganda that King was being defeated by black groups demanding violent confrontations and punitive reparations. In retrospect, it is clear that both the media and the writers were very mistaken.

The struggle began with the riots in Watts, a black suburb of Los Angeles. There, in 1965, the police shut Negroes off in their slums, and proceeded to carry out a methodical massacre. In the following years, alienated Negro college students became strongly influenced by Communist tracts. The eloquent Negro Martiniquan author Dr. Frantz Fanon, a psychiatrist practicing in Algerian hospitals who studied Algerian victims of torture along with their French torturers, had published *The Wretched of the Earth,* which deals with the exploitative methods of colonial powers in Africa, and the defense by the native resistance. This impassioned book, with its celebration of violence, converted Carmichael; a year or two later, it converted Huey Newton, Bobby Seale, Rap Brown, and the Black Panthers to its credo of violence. Fanon's description of the typical West African colony exploited by Europeans, and of its revolution led by black guerrillas, became the model that Carmichael (though not Charles Hamilton) held up to replace King's notions of *agape* and the "beloved community." Just as Fanon was influenced by French theoretical Marxists, so Newton and Seale were guided by a book of Chairman Mao's maxims for guerrillas which Bobby Seale found in a Berkeley, California store. Mao's and Fanon's books thus guided the leaders of the Black Power groups as well as those of the Communist-inspired and Communist-financed Black Panthers. But since most blacks lived in industrial slums, they could not have adopted a more unrealistic strategy than one designed for rural or mountain guerrillas in China and Africa. Furthermore, the Black Power fighters were not recruited from the proletariat, but from high-school and city college youth. They, in

turn, proselyted, not workers, but street-corner groups and prisoners.

Television news departments, as Dr. John A. Davis has pointed
out, had always considered King's demonstrations to be "show
business" rather than documentaries of a social movement. The tension of the racial confrontations in the street, the unleashing of
fierce dogs, the police brutality, and the fallen Negro men, women,
and children made powerful tragic drama.

When Black Power and Carmichael came upon the scene shouting havoc and revolution, however, the television news departments quickly recognized a bigger show. A violent revolution! Those
who knew Negro life told them repeatedly there was no chance that
either working-class or middle-class Negroes would resort to violence, or that slum Negroes would organize guerrilla warfare. But
the television newsmakers would not listen, because they had their
own television "revolution" going, and it was the best show in town.
Everyone had a free ticket to see the announced downfall of the
"old" leader, King. Carmichael played this media game cleverly. The
Panther leaders added real revolutionary flavor with a minuscule
shoot-out with a few policemen.

The media kept pushing this fake revolution, with its fanatical
threats and even wilder demands for "reparations." Now, years later,
one can see that this scenario was as phony and as bloodless as a
typical revolution in a small South American country, but at that
time, from 1965 to 1968, television blew it up into a daily threat to
King's leadership.

During 1965 King won over the Chicago street gangs, the Cobras and Saints, to his *non*violent strategy, and they supervised his
second nonviolent march into Marquette Park in Chicago! But he
never won over his "friend" Carmichael, or the other Black Power
and Black Panther leaders. Since they were suicidal, they could learn
nothing from King. The Cobra leaders, on the other hand, who
recognized the great practical value of nonviolence, could and did
learn, and eighteen years later were working constructively, without

violence, in the Chicago West Side black ghettos to register voters against a racist mayor (1982).

The media were quick to report Carmichael's, Eldridge Cleaver's, Newton's, and Seale's cries for black violence, ignoring Charles Hamilton's expert sociopolitical-economic analysis, and his plea for peaceful political and community organization, which was what *he* meant by "black power." In early 1967, a year before King's assassination, the media had convinced most whites and blacks that these groups—the Communist student followers of Fanon, the Black Panthers, the Black Power leaders (who had no followers), and the Black Nationalists—were rising to arms, warring on the police, and rioting to get eight or ten or twelve billion dollars in "reparations" to compensate them for the miseries of the past 350 years of oppression! Most critics who wrote on King were taken in by this nonsense. Actually, there was never a time when Carmichael or Newton or any Black Nationalist had more than a small handful of followers, never a time, therefore, when they represented any important group in the black community, and never a time when they achieved any kind of gain for that community. After a few isolated shootouts with the white police in Chicago, Cleveland, and Oakland, the Black Panthers all but disappeared. As to the Black Power "leaders," they had no followers at all except other "leaders" making speeches. Even worse, they had no organization, and, of course, were of no help to Negroes.

How, then, could nearly all of King's biographers and critics have been convinced in 1965–1968 that he was losing the struggle with the radical and violent groups? Perhaps they were led astray by the reporters and commentators. It now seems more likely that some were led afield by their own desires, hoping for the downfall of a man who had achieved resounding success. At least one biographer and several social scientists have revealed their envy in using ridicule and irony to derogate King's intelligence, courage, and, in one case, even his Christianity!

It was King's confrontation with Lyndon Johnson and the Vietnam war party led by Dean Rusk, Walt and Eugene Rostow, and William P. Bundy, that did him the greatest damage. Even the heads of the national NAACP and the National Urban League attacked him for endangering the fight for Negro rights by joining the fight for peace. Not only would the Negro be called unpatriotic, they said, but King and the SCLC would waste their time trying to influence American-Asian strategy. In reply, King cited his duty to the black soldiers in combat in South Vietnam and to those killed or wounded; in terms of percentages, both figures were higher than those for American whites. As to economic loss, he pointed out that it was precisely the Vietnam War that was taking the money needed for Johnson's "War on Poverty." The war was starving out the slums. Vietnam took $20 billion, he charged, which should have been used to rehabilitate the United States slums with their 66 million inhabitants—half of whom were white.

But many of his SCLC staff were not satisfied. For a long time, he struggled with himself, reviewing the situation again and again, and contemplating its many facets. Would he irrevocably damage the Movement by opposing Johnson's war and by not supporting Johnson's candidacy for President? But he had never supported any party's candidate. The SCLC always had been nonpartisan. But was not the antiwar movement a *white* one, led by the Students for a Democratic Society, the National Committee on a Sane Nuclear Policy (SANE), and Eugene McCarthy, all of whom had done nothing for the black Movement? No, since Negro boys were bearing the brunt of combat, peace could not be a white issue. (Evading the draft was both a white and black middle-class issue; the draftees came predominantly from white and black working-class and slum groups.)

He suspected, on the one hand, that the white antiwar groups were trying to use him to pull their chestnuts from the fire. On the other hand, SDS and many of the white antiwar people had helped in the Mississippi voters' registration drive. Negroes and whites clearly had an urgent common goal: to stop the killing. But Mc-

Carthy had done nothing for Negro rights—he had a lily-white standoffish image; he was an ascetic, who would not understand or trust black vitality, especially sexual vitality. (He seemed more suited to a mission that called for being sacrificed on an altar or retiring to a seminary.) But he had a highly analytic intelligence, and—something nobody else of his status seemed to have—the guts to stand up to Johnson. With McCarthy, the antiwar people didn't need King. McCarthy might even oust Johnson, whose position in 1967 was quickly deteriorating.

But clearly the peace leaders still wanted King. They saw he was drawing vast crowds; for *millions of white people who were suspicious of SANE, SDS, McCarthy, and the leftist groups,* King still possessed the aura and the charisma of a messenger sent by God.

The choices became clear to him. They were either (1) to devote himself even more thoroughly to "massive" nonviolent protests against racial discrimination in industry, housing, and education, or (2) to devote himself fully to converting the Black Power and Black Panther groups, or (3) to use all his prestige and influence to stop the carnage in Vietnam once and for all, and redirect America's attention to the War on Poverty at home. As a minister, he should work to stop the organized mass murder in Vietnam, but he knew this would be the least popular choice. King remembered his idol, Du Bois, and the federal persecution he had suffered for his unpopular attacks on colonial wars. It was not too farfetched to imagine himself, like Du Bois, being charged with giving aid to the enemy. J. Edgar Hoover was capable of making such a charge. Moreover, the black middle class itself did not approve of endangering their gains in civil rights by exposing their leader to charges of treason. The black middle class was an easily intimidated group; most of them worked for either federal, state, or city governments, as teachers, Post Office employees, typists, or file clerks, and were therefore subject to "loyalty tests." As a matter of fact, the black middle class had not supported his campaign in Chicago because all knew full well that Mayor Richard Daley and his secret police, as well as federal agents, took photographs of those who attended King's meetings and marches. Negro physicians and dentists had not been supportive either, except for one or two of the most outstanding ones. At a night meeting for King held at one physician's magnificent home, Daley's secret police ducked in and out of the shrubbery to take pictures of everyone who entered. The pictures went into Daley's "Red File."

In the fight against the Vietnam War, King felt he would certainly lose the support of the black middle class. And who knew what the black working class thought about Vietnam? According to David Halberstam, they objected to King's attack on the war because their sons and brothers were fighting in Vietnam. (But Halberstam's only "evidence" on this matter, it seems, was a series of remarks overheard by a Negro friend in Harlem bars.) King decided that he would have to lose the Southern black middle class; as to the Northern black middle class, it never had supported him. He realized furthermore that Communists were influential in the white SDS and other organizations within the antiwar movement. He knew, too, that black student groups had refused to unite with the white SDS and would not approve of his doing so.

With his eyes wide open, therefore, King persisted in his struggle with Johnson and J. Edgar Hoover for peace in Vietnam. Knowing he had nothing to gain politically, he followed his convictions, his conscience, and the Presence and Voice to which he prayed. As he had done in every previous situation when his life was threatened, he did "what he had to do." As at Montgomery, Birmingham, Selma, and finally Memphis, he knew he was facing death.

He had learned long ago, however, to give up expecting exhilaration and praise. As the responsibilities of leadership grew increasingly complex and trying, the chances of being misunderstood and rejected by one's followers became greater. But he felt his duty was to follow his insight, even though he had to admit that it could lead to death for him. The call of a greater human need had to be answered. He could make high-sounding excuses for not venturing into this more universal field; in fact, his followers themselves provided him with such excuses. But he had learned that mankind everywhere is one. The hands which dropped the bombs upon Vietnamese women and children were his hands and the hands of his fellow Americans. It was his duty to God and to mankind to stop what he and thousands of American boys—black and white—were doing to the Vietnamese people.

His decision was to tell America it could not win, was not winning, and should seek a negotiated peace. It proved to be excellent advice. Had Johnson or Nixon followed it during the next six years, they would have been saved from total defeat "without honor."

Was King's steadfast decision to oppose Johnson's Vietnam policy evidence of a basic suicidal or masochistic trend in him? Or was it loyalty to his God, and to his own best self? Since we know that King was seen by his wife, his staff, and by outsiders as a hearty, cheerful man who loved telling jokes and tall tales and being with people, it is clear that he was far from masochistic, even in the popular use of this term.* His family and staff still hold that he loved life; the strongest evidence of this was his powerful desire to win, for the basic force in the healthy ego is the desire for self-preservation. King risked his life, not out of any suicidal drive, but as part of his "service to God"; it was part of his strategy in the battle, as it had been for Frederick Douglass and for Malcolm X. He did not take his own life. He calmly "put it on the line" to be true to his convictions, to his Vision.

King saw the Vietnam War with a vision that has since proved accurate. The war was *not* won; it nearly bankrupted the govern-

---

*Psychiatrists and analysts use the term "masochistic" to refer strictly to sexual behavior. We know King was not a sexual masochist; his wife attests to the opposite. He had four children and, according to J. Edgar Hoover, had affairs with women. Could one say he had an unconscious need to be punished? This need was identified by Freud in convicted criminals. Even if King did have such a need, we must remember that King's *decision to suffer* imprisonment was a *conscious* act taken after long thought, and a part of his strategy against white segregation laws.

ment, and caused havoc and waste in the slums, and—since we did not leave when King implored the President to do so—we were forced to flee in disarray. The next President, who took four more years to withdraw from Vietnam, ended in an utter debacle and had to resign in disgrace. King came out vindicated.

When the smoke cleared, however, few except his biographers David Lewis and Stephen Oates noticed that King had been correct all along and that all those who had said his antiwar speeches were misdirected because he was out of his field were themselves completely incorrect. His priorities were unimpeachable, both morally and practically. He told it, as blacks say, "exactly like it was," although he knew that in doing so he was risking his position and his life. Today it is a fair supposition, as we shall see, that he paid for his attack on the Vietnam War with his own life.

After Selma, King so rapidly had lost favor with Lyndon Johnson over the Vietnam War that in 1965 Johnson instructed J. Edgar Hoover to spy on him. Hoover and the FBI conducted a smear campaign to denounce him in any way possible; preferably by claiming King was controlled by Communists—the very people he was fighting in the Black Panther and Black Power groups. By June 1966, when Johnson's fraudulent and censored Civil Rights Committee met, Johnson had turned the overwhelming power of the federal government upon King, as Truman had done with Dr. Du Bois in 1951. The effect upon the Negro middle class and on King's own SCLC colleagues was the same as the earlier effect on the NAACP and on middle-class Negroes when Du Bois was indicted as a foreign agent in 1951. His SCLC aides were terrified for King, and most of the middle class—white and black—became frightened to be associated with him. The old liberals turned against him, as did the NAACP and the National Urban League, which they controlled. But, amazingly, later contributions to SCLC increased slightly.

Beginning in 1965, while living in a West Side Chicago Negro slum with his family for several months, King initiated talks with the black left-wing leaders. From them he learned about the eight million Negroes who lived at the very bottom of black society, far below the "poverty line." With more than 60% of their youth unemployed, this *underclass,* as I first described them in 1972, was a tinderbox set to ignite. First King learned that his civil-rights laws, which abolished segregation in public places but not in housing or schools, did them no good. The laws provided these people with no jobs, no money, no improvement in their segregated slum schools, and no escape from the ratholes to which racism had exiled them. After seeing the environment in which they were trapped, he understood the roots of the Black Panthers.

Black slum youth, those whom middle-class whites and Negroes call "savages," actually do live in a white-created and white-controlled "jungle," penned off from the rest of society by real-estate companies and just barely fed by the federal, state, and city governments. No force in government or in the economy is working toward—or envisages—a time when there will be a breakthrough (more accurately, a "breakout") for these eight millions. The "democratic ladder," that is, the ladder of upward socioeconomic mobility, stopped working for them long ago. Mechanization and automation will completely finish them off. Unless there is some kind of powerful intervention by industry or government, they will remain a permanently outcast group. But they are constantly stimulated by the sight of a better life—cars, houses, clothes, food—and are, therefore, constantly frustrated. The result is severe alienation, powerful and barely suppressed anger, hatred of the black middle class, fear of whites, social disorganization, and crime—the "jungle" with its young "savages."

This is the picture black slum leaders drew for King. His observations in Chicago, Oakland, Los Angeles, Cleveland, Harlem, and elsewhere confirmed it. He changed his social goals, but not his belief in cooperation and nonviolence. In time, plans for a campaign for the poor began to take shape in his mind. This idea was rejected by his critics and most middle-class Negroes. Here again, as in his campaign against the war, his critics proved almost uniformly obtuse. King's goal was not simply to feed and house the poor of all groups; it was to give them an economic base in jobs, and in housing. The poor, he had seen, are being turned into desperate ravening creatures. To start with, they must be fed and housed; but that alone will not stop the murder, robbery, and gang killings. To turn the jungles of Harlem or Chicago's West and South sides into living space, and to generate a rebirth, the poor must have jobs. To regenerate the slum dwellers by transforming their previously unsocialized youth was the real goal King shared with his top Northern lieutenants, James Bevel, C. T. Vivian, and Jesse Jackson. But the media, and his incredibly biased critics, hounded him, talking of the program for the poor as if it meant to establish soup kitchens in the White House "rose garden." During that time of high inflation and "prosperity"—1967 and 1968—few middle-class people believed the poor were desperate. In 1983, in the worst economic depression in fifty years and with the highest rate of unemployment and bankruptcy, we begin to understand what King was trying to avoid for the Negro community.

In 1966–1967, the proliferation of the Vietnam War brought King face to face with disaster. During this period, he seemed to be losing the support of all Negro leaders (including Roy Wilkins and Whitney Young) as well as the approval of his closest friends and colleagues. As Abernathy, Young, and his staff in the SCLC increasingly objected to his active campaign against the Vietnam War, King had to question his own motives even more deeply. (Why, he asked himself, was he opposing Johnson—a man who had cited the events in Birmingham and Selma to promote the powerful Civil Rights Act of 1964 and the even more effective Voting Rights Act of 1965?) But he had seen Johnson change radically and horribly. Always tough, sympathetic to minorities, and intelligent, the President had become obsessive about his war, and paranoidal. He was then, in early 1966, compulsively reiterating that his war, like the Civil War, was a war of emancipation and liberation; that he, like

Lincoln, was being persecuted by his own fellow Americans, and had been called a tyrant simply for trying to end the Communist threat to America's freedom. He had woven a purely hallucinatory myth. King had heard him recite this self-absolving myth to a group of Negro advisers on civil rights in March 1966. For twenty minutes at the beginning of the meeting, Johnson had talked more understandingly than any other white man could on the position of the Negro American. Then, for an hour, he gave a pep talk for the all-out prosecution of the war. It was so blatant as to have been unbelievable. There had been no applause. Surely Johnson didn't really believe he was a new Lincoln fighting the Civil War—against Communists 12,000 miles away. What he meant, clearly, was that the Negro leaders should remember that he, Johnson, had freed them a second time, and that they owed him their support now. King decided he could not join such an alliance. He would not act as if he had been bought and paid for.

On March 25, 1967, King led his first peace march, declaring: "We must combine the fervor of the civil rights movement with the peace movement." James Bevel, one of his top lieutenants in Chicago, was given leave of absence to work for peace, and King joined the Spring Mobilization for Peace campaign, along with Dr. Benjamin Spock and William Sloane Coffin. King announced his opposition to "my government's" war policy; he denounced a "cruel manipulation of the poor" carried out by a government that sent blacks to Vietnam as cannon fodder after having promised them a "war on poverty" in their communities. At Riverside Church in New York City, on April 4, he called for the organization of massive, nonviolent protests to oppose the war.

He received a tremendous ovation from a crowd of more than 125,000 in New York City on April 15. King's "word-picture of the indiscriminate American devastation in Vietnam" that killed twenty South Vietnamese (our allies), to every one Viet Cong, and his description of our own poor in American slums, riddled by poverty, unemployment, and the lost War on Poverty, led to the manifesto of a "Vietnam Summer," during which thousands of volunteers would work to stop the war. His father later wrote that during the last months of 1967 Martin received continual threats upon his life by letter and telephone. After his April 4 speech that spring, his father, who had opposed his work against the war, finally agreed with his son. "I know—the whole audience knew—the man was right."

Carl T. Rowan—the most widely read black journalist, who had been the director of the United States Information Agency, a government foreign-propaganda arm—advised King to disassociate himself from the antiwar movement. When King refused, Rowan wrote an article about King in the 14 April 1967 issue of the *Cleveland Plain Dealer*. The article stated that King was conceited, Communist-influenced, and a "persona non grata to Lyndon Johnson" (David B. Garrow, *The FBI and Martin Luther King, Jr.,* p. 290, n. 13). Rowan's article was reprinted in the *Reader's Digest* and had tremendous circulation. It must be said in fairness to Rowan that by the time of President Gerald Ford's Administration, six years later, he had undergone a change of heart, which he expressed in his newspaper column calling for a renewed investigation of King's assassination. The eminent Edward Levi, the United States Attorney General at that time, considered reopening the investigation. Carl Rowan wrote:

> My suspicions grow daily that the killing of Dr. King was ordered by Americans who were convinced by Hoover that King was harming the United States and helping the Soviet Union. . . . So now we have the eerie—and unproven—allegations by Roy H. Frankhouser, a former paid government informer who operated inside the Ku Klux Klan and the American Nazi Party, that the FBI tried to use the Klan to kill Dr. King in 1966. Frankhouser makes the equally inflammatory and unproven charge that James Earl Ray was "handpicked out of the FBI files" to kill Dr. King in 1968.
>
> Frankhouser's allegations deepen the suspicions of those of us who've always wondered about Ray's mysterious escape from prison in Missouri; or how he got the passport of a Royal Canadian

Mounted Police sergeant, with which he escaped to Europe; or who bankrolled him. Or why such an effort was made to imprison Ray without a trial.

In one last push, the Negro left—the Black Power leaders and the Black Panthers—redoubled their effort to discredit King. The media gave them full support; and the intellectuals ridiculed his last book, *Where Do We Go from Here: Chaos or Community?* The once liberal Southerner Professor C. Vann Woodward asked querulously, "What more do they want?," in a *Harper's* article; other scholars followed suit. Nevertheless, *Fortune* and the Louis Harris polls in 1967 showed that both Negroes and whites still overwhelmingly supported King's nonviolent methods and his demand for economic justice and redress.

But conservative Negro leaders continued to attack him, claiming he was defeated. They failed to acknowledge that King's and Johnson's Civil Rights Act of 1964 and their Voting Rights Act of 1965 were the most important advances—with the exception of school desegregation—toward insuring Negro rights made in ninety years; their charges smacked of jealousy and rivalry. Such jealousy—as within any ethnic group where the chances for national and worldwide attention are slim—was to be expected. King understood it because he had read Booker T. Washington's simile of crabs caught in a basket; each one tries to climb out, only to be pulled back by another crab clambering over. The charges of failure angered and depressed him, nevertheless.

The fight against the war gained increased momentum when Senator Eugene McCarthy, backed by the Conference of Concerned Democrats, announced on November 30, 1967 that he would be a candidate for the Presidency. In two months, by February 1968, the news from Vermont was that Johnson was not likely to do well in that primary.

The next four months, the last of King's life, were probably his most difficult. David Lewis has followed them in detail, but has not understood King's depression. The constant attacks by the Negro "left" made him angry, and anger leads to depression *unless expressed*. Against them, however, he could not express his anger by civil disobedience or nonviolent demonstrations. He was the very power they were opposing! He found himself in a constantly ambivalent position and mood. Trying to maintain his leadership and power against leftist attacks, he would become angry; then he would become repentant for his anger.

Most of his friends in the SCLC also were opposed to his campaign against the war; they, too, thought he was failing against the left—which cried for violence and called him "Uncle Tom." It came as a shock to him to realize that he was also angry with his own staff and friends. He was still vulnerable to anger. Well, he was not perfect. He was not God!

In his very last days, it became apparent that they could not see as far ahead or with as deep insight as he. Nor were they as patient, as stubborn, and as committed to the love of mankind—*all* mankind—as he was. And perhaps, except for Hosea Williams, Abernathy, and very few others, their faith in him was not as resolute as his faith in them. But he had taught them the invaluable truths by which they would learn to live: that they need not be afraid of standing up to the powerful and the mighty; that there are no giants and no dragons capable of withering us with fire and brimstone. He had taught them not to feel timid or frail simply because they were black, or female, or young, or old, or uneducated, or cloistered, or "powerless." He called upon them to use whatever strength they possessed and to profit by the miracle of growth. The only difference between people that counts, he said, is that some will shake and quake and bow and tremble, and others will stand erect, assert themselves, and ask for their just due. The person to be admired, said King, is the one who throws off the bonds of color, sex, class, age, and nationality to join hands with all mankind.

He may have been depressed during these months, but he worked hard enough for three men, speaking at leading universities and cathedrals. He was invited by the antiwar left to run for President; he declined. When he addressed the wealthy community adjacent to Detroit, Grosse Point, the elite of the automotive industry attacked him angrily for his opposition to the war. He was enthusiastically greeted by Berkeley students, including Negroes. *Life* attacked his proposals on Vietnam, and the U.S. Supreme Court sent him to jail in Birmingham on an old 1963 charge of demonstrating without a license.

Deciding to extend his Poor People's Campaign to include Puerto Ricans, Mexican Americans, American Indians, and Appalachian whites, he held a series of meetings in Southern and Northwestern cities to win support and plan a march to Washington. As he began to see the national and multiethnic possibilities of a poor people's union, he threw himself into the preparation for the march. His widow writes that, as always, he was lifted by the enthusiasm of his followers. Nevertheless, he interrupted the planning and organization of this demonstration to attend a memorial service for the Vietnam dead, speak at a peace rally in Carnegie Hall in New York in memory of W. E. B. Du Bois, and visit the scenes of the proliferating race riots.

Mrs. King, who naturally is our best informant on his behavior in these last days, writes that his depression during his last months was caused by recurrent riots in Negro urban slums (Detroit, New York City, Birmingham, and even New Britain, Connecticut, and Rochester, New York). He felt that the Poor People's March was their last chance to save the nation from chaos. The riots were usually reactions against unnecessary killings by the police. They were not planned by Panthers or by Black Power leaders. King knew these chaotic outbursts firsthand. In Chicago, in 1965, he had spent nights keeping vigil over riots on the West Side, trying to stop gangs from breaking into Jewish stores and looting. He dealt personally with the Cobras and the Vice Lords, finally persuading them to accept him and his white aides. He learned their needs and included them in the list of demands he nailed to the doors of Daley's City Hall.

His depression, then, was caused in part by external realities—the riots—and to that extent it was beyond his healing. His only option was to continue in his quest to change the complex environment. His enthusiasm for the Poor People's Campaign was unrealistically high perhaps because it gave him hope of organizing the poor to work on their *own behalf.* No one could "free" them or lift them; they would have to do that for themselves, as his followers in Montgomery, Birmingham, and Selma had. He had been studying Du Bois's accounts of alliances during the early Reconstruction period between the black and white poor in the South; to King they suggested that what was needed was an interracial and multiethnic union of the poor. "It is not *now* a matter of race, but of class," Coretta quotes him. This exciting and creative plan fought his depression; part of his anger was converted into planning and initiative. His SCLC staff dragged along; some unwillingly.

I trust that nothing I have said in this book about the possibility of transforming anger into initiative and achievement will lead the reader to underestimate the destructive power of unleased anger. In its "raw" state, anger is part of what Freud late in his life called the "death drive." Turned against others, it can lead to murder; turned against the self—as self-anger or self-hatred—it can lead to suicide. We have studied anger's course in three angry men: the young Frederick Douglass, William Edward Burghardt Du Bois, and Richard Wright; but we have seen "raw" anger only rarely and then only in stories, like Douglass's accounts of the whippings of his aunt by her enraged and jealous master. The anger we see in a story, however, is a thousand times *less* forceful than anger we *feel* in our own lives. The human being caught up in his own fury is an unpleasant sight. He stands choking with rage, shaking with an elemental effort to restrain himself from attacking. It is, in fact, a tremendous victory to be able to express his anger even in words of hate rather than to hit or kill.

Man in our society, as Freud said in his "War and Death," has a drive to kill, and it is closely related to his drive to love. If he is not to hurt or kill those with whom he is angry, he must *express* his anger verbally and not swallow it. For if the anger is dammed up within him, it will lash out someday, either against the cause of the anger or against himself. From childhood, King had successfully handled his anger by discussion and negotiation; with his father as well as with the white establishment. After the advent of Carmichael's Black Power group and the radical Black Panthers, however, he had swallowed much of his anger, trying to pacify and win them over. His endless "patience" began to wear thin.

Mrs. King clearly remembers that he was also impatient (angry) with his staff's disagreements over the war and the Poor People's Campaign. The more patient he was, the more angry he undoubtedly became. The more angry he grew, the more depressed. He would have done well to express his anger toward them. He should have vented his anger toward Carmichael (who claimed to be a friend—a "joking friend"), and certainly toward the Panthers, who called him "Uncle Tom." But he wanted to convert them; and he depended upon his tactics of peaceful negotiation and reconciliation to win them over. Psychologically and emotionally, however, he was "turning the other cheek."

Near the end there was a change. His staff was inefficient in organizing the March 28 protest march in Memphis; violence resulted, led by a Negro gang, the Invaders. King angrily blamed his staff for incompetence. One staff member said to Coretta, "When Martin combined his penetrating criticism with his eloquence, it was *withering fire.*" Withering fire! *There* was the released anger. Immediately after this reaction, he cast off his depression and held a magnificent press conference. Even the press praised his vigor. Abernathy said afterward, "I saw a quality in Martin I hadn't seen before—*a kind of lion quality.*" Nobody kicks a lion.

This strong rebound from his depression showed King's ego was basically sound. The greatly expanded activities into which he had led the SCLC throughout that year—including not only the massive organization of the Poor People's Campaign, but also the expanding work of Operation Breadbasket and the voters' registration campaign in Cleveland, Ohio, where the SCLC registered 50,000 voters for the black Carl Stokes, insuring his election as mayor of Cleveland—were all clear evidence that King could work hard and long and well. Such effective work is one mark of a basically strong ego.

"Amid the enormous activity in connection with the Poor People's Campaign, there appeared a small but troublesome cloud on the horizon," wrote Coretta. The Sanitation Workers Union of Memphis, Tennessee, had asked for recognition by the city, a small raise of 5% a year for two years, and fringe benefits. The union was 80% Negro. Mayor Henry Loeb rejected the union's three major demands, and issued an ultimatum that all strikers would be discharged two days later. The local NAACP and the Negro ministers supported the union, and organized the community behind the strikers. Leaders of local and national unions supported the Negro garbage workers, and Walter Reüther offered material aid from the United Automobile Workers. Bayard Rustin and Roy Wilkins addressed 9,000 people in a Memphis church. But Mayor Loeb used police-escorted nonunion workers to collect garbage in white neighborhoods, and the situation became deadlocked. The director of the SCLC's Memphis office, James Lawson, kept King advised of the situation.

The local ministers decided King was the only person who could move the strike to a constructive solution. He agreed to come, and arrived on the evening following his hostile reception by the automotive executives at Grosse Point. He addressed a crowd of 15,000 and called upon all groups to support a one-day general strike to show the Mayor that they could close down the city. His ideas had become tougher. Lewis writes that the speech "reflected the nonviolent revisionism of the last few months." King had said, "There is a need to unite *beyond class lines*. Negro 'haves' must join hands with Negro "have-nots.' "

He promised to return to lead a massive demonstration. In the meantime, his staff was to prepare the ground, train the marshals in methods of nonviolent protection from the police, and decide who might march. Their chief problem was a Black Power gang, the Invaders; although they finally agreed to a nonviolent march, the gang proved intractable. Such agreements are, after all, a strictly middle-class cultural trait.

King was in New York giving a series of speeches, but returned on March 28 for the march. It failed to start. While the parade was assembling, the sounds of breaking glass and disorder were heard. King immediately canceled the march. But as the 6,000 demonstrators went home or to their churches, the Invaders and militants marched and looted. The police killed a sixteen-year-old boy, injured fifty persons, and arrested 120. The Tennessee National Guard took over, and a curfew was established. Lewis writes, "by most accounts, the police were more indiscriminately violent than were the small number of looters." Last night I viewed motion pictures of this police action. It was *murderous;* it sought to brain peaceful Negro shoppers and adults along with the young Invaders.

King's depression returned, and with it, for some reason, his remorse. "He couldn't sleep. He agonized over the march as though he had committed the violence with his own hands," an SCLC aide said. But anyone who had organized a peaceful demonstration that ended in rampant violence could easily feel disappointed. The very next morning at his press conference, however, was the occasion on which, Abernathy said, he demonstrated his "lion" qualities.

Nationally, the response to the rioting was wholesale condemnation of King. In New York, Congressman Adam Clayton Powell called him "Martin Loser King," and Roy Wilkins called for the cancellation of the Poor People's March on Washington. President Johnson spoke on television the same night, deploring "mindless violence." Everywhere the middle and upper classes condemned his marches.

He had been tricked by the left and the hoodlums. Should he

have banned them from his marches, so as to protect himself and his cause? Had he tried too long to convert them, to win them over to peaceful demonstration and negotiation? Is not the law of the slum the fist and the gun? Only jobs, he knew, and the promise of "respectability" that jobs bring will change that. Ironically, he was trying to get them jobs, but his middle-class critics, as usual, understood nothing.

The following Sunday, March 31, was Passion Sunday, and he spoke at the Washington Cathedral. That evening, Lyndon Johnson, frightened off by—of all people—Eugene McCarthy, said he would not seek reelection. King was vindicated. Although his critics and detractors had been legion, they had all been wrong. He had not destroyed the civil-rights movement, he had given it new legitimacy. God grant he had taught the fainthearted to risk, to try, to fight for their just due.

Encouraged by Johnson's announcement, he returned to Memphis on Wednesday, April 3. He gave his last exhilarating sermon: "He's allowed me to go up on the mountain . . . and mine eyes have seen the glory of the coming of the Lord." He was exalted by the Presence, and he transmitted his exaltation to his audience. It was as if he were immolated and consumed by the Spirit.

The next afternoon, at the Negro Lorraine Motel, located in a slum, King walked onto a balcony facing a ramshackle rooming house. As he looked over the balcony-railing to ask the soloist to be certain to sing his favorite hymn that night, "Precious Lord, Take My Hand," an explosion was heard and a bullet penetrated his forehead. It left an ugly ragged hole, three inches wide.*

---

*A few days before, the Invaders and Panthers had objected to his going to a Holiday Inn outside the slum. They felt it showed his effort to get away from blacks! If he had not yielded in order to please these Negro racists, he very likely would not have been killed that day. The area of the Negro motel was open and offered a clear shot. Worst of all, King had no police guard, as he would have had in a "white" hotel.

In one of his sermons King had said:

> The only way we can really achieve freedom is to somehow conquer
> the fear of death. But if a man has not discovered something that
> he will die for, he isn't fit to live. Deep down in our nonviolent
> creed is the conviction there are some things so dear, some things
> so precious, some things so eternally true that they are worth dying
> for, and if a man happens to be 36 years old, as I happen to be, and
> some great truth stands before the door of his life, some great op-
> portunity to stand up for that which is right and that which is just,
> and he refuses to stand up because he wants to live a little longer,
> and he's afraid his home will get bombed, or he's afraid that he will
> lose his job, or he's afraid that he will get shot or beat down by
> state troopers, he may go on and live until he's 80, but he's just as
> dead at 36 as he would be at 80, and the cessation of breathing in
> his life is merely the belated announcement of an earlier death of
> the spirit. Man dies when he refuses to stand up for that which is
> right. A man dies when he refuses to stand up for justice.

As time passes, one is able to gain a more objective view of
King's achievements. He emerges increasingly as the wisest leader
of our age. He was not, of course, as powerful as Franklin Roosevelt, Lenin, Stalin, and Churchill, who commanded armies and ruled
great nations. He addressed more effectively, however, the central
problem of this time, the mutual hatred and violence between and
within nations. He exposed these hatreds and showed mankind the
way to reduce and heal them. That method was to recognize and
identify group anger and hatred, and then to convert these feelings
into cooperative and affiliative behavior. Neither revenge nor mastery was to be the goal of either group, but reconciliation.

To understand King, one must first know what he meant by
"love," "the discipline of love," and "changing hate to love." Sec-
ondly, one must also try to understand how he handled his own
aggression. When attacked or denigrated, did he respond with direct counteraggression, or displace his aggression to someone
weaker, or identify with the aggressor and try to be like him, or

sublimate his aggression into socially acceptable forms, or—frustrated in all these directions—turn his aggression inward upon himself?

Although in his battle against the Vietnam War, King occasionally used direct aggression in attacking President Johnson and his war policy, he chiefly handled his aggressive feelings by identifying with his effectively aggressive father. His father was persistent, strong, and determined in a fight, but also ready to bargain and negotiate. King took this behavior of his father into himself; he identified with his peacefully aggressive, strong, patient, forceful, and prevailing father. And indeed, he himself became a father figure to millions, and, in the end, even to his father!

What about his anger? The typical response by King to his own angry and aggressive feelings was to feel guilty, and to *turn his anger against himself as punishment for this guilt*. This mechanism was first shown in his childhood attempt at suicide following his beloved grandmother's death. He felt intolerably guilty because he had slipped away to watch a parade while she was dying. The same kind of irrational guilt indirectly led to his own miscalculations in Memphis. Instead of expressing his strong disagreement with the Black Panthers and Black Power groups and driving them out of the Movement (as the outraged Christ drove the moneylenders and hypocrites from the Temple), King "turned the other cheek," and put up with them for nearly four years. As a result he paid the price everyone pays for swallowing his anger; a deep depression, which later interfered with his effective work in Memphis. There was some deep compulsion in King to suffer, to sacrifice himself.

But there was also an even more powerful drive to *teach* men and women, and to help them change; to minister to them in the best sense of that word. To all those who understood him (and they were legion, since he spoke to the basic beliefs and feelings of scores of millions trained in the Christian ethic), he taught a truth which renewed their lives. *It was that hate kills the hater*. In "On Narcissism," Freud had written the same thing a great many years before: ". . . in the last resort we must begin to love in order that we may not fall ill, and *must fall ill if, in consquence of frustration, we cannot love.*" (Emphasis mine.) That is, hatred and anger toward another make us ill. Can anyone doubt that Bull Connor and the sheriff of Lowndes County and Lyndon Johnson in his Vietnam War years were ill?

Freud does not say how those who hate may learn to love. But as a psychiatrist who had to minister "to a mind diseased," he had discovered that repressed resentment and hatred make a human being sick. That sickness may consist either of constant suspicion, or the wish to murder, or constant guilt over one's hate, or chronic anxiety, or depression, or all of these combined. When the South was constantly generating hatred between whites and Negroes, it undoubtedly had the sickest population in America. Now the South is renewed, and growing in hope and vitality, while Chicago and many Northern cities are full of hate and segregation. They are sick societies.

No one has told us how King was able to turn hate into the affiliative, unifying drive of which Freud speaks in the passage quoted on the title page of this book; into that unity of feeling and understanding, that "great unity, the unity of mankind." This relationship (*agape*) clearly has nothing sexual about it, nor is it like *philia,* that feeling between close personal friends who invite each other into their homes.

King's biographers have followed his distinctions between (1) sexual love, *Eros,* and (2) affiliative love, *philia,* and (3) *agape,* Christian love, and let it go at that. But what King and Gandhi did not know was the relationship between one's self-destructive aggression and one's love. Both men held that one must suffer deeply, even allow oneself to be injured and "punished," *in order to win the respect of one's opponent.* Gandhi became extremely puritanical in punishing himself; he banned sex for himself and his *satyagrahis* (followers), he fasted and denied himself sleep. King repeatedly subjected himself to imprisonment, insults, and (in Chicago) physical attacks. According to this philosophy, respect from one's opponent was to be won by suffering at his hands, which led him to feel guilty. This belief verges upon the idea of self-sacrifice, and turning the other cheek, which Freud would have called sick.

It was not chiefly through his suffering that King won white and black converts, but through his teaching them to forgive, to *open themselves* up so as to learn about the opponent, and to be willing to negotiate, and gradually to renounce hatred and revenge. He performed the miracle of changing hate first into negotiation and then into reconciliation. He did so by appealing to their common humanity and their common religious ideals.

There is another even more powerful psychological force which can turn hate into love. It is universal, and occurs first in childhood. The child of two or three is likely to be selfish, cruel, jealous of his older or younger sibling, and unfair. All the while, his parents are trying to teach him that it is "bad" to be selfish, or cruel, or jealous, or unfair. In time, his developing conscience tells him the same thing. Finally, he or she learns to be relatively cooperative and merciful, and to overcome his jealousy of his brother or sister. This *change to the opposite behavior* (cruelty changed into mercy, selfishness into unselfishness) is called a *reaction-formation,* and the change is *motivated by unconscious guilt.* The change is unconscious and may have caused both King and his father, who deeply hated whites, to change to acceptance of whites (through guilt). The same process, no doubt, worked in millions of whites who had hated or disliked Negroes. Since men are not naturally loving or democratic, forgiveness or acceptance through reaction-formation is welcome enough, though not heroic. Acceptance and fairness, however they are gained, contribute to the unity of mankind.

We conclude that there are three processes by which hate may be transformed into some form of "love." (1) The first process is motivated by unconscious guilt over one's hatred. This change usually occurs in childhood. Martin Luther King, Jr. showed this reaction-formation early; therefore his grandmother called him a "child of God," and his father thought him a perfect little "gentleman." (2) The second process is a kind of nonsexual masochism, exhibited by most deeply religious people. Such "love" is self-sacrificing and self-punishing, and basically self-destroying. I do not think King's love was of this kind. He was a hearty, outgoing, enjoying person, like his maternal grandmother. He did not wear the hair-shirt. (3) The third type of love evolves from a rational understanding of the destructiveness of hatred, and a consequent rejection of hatred, and search for empathy with all men. This was King's and Freud's highest ideal, and King was the greatest proponent of such love in our time. Gandhi clearly was not a lover of his fellow man; he was too punitive and masochistic.

Finally, to appreciate fully the power of King's example, one must always remember that we still live in an age of continuous violence and nuclear threat. In 1982, television showed us the mangled bodies of children, women, and civilians massacred by the "Christian" Phalangist armed forces in western Beirut! As usual, world leaders were "horrified" by the enormity of this mass murder. But tomorrow they very likely will start their own war or own massacre. When I began this book six years ago, the massacres in Northern Ireland were at their height. A dozen others (in Vietnam, Cambodia, El Salvador) have followed. Evidently there is no end to men's hate and desire to murder.

King believed that men can save themselves from their own mutual hatreds, for they have the capacity to turn hatred into its opposite—*mercy and love of mankind*. He taught his followers to renounce hatred, to learn to deal with the enemy as fellow human beings, to give up the desire for personal revenge, and to forgive injuries once and for all. He was always willing to try again with people; he wholeheartedly asserted his faith in the human animal, who—however blinded, vindictive, and embittered—is capable of learning to love.

It follows that the cure for the world's repetitive hatred and revenge lies in seeking leaders who first can convert their own hatred into constructive initiative, and then can *direct their full efforts toward saving mankind from its hatred, which otherwise will destroy it.* Through this rare "sea-change"* of hatred into compassion, a "brave new world" of love does indeed seem possible.

* "Nothing of him that doth fade
But doth suffer a sea-change
Into something rich and strange."

William Shakespeare, *The Tempest,* I, 2.

Select Bibliography

FREDERICK DOUGLASS

The best works to read on Douglass are his second and third autobiographies, and the well-researched four-volume biography by Philip S. Foner. The first autobiography by Douglass is one of the most dramatic narratives in American literature, but at the behest of the Massachusetts Anti-Slavery Society he purposely misrepresents his life with his white relatives.

Books by Douglass

Life and Times of Frederick Douglass. New York: Collier Books, 1963. Originally published in 1881.

My Bondage and My Freedom. New York: Miller, Orton and Mulligan, 1855; New York: Arno Press, 1968.

A Personal Narrative: Narrative of the Life of Frederick Douglass, an American Slave. Written by Himself. Boston: Anti-Slavery Office, 1845; with subtitle as title, New York: Doubleday, 1963.

Biographies, Criticism, Background

Chesnutt, Charles W. *Frederick Douglass.* Boston: Small, Maynard & Co., 1899.

Curry, Leonard P. *The Free Black in Urban America, 1800–1850.* Chicago: University of Chicago Press, 1981.

Du Bois, W. E. B. *The Supression of the African Slave-Trade to the United States of America, 1638–1870.* New York: Shocken Books, 1969.

Elkins, Stanley M. *Slavery.* Chicago: University of Chicago Press, 1959.

Foner, Philip S. *Frederick Douglass.* New York: Citadel Press, 1964. The basic biography of Douglass. Well researched and indispensable. The author's Marxist ideas intrude only rarely and then are so obvious they can easily be discounted.

———. *The Life and Writings of Frederick Douglass.* 4 vols. New York: International Publishers, 1950–1955; supplementary vol., 1975.

Lane, Ann J., ed. *The Debate Over Slavery.* Urbana: University of Illinois Press, 1971.

Preston, Dickson J. *Young Frederick Douglass: The Maryland Years.* Baltimore: Johns Hopkins University Press, 1980. A fascinating and indispensable account of both the white and the Negro families of Douglass.

Quarles, Benjamin, ed. *Frederick Douglass.* Englewood Cliffs, N.J.: Prentice-Hall, 1968.

Weissman, Stephen M., M.D. "Portrait of a Black Militant." In *The Psychoanalytic Study of the Child,* vol. 25. New Haven: Yale University Press, 1975. The only psychological study of Douglass. A perceptive work, excellent on his relationships with his white family.

WILLIAM EDWARD BURGHARDT DU BOIS

The most helpful works in studying Du Bois's personality are his autobiographical writings, *Darkwater,* parts of *The Souls of Black Folk, Dusk of Dawn,* and *The Autobiography of W. E. B. Du Bois.* This last book as published in the United States is mangled. It is difficult to fathom why a distinguished historian should have published a work which is unworthy of Du Bois. For some unexplained reason, parts of Du Bois's diary of his early years of European study and travel have been eliminated; they are available in the University of Massachusetts (Amherst) Du Bois Collection. Nevertheless, Chapters X and XVI of the *Autobiography* are helpful.

Books by Du Bois

Africa in Battle Against Colonialism, Racialism, Imperialism. Chicago: Afro-American Books, 1960.

The Amenia Conference. Amenia, N.Y.: Troutbeck Press, 1925.

An Appeal to the World. New York: National Association for the Advancement of Colored People, 1947.

The Autobiography of W. E. B. Du Bois: A Soliloquy on Viewing My Life from the Last Decade of Its First Century. Edited by Herbert Aptheker. New York: International Publishers, 1968.

Black Reconstruction: An Essay toward a History of the Part Which Black Folk Played in the Attempt to Reconstruct Democracy in America, 1860–1880. New York: Harcourt, Brace and Co., 1935; New York: Meridian Books, 1964.

Color and Democracy. New York: Harcourt, Brace and Co., 1945.

Complete Published Works. Compiled and edited by Herbert Aptheker. Millwood, N.Y.: Kraus-Thomson Organization, 1980.

The Correspondence of W. E. B. Du Bois. Edited by Herbert Aptheker. 3 vols. Amherst, Mass.: University of Massachusetts Press, 1973–1978.

The Crisis Writings. Edited by Daniel Walden. Greenwich, Ct.: Fawcett, 1972.

Darkwater: Voices from within the Veil. New York: Harcourt, Brace and Co., 1920.

Dusk of Dawn: An Essay toward an Autobiography of a Race Concept. New York: Harcourt, Brace and Co., 1940.

The Gift of Black Folk: The Negroes in the Making of America. Boston: Stratford Co., 1924.

John Brown. Philadelphia: G. W. Jacobs, 1909; New York: International Publishers, 1962.

The Philadelphia Negro: A Social Study; Together with a Special Report on Domestic Service by Isabel Eaton. Publications in Political Economy and Public Law, no. 14. Philadelphia: University of Pennsylvania Press, 1899.

The Souls of Black Folk: Essays and Sketches. 15th edition, Chicago: A. C. McClurg, 1903; Gloucester, Mass.: Peter Smith, 1963.

The Suppression of the African Slave-Trade to the United States of America, 1638–1870. Harvard Historical Studies, vol. 1. Cambridge, Mass.: Harvard University Press, 1896; New York: Schocken Books, 1969.

Worlds of Color. Vol. 3 of *The Black Flame.* New York: Mainstream, 1961.

Biographies and General Works

Aptheker, Herbert. *Annotated Bibliography of the Writings of W. E. B. Du Bois.* Millwood, N.Y.: Kraus-Thomson Organization, 1973.

Broderick, Francis T. *W. E. B. Du Bois: Negro Leader in a Time of Crisis.* Stanford: Stanford University Press, 1959.

Clarke, John Henrik, and others. *Black Titan: W. E. B. Du Bois.* Boston: Beacon Press, 1970. Anthology with comment. Allow for Communist influence.

Graham, Shirley. *His Day Is Marching On: A Memoir of W. E. B. Du Bois.* Philadelphia: Lippincott, 1971.

Lacy, Leslie Alexander. *Cheer the Lonesome Traveler: The Life of W. E. B. Du Bois.* New York: Dial Press, 1970.

Lester, Julius, ed. *The Seventh Son.* 2 vols. New York: Random House, 1971. An unsatisfactory work in a pretentious format.

Logan, Rayford W. *W. E. B. Du Bois: A Profile.* American Profiles Series. New York: Hill & Wang, 1971. The best annotated bibliography of Du Bois.

Partington, Paul G. *W. E. B. Du Bois: A Bibliography of His Published Writings.* Whittier, Ca.: The Author, 1977.

Rudwick, Elliott M. *W. E. B. Du Bois: Propagandist of the Negro Protest.* With a new preface by Louis Harlan and an epilogue by the author. New York: Atheneum, 1968. A cantankerous book by a hostile witness.

———. *W. E. B. Du Bois: A Study in Minority Group Leadership.* Philadelphia: University of Pennsylvania Press, 1960.

Sterne, Emma. *His Was the Voice: The Life of W. E. B. Du Bois.* New York: Crowell-Collier Press, 1971.

RICHARD NATHANIEL WRIGHT

The most helpful book on Wright's personality is his own *Black Boy.* Later, after instruction by the prominent New York psychoanalyst Frederic Wertham, M.D., Wright organized his fiction around psychological themes. No other work on Wright provides help in understanding his personality. Fabre's biography is the most detailed and well researched. Gayle's is the best written and the best documented on his early Communist relationships.

Books by Wright

American Hunger. New York: Harper & Row, 1977.

Black Boy. New York: Harper & Bros., 1945.

Black Power. New York: Harper & Bros., 1954.

The Color Curtain. New York: World Publishing Co., 1956.

Eight Men. New York: World Publishing Co., 1961.

Native Son. New York: Harper & Bros., 1940.

The Outsider. New York: Harper & Bros., 1953.

Pagan Spain. New York: Harper & Bros., 1957.

Savage Holiday. New York: Universal Publishers & Distributing Corp., 1965.

"Two Million Black Voices," *New Masses* 18, no. 9 (February 25, 1936).

Twelve Million Black Voices. With Edwin Rosskam. New York: Viking Press, 1941.

Uncle Tom's Children. New York: Harper & Bros., 1938.

White Man, Listen! Garden City, N.Y.: Doubleday & Co., 1964.

Biographies and Criticism

Baldwin, James. *The Devil Finds Work.* New York: Dial Press, 1976.

———. *Notes of a Native Son.* Reissue, New York: Dial Press, 1963.

———. *Nobody Knows My Name*. New York: Dial Press, 1961.

Brignano, Russell Carl. *Richard Wright: An Introduction to the Man and His Works*. Pittsburgh: University of Pittsburgh Press, 1970.

Carr, Virginia Spencer. *The Lonely Hunter*. Garden City, N.Y.: Doubleday & Co., 1976.

Fabre, Michel. "Interview with Simone de Beauvoir," *Studies in Black Literature* 1 (Autumn 1970).

———. *The Unfinished Quest of Richard Wright*. New York: William Morrow & Co., 1973.

Gayle, Addison. *Richard Wright: Ordeal of a Native Son*. New York: Anchor Press, Doubleday, 1980.

Himes, Chester. *My Life of Absurdity*. Garden City, N.Y.: Doubleday, 1972.

Koestler, Arthur, and others. *The God That Failed*. New York: Harper & Row, 1963.

Webb, Constance. *Richard Wright*. New York: G. P. Putnam's Sons, 1968.

Wertham, Frederic, M.D. "An Unconscious Determinant in *Native Son*," *Journal of Clinical and Experimental Psychology* 6 (July 1944): 111–15.

"Why Richard Wright Came Back from France," *P.M. Magazine*, February 16, 1947.

MARTIN LUTHER KING, JR.

Works by King
(as listed with comment in William H. Fisher, *Free At Last*)

Beyond Vietnam. Palo Alto, Ca., Alton Press, 1967. Major antiwar statement, delivered at New York's Riverside Church on April 4, 1967.

Conscience for Change. Toronto, Canadian Broadcasting Company Publications, 1967. Five radio lectures, dealing with his philosophy of nonviolence, his antiwar stance, and the need for vigorous social action.

Declaration of Independence from the War in Vietnam. New York, n.p., 1967. Antiwar statement from Riverside Church under a different title.

A Drum Major for Justice. Bushey Heath, England: Taurus Press, 1969. His own eulogy, in a sermon delivered at Ebenezer Baptist Church in Atlanta.

I Have a Dream: The Text of the Speech Delivered August 28, 1963, at the Lincoln Memorial, Washington, D.C. Los Angeles: The John Henry & Mary Louise Dunn Bryant Foundation, 1963; New York: Time, 1968. The text of his most popular and often quoted work.

Letter from Birmingham City Jail. Philadelphia: American Friends Service Committee, 1963. Response to criticism of his activities by eight Alabama clergymen. Presents his most noted justification of the civil-rights movement and his nonviolent philosophy.

The Measure of a Man. Philadelphia: United Church Press, 1968. Presents his philosophical and theological ideas on man and how man can lead a more complete life.

Nobel Lecture by the Reverend Dr. Martin Luther King, Jr., Recipient of the 1964 Nobel Peace Prize, Oslo, Norway, December 11, 1964. New York: Harper & Row, 1964. Text of his acceptance at Nobel ceremonies.

Sermon, the Washington Cathedral, Sunday, March 31, 1968. N.p., 1968. One of his last major addresses. Speaks of America's potential to help eradicate world poverty and hunger.

Strength to Love. New York: Harper & Row, 1963. Deals with "Christian" answers to social problems in sermons delivered at the time of the Montgomery boycott.

Stride Toward Freedom: The Montgomery Story. New York: Harper & Row, 1958. His first book, in which he presents his story of the Montgomery boycott and his rationale for the use of nonviolence.

The Trumpet of Conscience. New York: Harper & Row, 1968. His Massey lectures, in which he deals with his philosophy of nonviolence, the war in Vietnam, the role of youth in the world, and hope for world peace.

Where Do We Go from Here: Chaos or Community? New York: Harper & Row, 1967.

Why We Can't Wait. New York: Harper & Row, 1964. Tells his story of the Birmingham campaign.

Biographies and Criticism

Bennett, Lerone. *What Manner of Man: A Biography of Martin Luther King, Jr.* Chicago: Johnson Publishing Co., 1964.

Carmichael, Stokely, and Charles V. Hamilton. *Black Power: The Politics of Liberation in America.* New York: Random House, 1967.

Fisher, William H. *Free at Last: A Bibliography of Martin Luther King, Jr.* Metuchen, N.J.: Scarecrow Press, 1977.

Garrow, David J. *The FBI and Martin Luther King, Jr.* New York: Holt, Rinehart & Winston, 1969; New York: W. W. Norton, 1981.

King, Coretta Scott. *My Life with Martin Luther King, Jr.* New York: Holt, Rinehart & Winston, 1969. In many ways, this is the most helpful and insightful book on Martin Luther King, Jr. Undoubtedly, Mrs. King, Reverend David Abernathy, and King's father understood him best and were with him most.

King, Martin Luther, and Clayton Riley. *Daddy King: An Autobiography*. New York: William Morrow & Co., 1980.

Lewis, David L. *King, A Critical Biography*. New York: Praeger, 1970. Reprinted, Urbana: University of Illinois Press, 1978. Well researched by an able scholar.

Lincoln, Charles Eric., ed. *Martin Luther King, Jr.: A Profile*. New York: Hill & Wang, 1970.

Littleton, A. C., and M. W. Burger, eds. *Black Viewpoints*. New York: New American Library, 1971.

Marine, Gene. *The Black Panthers*. New York: New American Library, 1969.

Oates, Stephen B. *Let the Trumpet Sound: The Life of Martin Luther King, Jr.* New York: Harper & Row, 1982. This discussion of King's philosophical and theological reading is the best available. It is also the best account of his attack on the Vietnam War, and the best-written biography.

Reddick, Lawrence Dunbar. *Crusader Without Violence: A Biography of Martin Luther King, Jr.* New York: Harper & Bros., 1959. The best account of his first years, by his Boswell through the Montgomery bus boycott and his trip to India in 1959. All other biographers have depended upon Reddick's book for a knowledge of King's first thirty years.

Index